Better Homes and Gardens®

1987 BEST-RECIPES YEARBOOK

ISSN: 8755-3090
ISBN: 0-696-02129-3

Better Homes and Gardens®

Editorial Director DORIS M. EBY
Editor DAVID JORDAN
Managing Editor KATE GREER   Art Director ROBERT C. FURSTENAU

Food and Nutrition Editor NANCY BYAL
Department Head—Cook Books SHARYL HEIKEN
Senior Food Editor—Magazine JOY TAYLOR
Senior Food Editor—Special Interest Publications JOANNE JOHNSON
Associate Department Heads JANET FIGG   SANDRA GRANSETH
ROSEMARY HUTCHINSON   ELIZABETH WOOLEVER
Senior Food Editors BARBARA ATKINS   LYNN HOPPE   JULIA MALLOY
MARCIA STANLEY   PAT TEBERG   JOYCE TROLLOPE
Associate Food Editors LINDA HENRY   MARY MAJOR   DIANA MCMILLEN
MARY JO PLUTT   MAUREEN POWERS   MARTHA SCHIEL   LOIS WHITE   TERRI PAUSER WOLF
LINDA FOLEY WOODRUM   DIANE YANNEY

Editorial Marketing Services Director MARGARET McMAHON
Editorial Management Trainee DAVID S. JOHNSON

Copy Chief ELIZABETH HAHN BROOKS   *Makeup Editor* LINDA R. THOMAS
Associate Makeup Editors KATHRYN DAVIDSON   JUDY HUNSICKER

Managing Art Director GERALD PREATOR
Associate Art Directors BRADFORD W. S. HONG   ALISANN DIXON   JERRY J. RANK
Senior Graphic Designer KIMBERLY B. ZARLEY
Graphic Designers KELLY BARTON   NANCY N. KLUENDER   KEVIN S. LUDGATE

Executive Director Editorial Services DUANE L. GREGG
Director, Editorial Planning DAVID R. HAUPERT
Director, Editorial Research C. RAY DEATON   *Research Assistant* SCOTT R. TOLAN
Administrative Editor ROSE ANDERSON   *Art Business Office Manager* DIANE BOYLE
Test Kitchen Director SHARON STILWELL   *Photo Studio Manager* DON WIPPERMAN
Test Kitchen Photo Studio Director JANET PITTMAN

Books *Editor* GERALD KNOX   *Managing Editor* DAVID A. KIRCHNER
Art Director ERNEST SHELTON
Associate Art Directors LINDA FORD VERMIE   NEOMA ALT WEST   RANDALL YONTZ
Editorial Project Managers JAMES D. BLUME   MARSHA JAHNS
ROSANNE WEBER MATTSON   MARY HELEN SCHILTZ
Assistant Art Directors LYNDA HAUPERT   HARIJS PRIEKULIS   TOM WEGNER
Senior Graphic Designers JACK MURPHY   STAN SAMS   DARLA WHIPPLE-FRAIN
Graphic Designers MIKE BURNS   W. BLAKE WELCH   BRIAN WIGNALL

MAGAZINE GROUP PRESIDENT **JAMES A. AUTRY**
Magazine Group Vice President DORIS M. EBY, Editorial Director

Vice President–Publisher, Better Homes and Gardens J. WESLEY SILK
Publishing Services Director TERRY UNSWORTH
Advertising Sales Director LENNOX E. H. STUART
Associate Publisher/Development DEL RUSHER

CORPORATE OFFICERS: **Chairman of the Board E. T. MEREDITH III**
President ROBERT A. BURNETT
Executive Vice President JACK D. REHM, Corporate Services
Group Presidents: JAMES A. AUTRY, Magazines   **FRED STINES**, Books
W. C. McREYNOLDS, Broadcasting   **ALLEN L. SABBAG**, Real Estate
Vice Presidents: DONALD L. ARNOLD, Corporate Relations
THOMAS G. FISHER, General Counsel and Assistant Secretary
NEIL KUEHNL, Product Development   **HERB SCHULTE**, Corporate Planning
WILLIAM H. STRAW, Finance   **GERALD D. THORNTON**, Administrative Services
Secretary BETTY CAMPBELL MADDEN   Treasurer MICHAEL A. SELL
Corporate Controller LARRY D. HARTSOOK

Our seal assures you that every recipe in the *1987 Best-Recipes Yearbook* has been tested in the Better Homes and Gardens® Test Kitchen. This means that each recipe is practical and reliable, and meets our high standards of taste appeal.

CONTENTS

Month after month,
Better Homes and Gardens magazine
comes up with winning ideas
and recipes to meet your changing
life-style. Whether you're too busy to
cook, concerned about nutrition, or
looking for new foods, we've got
the recipes you can make and share
with your family. Leaf through
this volume, our fifth annual recipe
yearbook, to rediscover the best of the
recipes we published in 1986.

LOW-CAL DISHES

FOR POST-HOLIDAY DIETS

After a holiday season of irresistible foods, it's time to pare calories from meals. Merge your determination to shed those pounds with either a nutritious family-size entrée or a satisfying single-serving freeze-ahead meal.

PORK CHOP BULGUR BAKE

- 2 tablespoons bulgur wheat
- 2 tablespoons shredded carrot
- 2 tablespoons sliced celery
- ½ teaspoon instant chicken bouillon granules
- ¼ teaspoon dried minced onion
- ⅛ teaspoon dried tarragon, crushed
- 1 small pork rib chop, cut ½ inch thick (about 4 ounces)
- 1 cup frozen broccoli cuts
- 1 tablespoon catsup
- 2 teaspoons dry red wine

Combine bulgur, carrot, celery, bouillon, onion, tarragon, and ¼ cup *water;* bring to boiling. Pour into a shallow individual baking dish. Top with pork chop and broccoli. Cover tightly with foil. Bake, covered, in a 375° oven 45 minutes or till meat is done. Combine catsup and wine; spread over chop. Bake, uncovered, 5 minutes. Serves 1.

Nutrition info per serving: 347 cal., 21 g pro., 25 g carbo., 18 g fat, 56 mg chol., 430 mg sodium. U.S. RDA: 85% vit. A, 156% vit. C, 48% thiamine, 21% riboflavin, 10% calcium, 30% phosphorus, 26% niacin, 22% iron.

FOR ONE

Pork Chop Bulgur Bake—a satisfying meal just right for one, and under 400 calories! To fix ahead and freeze, partially bake the entrée in an oven-to-freezer baking dish in a 375° oven 30 minutes. Cool. Seal, label, and freeze. To serve, bake, covered, in a 375° oven 1 hour. Combine catsup and wine; spread over chop. Bake, uncovered, 5 minutes more.

FOOD STYLIST: JUDY TILLS

FIESTA FISH AND SHELLS

- 1 11½- or 12-ounce package individually frozen fish portions
- 1 cup tiny shell macaroni
- 1 16-ounce can tomatoes, cut up
- ½ cup chopped onion
- ½ of a 1¼-ounce package (2½ tablespoons) taco seasoning mix
- 1 medium green pepper, cut into strips
- ¼ cup shredded cheddar cheese (1 ounce)

Allow unwrapped frozen fish to stand at room temperature about 20 minutes. Meanwhile, cook macaroni according to package directions; drain thoroughly. In a medium saucepan stir together *undrained* tomatoes, onion, and taco seasoning mix. Add macaroni and green pepper strips; bring mixture just to boiling. Pour tomato-macaroni mixture into a 10x6x2-inch baking dish. Fold each fish portion as necessary to fit in pan; place over the mixture.

Spoon some of the sauce over fish. Bake, covered, in a 350° oven 35 minutes or till fish flakes easily when tested with a fork. Uncover; sprinkle cheese over fish. Bake 5 minutes more or till cheese melts. Makes 4 servings.

Nutrition information per serving: 261 cal., 29 g pro., 20 g carbo., 7 g fat, 77 mg chol., 765 mg sodium. U.S. RDA: 27% vit. A, 89% vit. C, 13% thiamine, 12% riboflavin, 19% niacin, 10% calcium, 12% iron, and 31% phosphorus.

FOR THE FAMILY

Fiesta Fish and Shells—a family-size dinner for an investment of just 261 calories per serving! You and your family can enjoy this hearty meal that's long on flavor and low in fat. Calorie-cutting was easy—the fish cooks in a taco-seasoned tomato sauce for flavor. The vegetables add crunch plus a lot of valuable vitamins and minerals.

ASIAN-STYLE
HOME COOKING
THREE FAMILIES SHARE THEIR RECIPES

**Across America the foods of Asia are on the front burner!
Asian restaurants (Thai, Vietnamese, even Burmese) are thriving, and
supermarkets are stocking ingredients indigenous to Asian countries. Experiment
with these readily available foods, and enjoy the refreshing tastes of hoisin sauce,
lemon grass, rice cake, and more at your own meals. With help from three families,
you'll soon agree that the flavorful recipes of Asia suit your busy lifestyle.**

By Mary Gunderson

CHINESE: FAST AND HEALTHFUL

MIKE JENSEN

DOUG AND LINDA LEW dine on Chinese food several times a week, either
alone, with their two children, or with friends.

Doug Lew introduced Linda, his wife, to the food of his native China in the early 1950s. Ever since that first taste, Linda has loved the pungent flavors, tender bits of meat and fish, and fresh vegetables.

Linda, who grew up on hearty Illinois fare, learned to cook Chinese style from Doug's mother and sisters. Over the years she has adapted the recipes (for instance, using less soy sauce), because she and Doug prefer lighter-tasting foods.

The Lews have found any number of ways to improvise—Chinese cooking allows for endless combinations of vegetables, meats, and seasonings. They can cook a Chinese meal with almost any ingredient available to them.

For first-time Chinese cooks, Linda recommends starting with mildly seasoned dishes (some Chinese foods use hot peppers liberally), and gradually introducing such unfamiliar ingredients as black mushrooms and lotus root.

SHRIMP-BACON STIR-FRY

After cooking the bacon, seafood, peas, and bamboo shoots, pour the sauce ingredients into the middle of the wok, skillet, or Dutch oven. Cook and stir the mixture till thickened and bubbly.

The Lews almost always cook Chinese for friends, because it's easy to expand the number of dishes as the guest list increases. Serve 6 to 8 with this menu: *Shrimp-Bacon Stir-Fry (front), Vegetable Beef with Rice Cake (center),* and *Chinese Buns (back).*

CHINESE BUNS

Press the soft yeast dough into ten 4-inch circles. Top each circle with about ¼ cup of the spiced pork filling, then bring up the edges of the dough to seal in the meat. Ready, set, steam!

VIETNAMESE
FAST AND FLAVORFUL

ERNIE BRAUN

DIEP LE AND THO X DO with their daughters, Dee and An, at home in northern California.

The way Diep Le learned to cook in her native Vietnam fits well with her family's busy life in the United States. Though the family has lived here for more than six years, they still prefer fast-to-fix Vietnamese-style meals at home.

The actual cooking times for Vietnamese dishes are short—stir-frying, steaming, and grilling are Diep's favorites. "Most of the time you spend preparing a meal is for chopping vegetables and assembling foods," she says.

Diep's cooking draws on all regions of Vietnam: fish, seafood, vegetables, and fruits from the south; chilies from the central region; and Chinese seasonings, stir-frying, and steaming from the north.

Diep and Tho, her husband, consider the evening meal an important part of the day. "The first pleasure in the world is eating," Tho says.

Their simple meal plans could easily adapt to yours. For weekday dinners, the family usually enjoys a soup, a vegetable, and a meat or fish dish, such as the Chicken Curry pictured. Rice is the most common side dish, but is sometimes replaced by French bread, an item that was introduced to Vietnam while the French had colonial control of Indochina.

Most often Diep and Tho skip dessert, but they sometimes reach for bananas, papayas, or mangoes.

Field editor: Helen Heitkamp

MIKE JENSEN

VEGETABLE AND BEEF ROLLS
Diners cook thin beef strips in hot broth for 1 to 2 minutes, then assemble their own bundles using rice paper, an edible Vietnamese wrapper. Each bundle holds cooked beef, mint and cilantro leaves, lettuce, cucumber, and red onion. Dip the finger food in a lime-seasoned sauce.

From Diep's kitchen to yours: *Chicken Curry* (*lower right*) is often served for family meals because it's quick to prepare. The *Vegetable and Beef Rolls* (*upper center*) are festive and fun because the diners get in on the cooking action.

10

INDONESIAN
ROBUST AND EASY

LIAN AND JAMES GOEI, SR., share recipes with grandchildren (from left) Michéle, Michael, and Nicole.

"The grandchildren always say, 'Grandma, please, make saté,'" says Lian Goei. Her 23 grandchildren know what's good. Now you can sample a taste of Indonesia with Lian's saté (sa-TAY)—marinated strips of grilled beef, pork, or chicken served with crunchy vegetables and dipping sauces.

Lian and her husband, James, have passed on the family recipes to their six sons and one daughter. She says that her daughters-in-law, who didn't grow up eating Indonesian foods, are now very enthusiastic about the specialties.

"Everybody likes saté and noodles—anything that's not spicy hot," Lian says. Since moving to the United States in 1960, Lian has introduced many friends to appealing Indonesian seasonings, herbs, and spices. For entertaining, she likes the easy, fast-to-make quality of Indonesian foods.

In her own home, Lian and James eat spicy Indonesian meals daily with an occasional switch to Dutch, Chinese, or typically American foods. Asian markets abound in the Los Angeles area where the Goeis live, but Lian finds the cilantro (coriander) and ginger at the neighborhood supermarket. She occasionally asks friends to bring hard-to-find items from Indonesia. However, there's an Americanized touch to her cooking, too; she uses catsup in the sweet and sour sauce for Foo Yong Hay.

Field editor: Joan Dektar
Food stylist: Judy Tills

The Goei's dine on *Foo Yong Hay* (*front*), a hearty meal, for a busy weeknight. Along with *Chicken Saté* and *Pork Saté* (*center back*) Lian serves *Peanut Sauce* (*far back*), chopped onions, and hot peppers to spoon over the meat.

FOO YONG HAY
Pork, shrimp, eggs, and seasonings are the basics of this entrée. For each patty, drop ⅓ cup of the batter onto a hot griddle or skillet. Cook the patties just 2 minutes on 1 side or till they bubble and become slightly dry around the edges. Flip and cook 2 minutes more.

THE FLAVORS THAT MAKE THE DIFFERENCE

Tofu   Cloud ears   Lotus root

CHINESE

The Chinese stand out among the world's most resourceful cooks. From their almost limitless choices of ingredients, we selected three for you to sample.

Tofu, also called soybean curd, is an inexpensive protein source to people throughout the world. Mild-flavored and cream-colored, tofu absorbs the tastes of saucy mixtures.

Many kinds of mushrooms flavor Chinese cooking. The dried **cloud ear** must be softened in water before cooking. Try its assertive flavor in stir-fried dishes.

Lotus, a water plant, offers roots, leaves, paste, flour, seeds, and buds for cooking. Raw, the *lotus root* can give crunch to a recipe; cooked, it can replace potatoes in soups and stews. It's good for pickling, too. The most widely available forms are canned, dried, and sugared.

Lemongrass   Fish sauce   Coconut milk

VIETNAMESE

Vietnamese cuisine combines influences of China, India, all of Southeast Asia, and France. Foods in the north are rich with chilies. In the south there's an abundance of fruits and seafood. Though similar to Chinese food, Vietnamese cooking relies on French seasonings.

Lemongrass looks like a fibrous green onion and lends its pungent, lemonlike flavor as a seasoning to main dishes. Buy it fresh or dried.

Fish sauce is an ever-present seasoning used both in cooking and at the table. It has a bold, salty flavor.

Coconut milk, a smooth, rich liquid made from the meat of fresh coconuts, is a favorite ingredient in sauces, desserts, and beverages. You can make coconut milk from fresh coconut or buy the milk in cans.

Shrimp crackers   Laos   Sweet soy sauce

INDONESIAN

The cuisine of Indonesia, a nation of islands, delights the senses: sweet, sour, salty, and sometimes hot! Foods are laced with the delightful variety of seasonings found throughout the Spice Islands.

Shrimp crackers often are served with meals. Made from dried shrimp and egg white, the crackers swell into crisp and puffy wafers when deep-fried. You can purchase them prefried, too.

Laos (galanga root) looks like ginger; its mild flavor enhances curries and fritters. You can buy it frozen or dried.

Indonesian **sweet soy sauce** is sweeter, darker, and thicker than the soy sauce with which most Americans are familiar. Called *ketjap* by Indonesians, sweet soy sauce is used to flavor a variety of foods, including grilled meats.

Coriander   Hot chilies   Shrimp paste

THAI

Thai and Indonesian cookery are closely related. Cooks take advantage of the tropical abundance in both countries to make outstanding food. The most distinctive ingredient in Thai cooking is **coriander root.** In addition, the *coriander leaves* (cilantro) and *seeds* are used extensively in Thailand as they are in other Southeast Asian countries. Add the hearty flavor of the root, leaves, or the crushed seeds to soups, stews, and sauces.

Hot chilies belong to almost every Asian cuisine. In Thailand they are used both in cooking and as a condiment. Use chilies sparingly until you find the hotness level you like best. Handle chilies with gloved hands; they may cause a burning sensation on your skin.

Shrimp paste is a thick mixture of shrimp, chilies, and curry. Use it sparingly in meat mixtures.

SHRIMP-BACON STIR-FRY

Whole gingerroot can be wrapped in moisture- and vaporproof wrap and stored in the freezer. Grate it without thawing, using the finest blade of a grater as you would to finely shred orange or lemon peel—

- 1 **pound fresh *or* frozen peeled and deveined medium shrimp**
- ¼ **cup bias-sliced green onions**
- 3 **tablespoons dry sherry**
- 1 **teaspoon finely grated gingerroot**
- ¼ **cup chicken broth**
- 2 **teaspoons cornstarch**
- 4 **slices bacon, cut into small pieces**
- 1 **tablespoon cooking oil**
- 1 **cup frozen peas**
- ½ **of an 8-ounce can (½ cup) bamboo shoots, cut into julienne strips**

Hot cooked rice

Thaw shrimp, if frozen. In a large mixing bowl stir together green onions, sherry, and gingerroot. Add shrimp; toss to coat. Cover and marinate in the refrigerator for 2 hours.

Drain shrimp and onions, reserving marinade. In a small mixing bowl combine the reserved marinade, chicken broth, and cornstarch.

Preheat a wok or large skillet over high heat. Add bacon and stir-fry for 1 to 2 minutes or till crisp. Remove bacon and set aside; discard drippings. Add cooking oil to wok. Stir-fry shrimp and onions, *half* at a time, over medium-high heat for 2 to 3 minutes or till done. Return all shrimp and onions to wok. Stir in bacon, peas, and bamboo shoots; push mixture to sides of wok.

Add marinade mixture to center of wok (see how-to photo, page 9). Cook and stir till thickened and bubbly. Push shrimp-vegetable mixture into the sauce. Cook and stir for 2 minutes more. Season to taste with salt and pepper. Serve over hot cooked rice. Pass soy sauce, if desired. Makes 4 servings.

Nutrition information per serving: 351 cal., 29 g pro., 36 g carbo., 9 g fat, 188 mg chol., 767 mg sodium. U.S. RDA: 16% vit. C, 22% thiamine, 31% niacin, 10% calcium, 22% iron, and 28% phosphorus.

CHINESE BUNS

If your steamer rack is too small for all 10 buns at once, refrigerate half while the others steam. Or, in place of a steamer, invert a heat-proof bowl in a Dutch oven. Add water to almost cover bowl; bring to boiling. Set a round wire cooking rack or foil pie plate punched with holes on top of bowl to hold the buns—

- 3¼ **to 3¾ cups all-purpose flour**
- 1 **package active dry yeast**
- 1 **cup milk**
- 2 **tablespoons sugar**
- 1 **tablespoon shortening**
- ½ **teaspoon salt**
- 2 **egg whites**
- 10 **dried black mushrooms**
- 2 **tablespoons oyster sauce**
- 1 **tablespoon water**
- 1½ **teaspoons cornstarch**
- 1 **tablespoon cooking oil**
- 1 **teaspoon grated gingerroot**
- 2 **green onions, sliced**
- ½ **pound lean boneless pork, diced**
- 1 **teaspoon sugar**
- 1 **teaspoon soy sauce**
- ¼ **teaspoon white pepper**
- ½ **of an 8-ounce can bamboo shoots, drained and chopped**

For dough, in a large mixer bowl stir together *1 cup* of flour and yeast. In a small saucepan heat milk, 2 tablespoons sugar, shortening, and salt till just warm (115° to 120°) and shortening is almost melted, stirring constantly. Add to flour mixture. Add egg whites.

Beat with an electric mixer on low speed for ½ minute, scraping sides of bowl constantly. Beat on high speed for 3 minutes. Using a spoon, stir in as much remaining flour as you can.

Turn dough out onto a lightly floured surface. Knead in enough of the remaining flour to make a moderately stiff dough (6 to 8 minutes). Place dough in a greased bowl; turn once to grease surface. Cover and let rise till nearly double (about 1 hour).

Meanwhile, prepare filling: In a small bowl soak mushrooms in enough hot water to cover for 30 minutes. Remove stems. Rinse, drain, pat dry, and finely chop mushroom caps; set aside. Combine oyster sauce, water, and cornstarch; set aside.

Preheat a wok or large skillet over high heat; add cooking oil. Stir-fry gingerroot in hot oil for 15 seconds. Add green onions; stir-fry for 1 minute. Add more oil to wok, if necessary. Add pork, 1 teaspoon sugar, soy sauce, and pepper to the hot wok. Stir-fry about 3 minutes or till meat is no longer pink. Push mixture to sides of wok.

Stir oyster sauce mixture; add to center of wok. Cook and stir till thickened and bubbly. Cook and stir for 2 minutes more. Stir in mushrooms and bamboo shoots. Remove wok from heat.

Punch dough down. Divide into 10 pieces. Flatten each into a 4-inch circle. Place a scant *¼ cup* of the pork filling in the center of 1 piece of dough. Bring up edges, seal seams, and place, seam side down, on a 2-inch square of waxed paper (see how-to photo, page 9). Repeat with remaining dough and filling. Cover and let rise in a warm place about 20 minutes or till double.

Meanwhile, in a steamer bring water for steaming to boiling over high heat. Place buns and waxed paper on steamer rack so sides don't touch. Place steamer rack over boiling water. Cover and steam about 15 minutes or till done. Serve immediately. Makes 10.

Nutrition information per bun: 282 cal., 11 g pro., 37 g carbo., 10 g fat, 19 mg chol., 457 mg sodium. U.S. RDA: 33% thiamine, 20% riboflavin, 20% niacin, 13% iron, and 13% phosphorus.

VEGETABLE BEEF WITH RICE CAKE

Rice cake rolls are a compressed rice-flour product found in the frozen food case of Oriental food markets. Cooked rice cakes have a chewy texture and may become sticky while cooking. Cooking the rice cake rolls in broth helps prevent them from becoming too sticky—

  8 **ounces frozen rice cake rolls**
  ½ **pound beef round steak, cut ½ inch thick**
  2 **tablespoons soy sauce**
  2 **tablespoons dry sherry**
  2 **green onions, sliced**
  ½ **teaspoon grated gingerroot**
  3 **tablespoons cooking oil**
  1 **bunch bok choy, sliced (about 4 cups)**
  1 **15-ounce can straw mushrooms, drained**
  1 **8-ounce can bamboo shoots, drained**
  2 **green onions, sliced**
  2 **tablespoons fresh *or* frozen snipped chives**
Chicken broth

Thaw rice cake rolls in refrigerator overnight. Let stand at room temperature for 2 hours before cooking. Partially freeze beef. Bias-slice beef across the grain into thin bite-size strips.

Place beef in a plastic bag set in a deep bowl. Combine soy sauce, sherry, 2 green onions, and gingerroot. Pour over beef. Close bag. Marinate in the refrigerator for 1 to 2 hours, turning the bag occasionally to distribute marinade. Drain well, reserving marinade.

Bias-slice rice cake rolls into ¼-inch slices; set aside. Heat *2 tablespoons* of the oil in a wok. Add bok choy, mushrooms, bamboo shoots, 2 green onions, and chives. Stir-fry for 3 minutes or till bok choy is crisp-tender. Remove vegetables and juices from wok.

Heat remaining oil in wok. Add beef to wok. Stir-fry for 3 minutes or till no longer pink. Remove from wok.

Add ¼ cup chicken broth and reserved marinade to wok. Add bias-sliced rice cake rolls. Stir constantly for 2 to 3 minutes or till rice cake slices soften, adding more chicken broth as necessary to prevent rice cake slices from sticking together. Return beef and vegetables to wok. Heat through. Serve immediately. Makes 4 servings.

Nutrition information per serving: 378 cal., 24 g pro., 36 g carbo., 15 g fat, 52 mg chol., 1,236 mg sodium. U.S. RDA: 45% vit. A, 42% vit. C, 22% thiamine, 24% riboflavin, 41% niacin, 16% calcium, 28% iron, 30% phosphorus.

VEGETABLE AND BEEF ROLLS

If you prefer, heat beef broth, vinegar, and pepper to boiling in a 10- or 11-inch electric skillet and place it in the middle of your dining table. Reduce heat to simmer and cook meat as directed—

  1 **pound beef top round *or* sirloin steak, cut 2 inches thick**
  1 **package 8-inch-round dried rice papers, halved**
  4 **cups beef broth**
  2 **cups rice *or* white vinegar**
Black pepper
Lettuce leaves (Boston, green, *or* red leaf lettuce)
  1 **small cucumber, sliced and cut into strips**
  ⅓ **cup fresh cilantro *or* parsley sprigs**
  ⅓ **cup fresh mint leaves (optional)**
  1 **red onion, sliced and separated into rings (optional)**
  1 **recipe Dipping Sauce (see recipe, right)**

Partially freeze beef. Bias-slice beef across the grain into thin bite-size strips. Separate rice papers; soak in water for 2 minutes. Drain on a dish towel.

About 20 minutes before serving, in a large saucepan combine beef broth, rice or white vinegar, and pepper to taste. Transfer enough broth mixture to a fondue pot or an electric skillet to fill to a depth of about 2 inches. (Keep remaining mixture warm over low heat to refill fondue pot during serving.)

Place the fondue pot over heating unit. On a large serving platter arrange meat strips, rice papers, lettuce leaves, cucumber slices, cilantro or parsley, and mint, if desired.

To serve, allow each diner to use chopsticks or forks to dip meat and onions, if desired, into the simmering broth. (Allow 30 to 60 seconds cooking time for the meat; 2 minutes for the onion.) Remove from the broth.

Place meat and lettuce, cucumber, cilantro or parsley, and mint, if desired, onto rice paper (see how-to photo, page 10). Roll up and serve with Dipping Sauce. Makes 4 to 6 servings.

Nutrition information per serving with Dipping Sauce: 508 cal., 31 g pro., 62 g carbo., 16 g fat, 81 mg chol., 1,135 mg sodium. U.S. RDA: 46% vit. A, 160% vit. C, 13% thiamine, 18% riboflavin, 35% niacin, 29% iron, and 32% phosphorus.

DIPPING SAUCE

When you look for fish sauce at the Oriental market, you may need to ask for it by its Vietnamese name, nuoc cham—

  3 **tablespoons sugar**
  2 **red *or* green chili peppers, seeded and finely chopped**
  4 **cloves garlic, minced**
  ⅓ **cup lime juice**
  2 **tablespoons white vinegar**
  2 **tablespoons fish sauce *or* soy sauce**
  2 **teaspoons water**

In a small mixing bowl stir together sugar, red or green chili peppers, and garlic. Stir in lime juice, vinegar, fish sauce or soy sauce, and water. Makes about ⅔ cup sauce.

CHICKEN CURRY

Fresh lemongrass has the appearance of a fibrous green onion. Remove the tough outer layers to reveal a tender white center and chop into fine pieces—

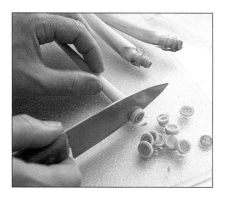

- ½ cup water
- 2 teaspoons brown sugar
- 2 teaspoons curry powder
- 2 teaspoons sesame oil
- 1 teaspoon salt
- ¼ teaspoon pepper
- 1 tablespoon cooking oil
- 1 small onion, finely chopped (¼ cup)
- 5 cloves garlic, minced
- 1 stalk fresh lemongrass, chopped (1 tablespoon), *or* 1 teaspoon finely shredded lemon peel
- 1½ pounds chicken breasts and thighs, skinned, boned, and cut into bite-size strips
- 1 tablespoon cooking oil
- 3 medium sweet potatoes, peeled and cut into julienne strips (about 4 cups)
- 3 carrots, thinly bias sliced
- 1 14-ounce can coconut milk
- French bread slices *or* hot cooked rice (optional)

In a small mixing bowl stir together water, brown sugar, curry, sesame oil, salt, and pepper; set aside.

Preheat a wok or large skillet over high heat. Add 1 tablespoon cooking oil. Add onion, garlic, and lemongrass or lemon peel; stir-fry in hot oil for 1 minute. Remove from the wok or skillet.

Stir-fry chicken, *half* at a time, for 2 to 3 minutes or till chicken is tender. Remove chicken from the wok or skillet; set aside.

Add 1 tablespoon oil to the hot wok or skillet. Add sweet potatoes; stir-fry about 3 minutes or till sweet potatoes are light brown. Add carrots.

Stir curry mixture into the vegetable mixture in the wok or skillet. Bring to boiling; reduce heat. Simmer, covered, for 10 to 15 minutes or till sweet potatoes and carrots are tender.

Gently stir onion mixture, chicken, and coconut milk into the vegetable mixture in the wok or skillet. Cook and stir over medium heat till mixture is heated through. Serve immediately with French bread slices or hot cooked rice. Makes 4 to 6 servings.

Nutrition information per serving: 586 cal., 24 g pro., 37 g carbo., 39 g fat, 66 mg chol., 647 mg sodium. U.S. RDA: 299% vit. A, 51% vit. C, 14% thiamine, 14% riboflavin, 42% niacin, 23% iron, and 33% phosphorus.

SWEET AND SOUR SAUCE

Sweet soy sauce is thicker and more syruplike than ordinary soy sauce. Look for bottles of it in Oriental markets—

- ⅓ cup cold water
- 2 teaspoons cornstarch
- 2 teaspoons brown sugar
- ⅓ cup catsup
- 2 teaspoons white vinegar
- 1 teaspoon sweet soy sauce *or* soy sauce
- Dash salt

In a small saucepan stir together water, cornstarch, and brown sugar. Stir in catsup, white vinegar, sweet soy sauce or soy sauce, and salt. Cook and stir till thickened and bubbly. Cook and stir for 2 minutes more. Serve warm. Makes about ⅔ cup sauce.

FOO YONG HAY

When you have leftover pork, but no cooked shrimp, use a 4½-ounce can shrimp, drained, for the fresh shrimp—

- 3 eggs
- 1 tablespoon brown sugar
- ½ teaspoon garlic powder
- ¼ teaspoon pepper
- ¾ pound ground pork, cooked
- ¼ pound cooked, shelled shrimp, finely chopped (about ¾ cup)
- ½ cup chopped celery
- 1 medium onion, chopped (½ cup)
- 4 green onions, thinly sliced (¼ cup)
- ¼ cup all-purpose flour
- 1 tablespoon cooking oil *or* peanut oil
- Boston lettuce leaves
- 1 medium tomato, sliced
- 1 recipe Sweet and Sour Sauce (see recipe, below left)
- ½ cup hot cooked peas

In a large bowl beat together eggs, sugar, garlic powder, and pepper. Stir in cooked ground pork, cooked shrimp, celery, chopped onion, and green onions. Stir in flour.

Heat cooking or peanut oil on a griddle or in a 10-inch skillet. For *each* patty, drop a scant ⅓ *cup* pork mixture onto the hot griddle or skillet. Cook over medium-low heat about 2 minutes on each side or till light brown (see how-to photo, page 11).

To serve, arrange patties down center of a lettuce-lined platter. Tuck tomato slices between patties. Spoon Sweet and Sour Sauce down the center of patties. Sprinkle with hot cooked peas. Makes 4 servings.

Nutrition information per serving with sauce: 445 cal., 29 g pro., 26 g carbo., 25 g fat, 283 mg chol., 521 mg sodium. U.S. RDA: 28% vit. A, 34% vit. C, 49% thiamine, 22% riboflavin, 27% niacin, 10% calcium, 29% iron, 37% phosphorus.

PORK SATÉ

The marinade gives the pork strips a deep, rich mahogany glaze—

- 1½ **pounds boneless pork loin** *or* **beef sirloin, cut 1 inch thick**
- ½ **cup sweet soy sauce**
- 3 **tablespoons lime juice (1 to 2 limes)**
- 1 **tablespoon finely chopped cilantro** *or* **parsley**
- 4 *or* 5 **cloves garlic, minced**
- ½ **teaspoon pepper**
Fresh fruit (optional)

Partially freeze the pork or beef. Bias-slice meat across the grain into 3x¼-inch strips. Loosely thread the meat strips accordion-style onto 12 skewers. Set aside.

For soy marinade, in a small mixing bowl stir together sweet soy sauce, lime juice, chopped cilantro or parsley, garlic, and pepper.

Pour marinade into a large shallow baking dish. Place the 12 skewers in marinade, turning to coat all sides.

Cover and marinate for 2 hours in the refrigerator, turning skewers several times and spooning marinade evenly over meat. Drain, reserving marinade.

Place skewers on unheated rack of a broiler pan. Broil 4 to 5 inches from the heat for 6 to 8 minutes or till meat is tender, turning and brushing often with the reserved marinade. (Or, grill skewers over *medium-hot* coals for 6 to 8 minutes, turning and brushing often with reserved marinade.)

Serve immediately with fresh fruit, if desired. Makes 6 servings.
Nutrition information per serving: 383 cal., 20 g pro., 11 g carbo., 28 g fat, 70 mg chol., 954 mg sodium. U.S. RDA: 63% thiamine, 15% riboflavin, 26% niacin, 20% iron, and 24% phosphorus.

CHICKEN SATÉ

For your ease and convenience, you can purchase chicken already skinned and boned. You'll need about 1 pound of chicken breast meat and 12 ounces of chicken thigh meat—

- 2 **whole large chicken breasts, skinned and boned**
- 3 **chicken thighs, skinned and boned**
- ½ **cup sweet soy sauce**
- 3 **tablespoons lime juice**
- 1 **teaspoon garlic salt**
Lime *or* **lemon wedges (optional)**
- 1 **recipe Peanut Sauce (see recipe, below right)**
Sweet soy sauce (optional)
Ground black pepper (optional)
Chopped green onions (optional)
Chopped fresh chili peppers (optional)

Cut chicken into 2x½-inch strips. Loosely thread chicken strips accordion-style onto 12 skewers. Set aside.

For soy marinade, in a small mixing bowl stir together ½ cup sweet soy sauce, lime juice, and garlic salt.

Pour soy marinade into a large shallow baking dish. Place the 12 skewers in the marinade, turning to coat all sides. Cover the baking dish and marinate for 2 hours in the refrigerator, turning the skewers several times and spooning marinade evenly over chicken. Drain, reserving marinade.

Place the skewers on the unheated rack of a broiler pan. Broil 4 to 5 inches from the heat for 5 to 7 minutes or till chicken is tender, turning and brushing often with the reserved soy marinade. (Or, grill skewers over *medium-hot* coals for 5 to 7 minutes or till chicken is tender, turning and brushing often with marinade.) Transfer the skewers to a serving platter. Garnish with lime or lemon wedges, if desired.

Serve immediately. To serve, remove the chicken from the skewers. Squeeze lime or lemon wedges over chicken. Spread Peanut Sauce on the chicken. Top with desired condiments. Makes 6 servings.
Nutrition information per serving with sauce: 518 cal., 49 g pro., 21 g carbo., 28 g fat, 41 mg chol., 1,714 mg sodium. U.S. RDA: 23% riboflavin, 92% niacin, 21% iron, and 54% phosphorus.

PEANUT SAUCE

Not only does this sauce add character to Chicken Saté; it's also delicious on fresh fruit—

- 1 **cup creamy peanut butter**
- 1 **tablespoon brown sugar**
- 1 **tablespoon soy sauce**
- 1 **tablespoon milk**
Peanuts (optional)

In a small skillet heat peanut butter. Stir in brown sugar, soy sauce, and milk. Cook and stir to a thick paste over medium heat. Transfer to a serving dish. Sprinkle peanuts over peanut butter mixture, if desired. Makes about 1 cup sauce.

FEBRUARY

CHOCOLATES
Homemade Candies That Say 'I Love You!'
♥ ♥ ♥   By Diana McMillen   ♥ ♥ ♥

BE-MINE
BONBONS

FORGET-ME-NOT FUDGE

18

C hocolate... luscious, rich, decadent! Treat your sweetheart to these homemade candies—a food gift from the heart. You'll discover what fun (and how easy) it is to dip and mold sweets.

Photographs: Scott Little
Food stylist: Janet Pittman

Use a wooden toothpick to gently remove Forget-Me-Not Fudge from candy molds.

Use a fork or chocolate dipper to dip candy in coating. Drag across edge of pan to remove excess chocolate.

FORGET-ME-NOT FUDGE

 2 cups sugar
 1 5⅓-ounce can evaporated milk
 ½ cup butter *or* margarine
 1 6-ounce package semisweet chocolate pieces
 ½ of a 7-ounce jar marshmallow creme
 ½ cup finely chopped almonds, toasted
 ¼ teaspoon peppermint extract

Lightly oil individual plastic or metal candy molds. In a buttered heavy 3-quart saucepan combine sugar, milk, and butter or margarine. Cook over medium-high heat to boiling, stirring constantly to dissolve sugar (about 6 minutes). Avoid splashing mixture on sides of pan. Carefully clip candy thermometer to saucepan. Cook over medium heat, stirring frequently, till thermometer registers 236°, soft-ball stage (9 to 10 minutes). The mixture should boil at a moderate, steady rate over entire surface.

Remove from heat; remove thermometer from pan. Add remaining ingredients, stirring to melt chocolate. Let stand 15 minutes. Using buttered hands, form mixture into small balls. Working quickly, press balls into molds. After all molds are filled, unmold candies using a wooden toothpick. Let stand on waxed paper till firm. Cover tightly; store in refrigerator. Makes 1½ pounds.

Per ½ ounce: 92 cal., 12 g carbo., 4 g fat, 8 mg chol., 28 mg sodium.

BE-MINE BONBONS

 ½ of a 6-ounce package dried apricots (1 cup)
 2 tablespoons orange juice
 ⅓ cup finely chopped pecans
 2 tablespoons butter *or* margarine, softened
 2 tablespoons light corn syrup
 1⅓ cups sifted powdered sugar
 8 to 10 ounces chocolate-flavored confectioners' coating

In a food processor or food grinder, finely grind apricots. In a small saucepan combine apricots and orange juice; cook till apricots are soft. Remove from heat. Stir in nuts. Cover and chill 30 minutes. Form mixture into ½-inch balls, using a slightly rounded ¼ teaspoon for each. In a medium mixing bowl combine butter or margarine and corn syrup. Stir in sugar; knead till smooth. Chill mixture if too soft to handle.

Shape about *½ teaspoon* of the sugar mixture around each apricot ball. Place on a baking sheet lined with waxed paper; chill till firm. In a medium saucepan melt confectioners' coating over low heat. Drop balls, one at a time, into melted coating. Use a dipping fork or table fork to lift candy out of the coating. Let excess coating drip off; pull fork across edge of pan to remove more coating. Place candies on baking sheet lined with waxed paper till firm. Store in a tightly covered container in a cool place. Makes about 45 candies, ¾ pound.

Per piece: 58 cal., 8 g carbo., 3 g fat, 2 mg chol., and 7 mg sodium.

Look for candy molds in kitchenware shops.

BE AN OUTSTANDING COOK!

By Diana McMillen

THE 6 SIMPLE SECRETS

Anyone can cook, but it takes some practice (and reliable recipes) to be a *great* cook. With these six cooking lessons in hand, you'll soon move to the front of the class.

HERBED LINGUINE WITH RED VEGETABLE SAUCE

Your goal: Tender pasta. How to achieve it: Properly mix, knead, roll, and cut the dough. Practice pasta making with Herbed Linguine. Next time, cut the dough into other pasta shapes, and top it with a cheese sauce.

Photographs: Scott Little. Food stylist: Janet Pittman

THINLY ROLL
Roll the dough thin for tender pasta. A scant 1/16-inch thickness is a good rule of thumb.

SLICE
Roll up the pasta dough jelly-roll style, then cut it into desired widths.

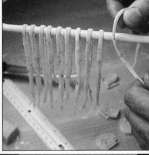

DRY
Drape the pasta over a coat hanger or drying rack; let dry several hours till it feels stiff to the touch.

Or, shape the dough with a pasta maker.

BE AN OUTSTANDING COOK!
SALMON WITH HOLLANDAISE

Patience and low heat ensure success when you prepare Hollandaise Sauce. Spoon the versatile sauce over cooked fish, chicken, vegetables, and eggs. You'll need only three ingredients to produce this sensational classic.

SLOW COOK
Slow, gentle cooking makes the difference. Use a double boiler to keep the heat low under the sauce. The water in the lower section should bubble gently without touching the top pan. Hollandaise Sauce will thicken as you cook and stir egg yolks and butter.

STIR, STIR
When all of the butter is melted, remove the top pan from water. Rapidly stir the sauce for 2 minutes, then stir in the lemon juice. Replace the sauce over the hot water. Continue cooking over low heat and stir constantly for 1 to 2 minutes more to thicken the sauce without curdling. Hollandaise should be thick but pourable.

DEEP-DISH CHERRY APPLE PIE

Your piecrusts and turnovers can be as irresistible as those found in pastry shops anywhere. Working with pastry dough is like working with clay—mold it gently but firmly. Try the technique on this two-fruit pie.

SPRINKLE
Too much water causes tough pastry. Add just enough water for the dough to cling together.

WORK GENTLY
Avoid stretching the dough! Ease pastry into pie plate so crust won't shrink.

DECORATE
A fluted edge on a piecrust is a pretty finish, but it also prevents the pie filling from seeping out.

Use either pastry or hors d'oeuvre cutters.

23

BE AN OUTSTANDING COOK!

BOURSIN-STUFFED CHICKEN

Try your hand at company-special stuffed meats. The culinary trick lies in how much you pound the meat. Begin with the chicken breast recipe below, then direct your mallet at beef round steak and veal.

POUND AWAY

Pound your choice of meat for an easy roll-up. Using the smooth side of a meat mallet, pound to the thickness or shape specified in the recipe. Strive to have the meat an even thickness, too, so it will fold around the savory filling.

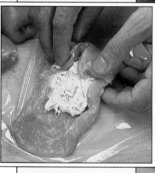

BE TIDY

Secure the meat into a bundle for a no-leak filling. To do so, spoon filling into the center of a flattened individual piece, or at 1 end of a large piece of meat. Fold in 2 opposite sides. Then roll up the meat, jelly-roll style. If the filling falls out, you may have too much of it. Secure the bundle with string or a toothpick if meat won't stay rolled up.

OAT-FRUIT MUFFIN SURPRISES

Muffins, like other quick breads, go together quickly—no creaming or kneading needed. Actually, the less you stir, the better your muffins will be. Follow the instructions on basic muffins and try some fun tricks, too.

BE CAREFUL!
Stir batter just till moistened. Overstir-ring causes tunnels and peaked tops.

FILL
Half-fill muffin cups with batter, add a surprise center, then add batter till ⅔ full.

BRUSH
For glistening muffins, brush baked ones with beaten egg white or melted butter; sprinkle with sugar.

25

DON'T GUESS
Use more than common sense to judge doneness—use a meat thermometer. The shape of meat affects cooking time; a long, thin roast cooks faster than a short, squatty one. Place thermometer in thickest meaty portion of roast so it's not touching bone.

BE AN OUTSTANDING COOK!
LA PETITE PORK ROAST
Scaled-down roasts meet the demand of today's families. They cook faster than large roasts, and leave no leftovers. The key is to roast the meat to the proper doneness.

ROASTING SMALL CUTS OF MEAT

Meat	Approx. Weight	Oven	Internal Temp.	Time*
BEEF				
Round tip roast	2 pounds	325°	160° (medium)	1¾-2 hours
Tenderloin	1 pound	425°	140° (rare)	½-¾ hour
Round rump roast	2 pounds	325°	160° (medium)	2-2¼ hours
Eye of round	2 pounds	350°	160° (medium)	1¼-1½ hours
PORK				
Tenderloin	¾-1 pound	325°	170° (well-done)	¾-1 hour
Boneless loin roast	1½-2 pounds	325°	170° (well-done)	1¼-1½ hours
LAMB				
Boneless leg	2-2½ pounds	325°	160° (medium)	1¼-1½ hours
Rib roast	2 pounds	325°	160° (medium)	1¼-1½ hours

*Roasting times may vary depending on the diameter of the roast.

SWEET-AND-SIMPLE REAL CHOCOLATE COATING

Any of the dipped candies here, as well as other dipped candy recipes, can be coated with semisweet chocolate instead of confectioners' coating. You'll need to allow extra preparation time for following these simple instructions—

  3 **cups semisweet chocolate pieces *or* miniature semisweet chocolate pieces**
  ¼ **cup shortening (*not* butter, margarine, *or* oil)**

In a 4-cup glass measure or 1½-quart glass mixing bowl stir together chocolate pieces and shortening. Set chocolate mixture aside.

In a large glass mixing bowl pour very warm tap water (100° to 110°) to a depth of 1 inch. Place glass measure or bowl containing chocolate mixture inside the large bowl. The water should cover the bottom half of the measure or bowl containing the chocolate mixture.

Stir chocolate mixture *constantly* with a rubber spatula until chocolate is completely melted and the mixture is smooth. This will take about 20 minutes; don't rush the process.

If water begins to cool, remove the bowl containing the chocolate mixture. Discard cool water and add more warm water. Return glass measure or bowl of chocolate mixture to the bowl containing water. (Be careful not to get *any* water in the chocolate mixture. Even one drop of water can cause the chocolate to become dull and gummy. If this happens, stir in additional *shortening,* 1 teaspoon at a time, until mixture becomes shiny and smooth again.)

Using a fork or chocolate dipper, dip desired candy, one at a time, into melted chocolate mixture as directed in candy recipe. Continue as directed.

If the chocolate becomes too thick while dipping, remove the glass measure or bowl of chocolate mixture from larger bowl containing water and replace water as directed above. Return glass measure or bowl of chocolate mixture to bowl containing water. Stir mixture constantly till it again reaches dipping consistency. Continue dipping.

Store coated candies, covered, in a cool, dry place between 65° and 70°. Use this coating in dipped candy recipes calling for 1 pound chocolate-flavored confectioners' coating.

CHERISH-ME CHERRIES

 60 **maraschino cherries with stems (about three 10-ounce jars)**
  3 **tablespoons butter *or* margarine, softened**
  3 **tablespoons light corn syrup**
  1 **tablespoon pink crème d'almond**
 2¾ **cups sifted powdered sugar**
  1 **pound chocolate-flavored confectioners' coating**

Drain cherries thoroughly on paper towels for several hours. In a small bowl combine butter or margarine, syrup, and crème d'almond. Stir in powdered sugar; knead till smooth. For easier shaping, cover and chill 1 hour.

Shape about ¾ *teaspoon* of the powdered sugar mixture around *each* cherry. Place coated cherries upright on a baking sheet lined with waxed paper; chill till firm.

In a double boiler melt about *one-fourth* of the confectioners' coating over hot, but not boiling, water. Add remaining coating, about *one-fourth* at a time, stirring till melted after each addition.

Holding the coated cherries by the stems, dip cherries, one at a time, into the melted confectioners' coating. Spoon coating over the cherries to coat; seal the cherries completely in coating to prevent any cherry juice from leaking out once the chocolate sets. Let excess coating drip off cherries. (Or, dip cherries following the procedure in Sweet-and-Simple Real Chocolate Coating recipe, left.)

Place dipped cherries, stem up, on a baking sheet lined with waxed paper. Let stand in a cool, dry place between 65° and 70° till coating is firm. If desired, decorate as directed on page 28.

Place cherries in a covered container. Let stand to ripen in a cool, dry place between 65° and 70° for 1 to 2 weeks. Store, covered, in a cool, dry place. Makes 60 covered cherries.

Nutrition information per candy: 65 cal., 0 g pro., 13 g carbo., 1 g fat, 2 mg chol., 23 mg sodium.

TRUE-LOVE TRUFFLES

  2 **cups sugar**
  ½ **cup water**
  ¼ **cup light cream**
  1 **tablespoon light corn syrup**
  2 **tablespoons amaretto *or* coffee liqueur**
  1 **pound chocolate-flavored confectioners' coating**

Butter the sides of a heavy 2-quart saucepan. In the saucepan combine sugar, water, cream, and corn syrup. Cook over medium-high heat to boiling, stirring constantly with a wooden spoon to dissolve sugar. This should take 5 to 6 minutes. Avoid splashing mixture on the sides of the pan. Carefully clip a candy thermometer to the side of the pan.

Cook sugar mixture over medium-low heat, stirring occasionally, till the thermometer registers 240°, soft-ball stage. The mixture should boil at a moderate, steady rate over entire surface. Reaching soft-ball stage should take 15 to 20 minutes.

Remove the saucepan from the heat. Cool, without stirring, to lukewarm (110°). (If necessary, tilt saucepan to 1 side so the thermometer bulb is covered with the mixture.) This should take 45 to 50 minutes.

Remove the thermometer. Add the amaretto or coffee liqueur; beat with a wooden spoon till creamy and slightly stiff. This should take 8 to 10 minutes. When mixture becomes too stiff to beat, turn it out onto a kneading surface. Form it into a ball and knead till soft and smooth. Shape mixture into 1-inch balls; place balls on a baking sheet lined with waxed paper. Let stand at room temperature at least 20 minutes or till surface is dry.

In a medium saucepan melt confectioners' coating. Use a fork to carefully dip balls, one at a time, into melted coating. Let excess coating drip off balls. (Or, dip balls following procedure in Sweet-and-Simple Real Chocolate Coating recipe, left.)

Place dipped balls on a baking sheet lined with waxed paper. Let stand in a cool, dry place till coating is firm. If desired, decorate as directed on page 28. Store, covered, in a cool, dry place between 65° and 70°. Makes 36.

Nutrition information per candy: 101 cal., 0 g pro., 21 g carbo., 2 g fat, 2 mg chol., 27 mg sodium.

February

DESIGNER CHOCOLATES

To add that extra personal touch to your homemade dipped candies, decorate them as shown on page 17—

Follow the instructions below to decorate Be-Mine Bonbons (see recipe, page 19), True-Love Truffles (see recipe, page 27), or Cherish-Me Cherries (see recipe, page 27). Place candies on a plate, waxed paper, or other movable decorating surface.

For coating, choose between leftover melted *chocolate-flavored confectioners' coating, Sweet-and-Simple Real Chocolate Coating,* 4 ounces melted *vanilla-flavored confectioners' coating,* or a small amount melted *milk chocolate.*

Spoon coating into a pastry bag fitted with a fine writing tip. (If coating has just been melted, let it cool slightly so the pastry bag doesn't become too hot to handle.)

For spirals: Start at the top-center of a dry, dipped candy and pipe a continuous spiraled line around the candy to its base. Let stand till dry.

For flowers: Start at the top-center of a dry, dipped candy and pipe 5 "petals" joining in the top-center of the candy. Let stand till dry.

For checkerboard: Start on 1 side of the base of a dry, dipped candy and pipe 3 or 4 parallel lines, ending lines at the base of the candy on the opposite side. Give the plate, waxed paper, or decorating surface a quarter-turn. Pipe 3 or 4 more parallel lines at a 90° angle to the first group of lines. Let stand till dry.

HERBED LINGUINE WITH RED VEGETABLE SAUCE

2⅓ cups all-purpose flour
1 teaspoon dried basil, marjoram, *or* sage, crushed
½ teaspoon salt
2 beaten eggs
⅓ cup water
1 teaspoon olive *or* cooking oil
1 recipe Red Vegetable Sauce (see recipe, below right)
Grated Parmesan cheese (optional)

Step 1: In a large mixing bowl combine *2 cups* of the flour, herb, and salt. Make a well in the center. In a small mixing bowl combine eggs, water, and oil. Add to flour mixture; mix well.

Step 2: Sprinkle the kneading surface with remaining flour. Turn dough out onto the floured surface. Knead till dough is smooth and elastic (8 to 10 minutes). Cover and let dough rest for 10 minutes.

Step 3: Divide dough into fourths. On a lightly floured surface roll *one-fourth* of the dough into a 12-inch square (see how-to photo, page 21). Keep remaining dough covered while working. Repeat rolling with remaining dough. Let stand for 20 minutes to dry surface slightly.

Step 4: Roll up dough jelly-roll style. With a sharp knife cut dough into ⅛-inch-wide slices (see how-to photo, page 21). Lift and shake to separate the strands. Cook fresh pasta immediately, as directed in step 8, or dry before cooking, as directed in step 5.

Step 5: To dry, hang the cut pasta on a pasta drying rack or over a plastic or wood coat hanger (see how-to photo, page 21). Let stand for several hours or till completely dry. Remove from rack.

Step 6: To store, wrap pasta in clear plastic wrap or foil or place in an airtight container. Store in refrigerator. (Or, to freeze pasta, let the cut pasta dry at least 1 hour. Wrap the cut pasta in moisture- and vaporproof wrap. Freeze for up to 8 months.)

Step 7: To serve, prepare Red Vegetable Sauce.

Step 8: Meanwhile, to cook pasta, in a large kettle or Dutch oven bring 3 quarts *water* and 1 teaspoon *salt* to a rolling boil. If desired, add 1 tablespoon *cooking oil* to keep pasta separated. Add *8 ounces* of the pasta (half of the recipe), a little at a time, so water does not stop boiling.

Reduce heat slightly and continue boiling, uncovered, till pasta is just tender (al dente), 1½ to 2 minutes for fresh pasta or 4 minutes for dry pasta, stirring occasionally. (Tasting the pasta is the best way to tell doneness. It should be tender, but still slightly firm. Cooking time will vary with the degree of dryness.) Immediately drain.

Transfer pasta to a heated serving dish. Spoon sauce on top. Sprinkle with Parmesan cheese, if desired. Makes 6 side-dish servings.

Nutrition information per serving with sauce: 210 cal., 6 g pro., 29 g carbo., 6 g fat, 42 mg chol., 420 mg sodium. U.S. RDA: 23% vit. A, 41% vit. C, 18% thiamine, 21% riboflavin, 20% niacin, 11% iron, and 12% phosphorus.

RED VEGETABLE SAUCE

3 cups sliced fresh mushrooms (8 ounces)
1 medium onion, chopped (½ cup)
1 clove garlic, minced
2 tablespoons olive *or* cooking oil
1 8-ounce can tomato sauce
1 7½-ounce can tomatoes, cut up
½ cup dry red wine
¼ cup snipped parsley
1 teaspoon sugar
¾ teaspoon dried basil, marjoram, *or* sage, crushed
1 medium zucchini, sliced (2 cups)

Step 1: In a 3-quart saucepan cook mushrooms, onion, and garlic in hot oil over medium-high heat about 5 minutes or till the onions are tender but not brown.

Step 2: Stir in tomato sauce, *undrained* tomatoes, wine, parsley, sugar, and herb. Bring to boiling; reduce heat. Cook, uncovered, for 20 to 25 minutes or till slightly thicker than desired.

Step 3: Stir in zucchini. Simmer, uncovered, about 5 minutes more or till zucchini is tender. Makes 3½ cups.

CLASSIC HOLLANDAISE SAUCE

Make this pretty, lemony sauce a part of your cooking repertoire—

- 4 **egg yolks**
- ½ **cup butter** *or* **margarine, cut into thirds and at room temperature**
- 2 **tablespoons lemon juice**

Dash salt

Dash white pepper

Step 1: In the top of a double boiler combine egg yolks and a *third* of the butter or margarine. Place pan over, but not touching, gently boiling water. (Water in the bottom of the double boiler should not touch the top pan.) Cook, stirring rapidly till butter melts.

Step 2: Add another *third* of butter or margarine; continue stirring rapidly. As butter or margarine melts and mixture thickens, add remaining butter or margarine, stirring constantly (see how-to photo, page 22).

Step 3: When butter or margarine is melted, remove the pan from water; stir rapidly for 2 minutes more. Stir in lemon juice, 1 teaspoon at a time (see how-to photo, page 22). Stir in salt and white pepper.

Heat again over gently boiling water, stirring constantly with a heat-proof rubber spatula or wire whisk for 1 to 2 minutes more or till thickened. Watch closely to avoid overcooking.

Step 4: Remove from heat at once. If sauce curdles, immediately beat in 1 to 2 tablespoons *boiling water.* To keep the sauce warm for a short time, pour sauce into a serving container; carefully set in a bowl of warm water. Serve over fish, poached eggs, or cooked vegetables. Makes ¾ cup.

Nutrition information per 3 table-spoons: 264 cal., 3 g pro., 1 g carbo., 28 g fat, 323 mg chol., 289 mg sodium. U.S. RDA: 30% vit. A, 10% phosphorus.

SALMON WITH HOLLANDAISE

Cooked broccoli and fresh lemon slices are a perfect addition to this scrumptious entrée—

- 1 **pound fresh** *or* **frozen salmon steaks**
- 1 **recipe Classic Hollandaise Sauce (see recipe, left)**

Step 1: Thaw salmon steaks, if frozen. If necessary, cut salmon into 4 serving-size portions; rinse. Measure the thickness of the salmon.

Step 2: In a 10-inch skillet bring 1 cup *water* to boiling; add salmon. Add more water, if necessary, to half-cover salmon. Return water to boiling; reduce heat. Simmer, covered, till salmon flakes easily when tested with a fork. Allow 4 to 6 minutes cooking time for each ½ inch of thickness.

Step 3: Meanwhile, prepare Classic Hollandaise Sauce. Transfer the cooked salmon to a plate. Spoon sauce atop. Makes 4 servings.

Nutrition information per serving with sauce: 440 cal., 24 g pro., 1 g carbo., 37 g fat, 385 mg chol., 348 mg sodium. U.S. RDA: 82% vit. A, 13% thiamine, 12% riboflavin, 17% niacin, and 41% phosphorus.

PERFECT PASTRY

Don't stop at pies! This two-crust pastry is versatile enough to appear in a variety of creative recipes—

- 2 **cups all-purpose flour**
- ½ **teaspoon salt**
- ⅔ **cup shortening** *or* **lard**
- 6 **to 7 tablespoons cold water**

Step 1: In a medium bowl combine flour and salt. Cut in shortening or lard till pieces are the size of small peas.

Step 2: Sprinkle *1 tablespoon* of cold water over part of the flour mixture; gently toss with a fork. Push to side of bowl. Repeat till all is moistened (see how-to photo, page 23). Divide flour mixture in half; form into 2 balls. Continue as directed in your recipe.

DEEP-DISH CHERRY APPLE PIE

- 2 **cups frozen pitted tart red cherries (10 ounces)** *or* **one 16-ounce can pitted tart red cherries**
- 1 **cup sugar**
- 3 **tablespoons quick-cooking tapioca**
- 4 **cups peeled, cored, and thinly sliced cooking apples (2 pounds)**
- 1 **recipe Perfect Pastry (see recipe, below left)**
- 2 **tablespoons butter** *or* **margarine**

Milk

- 2 **teaspoons sugar**
- ⅛ **teaspoon ground cinnamon**

Step 1: Thaw cherries, if frozen. *Do not drain.* For filling, in a large mixing bowl combine 1 cup sugar and tapioca. Add *undrained* cherries and apples; toss lightly to coat. Let stand for 20 minutes, stirring occasionally.

Step 2: Meanwhile, prepare Perfect Pastry. On a lightly floured surface flatten 1 ball of pastry. Roll from center to edge, forming a 13-inch circle. Ease into an 8x1½-inch round baking dish, being careful to avoid stretching (see how-to photo, page 23). Trim pastry to ½ inch beyond rim. Spoon filling into pastry; dot with butter or margarine.

Step 3: For top crust, roll out remaining pastry to a 10-inch circle. Make cutouts or cut slits for escape of steam. Place pastry over filling. Fold edges under. Seal and flute at 2-inch intervals. Make crisscross impressions with tines of fork between flutes (see how-to photo, page 23). Brush with milk. Combine 2 teaspoons sugar and cinnamon; sprinkle over top.

Step 4: To prevent overbrowning, cover edge with foil. Bake in a 375° oven about 60 minutes or till golden. Remove foil after half of the baking time. Makes 8 to 10 servings.

Nutrition information per serving: 450 cal., 4 g pro., 65 g carbo., 20 g fat, 10 mg chol., 173 mg sodium.

SAUSAGE APPLE TURNOVERS

Show off your pastry-making ability during the main course with these hearty individual pies—

- 1 **pound bulk pork sausage**
- 1 **small onion, chopped (⅓ cup)**
- 1 **medium cooking apple, cored and chopped (1¼ cups)**
- ½ **cup raisins**
- ½ **of an 8-ounce can tomato sauce**
- ¼ **teaspoon ground cinnamon**
- 1 **recipe Perfect Pastry (see recipe, page 29)**

Milk
Plain yogurt *or* **dairy sour cream**

Step 1: For the turnover filling, in a large skillet cook pork sausage and onion till sausage is brown and onion is tender but not brown. Drain sausage mixture well. Stir in apple, raisins, tomato sauce, and cinnamon.

Sausage Apple Turnovers

Step 2: Prepare Perfect Pastry. Divide the pastry into 5 portions. On a lightly floured surface roll each portion of pastry into a 7-inch circle. Place about ½ cup of the turnover filling in center of *each* circle. Fold the pastry over turnover filling, forming a half-moon shape. Moisten the edges and seal by pressing with the tines of a fork. Cut slits in the pastry to allow steam to escape. Brush pastry lightly with milk.

Step 3: Transfer turnovers to an ungreased baking sheet. Bake in a 375° oven for 45 to 50 minutes or till the pastry is golden. Serve warm with yogurt or sour cream. Makes 5 servings.

Nutrition information per serving: 709 cal., 15 g pro., 58 g carbo., 47 g fat, 41 mg chol., 804 mg sodium. U.S. RDA: 47% thiamine, 25% riboflavin, 23% niacin, 18% iron, 17% phosphorus.

BOURSIN-STUFFED CHICKEN

For added flair, serve the chicken bundles with cooked green beans tied in bundles with fresh chive tops—

- 2 **whole medium chicken breasts (1½ pounds), skinned, boned, and halved lengthwise**
- 1 **5-ounce package boursin cheese with garlic and herbs, softened**
- 1 **tablespoon all-purpose flour**
- ¼ **cup shredded carrot**
- ¼ **cup coarsely chopped walnuts**
- ¼ **cup snipped parsley**
- ⅓ **cup fine dry bread crumbs**
- 2 **tablespoons grated Parmesan cheese**
- 2 **tablespoons butter** *or* **margarine, melted**

Step 1: Place 1 chicken breast half, boned side up, between 2 pieces of clear plastic wrap. Using the smooth side of a meat mallet, pound lightly. Work from the center of the chicken breast half to the edges to form a 5½-inch square (see how-to photo, page 24). Remove the clear plastic wrap. Repeat with the remaining chicken breast halves.

Step 2: In a small mixer bowl beat together boursin cheese and flour till smooth. Stir in carrot, walnuts, and *2 tablespoons* of parsley. Place *one-fourth* of the cheese mixture on *each* pounded chicken breast half.

Step 3: To roll up the chicken, fold in 2 opposite sides, then roll up jelly-roll style (see how-to photo, page 24). Press edges to seal.

Step 4: For coating, in a small mixing bowl stir together remaining parsley, fine dry bread crumbs, and Parmesan cheese. Brush the chicken bundles with melted butter or margarine. Roll bundles in the coating mixture. Place chicken bundles, seam side down, on a wire rack in an 8x8x2-inch baking dish. Sprinkle with any additional coating mixture.

Step 5: Bake in a 350° oven for 40 to 45 minutes or till the chicken is tender enough to be easily pierced with a fork and the coating mixture is golden. Makes 4 servings.

Nutrition information per serving: 435 cal., 34 g pro., 11 g carbo., 28 g fat, 60 mg chol., 243 mg sodium. U.S. RDA: 39% vit. A, 11% vit. C, 22% riboflavin, 57% niacin, and 39% phosphorus.

Beef Roll-Ups Dijon

BEEF ROLL-UPS DIJON

*To drain spinach well, place it in a col-
ander and press firmly with the back of
a wooden spoon—*

- 1 **pound boneless beef top round
  steak, cut ½ inch thick**
- 1 **small onion, chopped (⅓ cup)**
- 1 **tablespoon butter *or* margarine**
- 1 **10-ounce package frozen
  chopped spinach, thawed and
  well drained**
- ½ **cup shredded carrot**
- ½ **cup shredded Swiss cheese
  (2 ounces)**
- ¼ **teaspoon pepper**
- 1 **tablespoon butter *or* margarine**
- ½ **cup dry white wine**
- ¼ **cup water**
- 1 **tablespoon Dijon-style mustard**
- 1 **teaspoon instant beef bouillon
  granules**
- 2 **tablespoons snipped parsley**

Hot cooked noodles

Step 1: Cut beef into 4 pieces. Using a
meat mallet, pound each piece to a ⅛-
inch thickness (about 8x4 inches each).

Step 2: For filling, in a 10-inch
skillet cook onion in 1 tablespoon hot
butter or margarine till onion is tender
but not brown. Cool onion slightly; stir
in thawed spinach, shredded carrot,
cheese, and pepper.

Step 3: Place *one-fourth* of the
spinach mixture on *each* of the flattened beef rectangles. Spread the spinach mixture to within ½ inch of the
edges. Roll up beef jelly-roll style, starting from 1 of the short sides. Secure
with a wooden toothpick. Repeat with
the remaining beef.

Step 4: In the same skillet cook
beef rolls in 1 tablespoon hot butter or
margarine over medium-high heat
about 5 minutes or till brown. In a
small mixing bowl combine wine, water, mustard, and bouillon granules;
add to skillet. Bring to boiling; reduce
heat. Simmer, covered, about 30 minutes or till beef is tender, turning the
rolls over once.

Step 5: Transfer beef rolls to a
heated serving platter. Cover with foil
to keep warm. In the skillet boil the
remaining juices rapidly about 5 minutes or till reduced to ⅓ cup. Strain the
juices. Stir in parsley. Serve juices over
the beef rolls and hot cooked noodles.
Makes 4 servings.

Nutrition information per serving:
463 cal., 32 g pro., 25 g carbo., 23 g fat,
131 mg chol., 435 mg sodium. U.S.
RDA: 130% vit. A, 27% vit. C, 23% riboflavin, 29% niacin, 23% calcium,
29% iron, 37% phosphorus.

OAT-FRUIT MUFFIN SURPRISES

- 1 **3-ounce package cream cheese**
- 1 **egg yolk**
- 1¼ **cups all-purpose flour**
- ½ **cup quick-cooking rolled oats**
- ¼ **cup packed brown sugar**
- 1 **tablespoon baking powder**
- 1 **teaspoon ground cinnamon**
- ¼ **teaspoon salt**
- 1 **beaten egg**
- ¾ **cup milk**
- 3 **tablespoons cooking oil**
- ½ **cup mixed dried fruit bits**
- 1 **egg white**
- 1 **tablespoon water**
- 3 **tablespoons sugar**

Step 1: For filling, in a small mixer
bowl combine cream cheese and egg
yolk; beat with an electric mixer on medium speed till combined. Set aside.
Grease 10 muffin cups or line with foil
or paper bake cups. Set aside.

Step 2: In a medium mixing bowl
combine flour, oats, brown sugar, baking powder, cinnamon, and salt. Make
a well in the center.

Step 3: In a small mixing bowl
combine whole egg, milk, and cooking
oil. Add all at once to flour mixture (see
how-to photo, page 25). Stir just till
moistened (batter should be lumpy).
Gently fold in fruit bits.

Step 4: Spoon *half* of the batter
into prepared muffin cups. Spoon about
½ tablespoon of the cream cheese filling into *each* cup (see how-to photo,
page 25). Spoon remaining batter into
cups, filling ¾ full.

Step 5: Bake in a 400° oven for 15
to 18 minutes or till golden. Remove
from pans; cool slightly.

Step 5: In a clean small mixing
bowl combine egg white and water; stir
with a fork till well mixed. Lightly
brush mixture onto muffin tops. Sprinkle tops of muffins with sugar (see how-
to photo, page 25). Makes 10 muffins.

Nutrition information per muffin:
222 cal., 5 g pro., 30 g carbo., 10 g fat, 62
mg chol., and 197 mg sodium.

MEXICAN CHEESE BREAD

- 1½ cups all-purpose flour
- ½ cup yellow cornmeal
- 2 tablespoons sugar
- 2 teaspoons baking powder
- ½ teaspoon chili powder
- ¼ teaspoon baking soda
- 1 beaten egg
- ¾ cup buttermilk *or* sour milk
- ¼ cup cooking oil
- ½ cup shredded Monterey Jack cheese with jalapeño peppers (2 ounces)

Step 1: Grease an 8x4x2-inch loaf pan. Set aside.

Step 2: In a large mixing bowl combine flour, cornmeal, sugar, baking powder, chili powder, and baking soda. Make a well in the center. Set aside.

Step 3: In a small mixing bowl combine beaten egg, buttermilk or sour milk, and cooking oil. Add egg mixture all at once to flour mixture. Stir just till dry ingredients are moistened (batter should be lumpy). Gently fold in shredded Monterey Jack cheese.

Step 4: Turn batter into the prepared pan. Bake in a 350° oven for 45 to 50 minutes or till golden. Cool in the pan for 10 minutes. Remove from the pan; cool on a wire rack. Makes 1 loaf (sixteen ½-inch-thick slices).

Nutrition information per slice: 116 cal., 3 g pro., 14 g carbo., 5 g fat, 20 mg chol., and 93 mg sodium.

MUSHROOM SALAD WITH MUSTARD VINAIGRETTE

Serve this as a first course, or as a side dish for grilled or roasted meat—

- ¼ cup Dijon-style mustard
- ¼ cup wine vinegar
- ½ teaspoon dried oregano, crushed
- ½ teaspoon dried tarragon, crushed
- ¼ teaspoon salt
- ¼ teaspoon pepper
- ½ cup olive *or* salad oil
- 12 ounces fresh mushrooms, sliced (4½ cups)
- ½ cup pitted ripe olives, halved
Tomato slices (optional)
Watercress sprigs (optional)

Step 1: For dressing, in a large mixing bowl combine mustard, vinegar, oregano, tarragon, salt, and pepper. Using a wire whisk, blend in oil. Stir in mushrooms and olives. Cover and chill at least 2 hours.

Step 2: To assemble salad, use a slotted spoon to spoon the marinated mushroom mixture onto plates. If desired, garnish with tomato slices and watercress sprigs. Makes 4 servings.

Nutrition information per serving: 318 cal., 3 g pro., 7 g carbo., 31 g fat, 0 mg chol., 727 mg sodium. U.S. RDA: 22% vit. C, 24% riboflavin, 20% niacin, and 12% phosphorus.

LA PETITE PORK ROAST

- 1 1½- to 2-pound pork loin sirloin roast
- 2 tablespoons soy sauce
- ¼ teaspoon dry mustard
- 2 tablespoons fennel seed
- 2 tablespoons caraway seed
- 1 recipe Savory Mustard Sauce
    Watercress (optional)

Step 1: Trim excess fat from the roast. Stir together soy sauce and dry mustard. Using your fingers, rub the soy mixture over the roast.

Step 2: Combine fennel seed and caraway seed; spread on waxed paper. Roll roast in seed to coat evenly. Wrap and chill for 2 hours or overnight so seasonings can penetrate the roast.

Step 3: Unwrap the roast. Place, fat side up, on a rack in a shallow roasting pan. Insert a meat thermometer so the bulb rests in the center of the thickest portion of the roast and doesn't rest in fat or touch bone (see how-to photo, page 26).

Step 4: Roast, uncovered, in a 325° oven for 1½ to 1¾ hours or till thermometer registers 170°.*

For easier carving, let meat stand for 15 minutes. Serve with Savory Mustard Sauce. If desired, garnish with watercress. Makes 4 to 6 servings.

*Note: Cooking times for small roasts vary with the shape and diameter of the meat. The wide end of a tapered roast cooks slower than the center of the roast and may register several degrees cooler. If that's the case, cook the roast a little longer until the wide end reaches the proper temperature.

Savory Mustard Sauce: In a small saucepan combine ¼ cup *water*, 2 tablespoons *dry mustard*, and 1 teaspoon *cornstarch*. Stir in 3 tablespoons *light corn syrup* and 1 tablespoon *vinegar*. Cook and stir till thickened and bubbly. Cook and stir for 2 minutes more. Makes about ⅓ cup.

Nutrition information per serving with sauce: 384 cal., 23 g pro., 13 g carbo., 26 g fat, 81 mg chol., 725 mg sodium. U.S. RDA: 56% thiamine, 15% riboflavin, 26% niacin, 25% phosphorus, and 22% iron.

Mexican Cheese Bread

The Idea Magazine for American Families

March 1986
$1.50

DESPERATION!
DINNERS
Tasty Meals From What's On Hand

Better Homes
and Gardens.

IN THIS ISSUE
• FOCAL POINT
  DECORATING
• ADVICE ON PARENTING
• EASTER EGG
  ENCORES

100 IDEAS UNDER $100

• STORAGE   • NEEDLEWORK
• TOYS   • FURNITURE
• CRAFTS   • DECORATING

EASTER EGG ENCORES

PHOTOGRAPHS: MYRON BECK. FOOD STYLIST: JANET MILLER

Has the Easter Bunny left your family more colored eggs than you know what to do with? Well, start crackin'— you can make quick and elegant dishes with your surplus of these springtime holiday treats.

By Terri Pauser Wolf

Keep Easter Eggs Fresh

After the Easter egg hunt, get your hard-cooked treasures into the refrigerator within 10 hours. You can store the eggs in the refrigerator for up to 7 days, and they'll be fresh for these recipes and more.

NESTED ITALIAN EGGS

- 2 10-ounce packages frozen chopped kale *or* spinach
- 6 hard-cooked eggs
- ½ cup creamy Italian salad dressing
- ½ cup shredded Swiss cheese (2 ounces)
- ⅓ cup grated Parmesan cheese
- ¼ cup fine dry bread crumbs
- 1 14½-ounce can stewed tomatoes

Cook kale according to package directions; drain well. Peel eggs; cut in half lengthwise. Remove yolks; set aside. Finely chop 4 of the egg white halves. Combine kale, chopped egg whites, ¼ cup of the salad dressing, the cheeses, and bread crumbs; spread in bottom of an ungreased 1½-quart oval baking dish. Using the back of a spoon, make 8 indentations in the kale-egg white mixture.

Mash yolks; combine with the remaining salad dressing. Fill egg white halves with yolk mixture; place in kale nests. In a small saucepan simmer *undrained* tomatoes, uncovered, for 5 minutes, stirring occasionally. Pour over eggs and kale mixture. Cover and bake in a 350° oven about 20 minutes or till heated through. Makes 4 servings.

Nutrition information per serving: 407 cal., 22 g pro., 19 g carbo., 27 g fat, 433 mg chol., 751 mg sodium. U.S. RDA: 210% vit. A, 70% vit. C, 13% thiamine, 31% riboflavin, 45% calcium, 20% iron, 38% phosphorus.

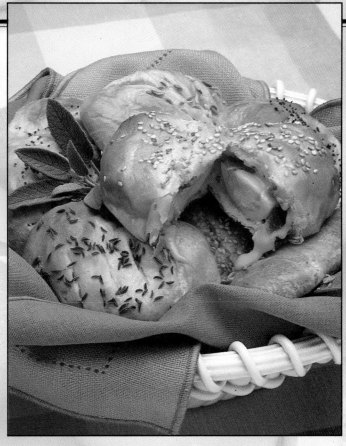

PEPPY MEXICAN EGG SPREAD

6 **hard-cooked eggs**
1 **medium tomato, finely chopped**
3 **green onions, sliced, or 1 teaspoon onion powder**
¼ **cup mayonnaise or salad dressing**
½ **of a 1¼-ounce package taco seasoning mix (about 2 tablespoons)**
Leaf lettuce
1 **recipe Tortilla Bowl (see recipe, page 41)**
½ **cup dairy sour cream (optional)**
½ **of a 6-ounce container frozen avocado dip, thawed (optional)**
Cilantro sprigs
Assorted crackers

Peel eggs; reserve 1 yolk for garnish. Finely chop remaining eggs. Combine chopped eggs, tomato, green onions or onion powder, mayonnaise or salad dressing, and taco seasoning. Cover an 8- or 9-inch round serving tray with the lettuce, removing any hard stems. Place tortilla bowl on lettuce; fill with egg mixture. Top with sour cream and avocado dip, if desired. Sieve reserved egg yolk over dip. Top with cilantro. Arrange crackers around bowl. Makes 1⅔ cups.

Nutrition information per tablespoon with 1 cracker: 39 cal., 1 g pro., 3 g carbo., 2 g fat, 42 mg chol., 46 mg sodium.

SCOTCH EGG BUNDLES

4 **slices bacon**
1 **package (8) refrigerated crescent rolls**
4 **1-ounce slices American cheese**
2 **hard-cooked eggs, peeled and halved lengthwise**
1 **tablespoon milk**
Caraway, poppy, or sesame seed

In a small skillet cook bacon till crisp. Drain bacon; crumble and set aside. Press seams of crescent rolls together to make 4 rectangles. Cut cheese slices in half lengthwise; place 2 halves on each rectangle, overlapping in the center. Sprinkle bacon over each. Place *1* egg half on 1 of the short ends of each rectangle. Roll up dough with egg, cheese, and bacon on inside. Pinch sides to seal well. Brush each bundle with milk. Sprinkle with desired seed. Bake in a 400° oven for 12 to 14 minutes or till golden brown. Makes 4 servings.

Nutrition information per serving: 385 cal., 15 g pro., 23 g carbo., 26 g fat, 169 mg chol., 1,003 mg sodium. U.S. RDA: 16% thiamine, 18% riboflavin, 20% calcium, 11% iron, 49% phosphorus.

DESPERATION DINNERS

By Terri Pauser Wolf

- **Tight on time?**
- **Short on dinner ideas?**
- **Too busy to shop?**
- **Want to eat in a hurry?**

Try our solutions to your dinner dilemmas!

FAST FOILED FISH

Individually wrap and bake all the makings for dinner and save on cleanup—

40 MINUTES

- **4** fresh *or* frozen fish fillets (½ inch thick)
- **½** cup bottled creamy buttermilk salad dressing
- **2** cups broccoli flowerets
- **1** sweet red *or* green pepper, cut into thin strips
- **1** small onion, thinly sliced

Place individual fish fillets on four 12-inch pieces of foil. Spoon *2 tablespoons* of the dressing over each fillet. Surround each fillet with ¼ of each vegetable. Seal each packet by rolling edges together. Place each packet on baking sheet or oven rack and bake in 450° oven for 20 to 25 minutes for fresh fillets, or about 35 minutes for frozen fillets. Let stand 1 to 2 minutes before serving. Makes 4 servings.

Nutrition information per serving: 284 cal., 24 g pro., 9 g carbo., 17 g fat, 57 mg chol., 350 mg sodium. U.S. RDA: 69% vit. A, 150% vit. C, 10% thiamine, 13% riboflavin, 16% niacin, 293% phosphorus.

FOODS TO KEEP ON HAND SO YOU'LL NEVER BE DESPERATE AGAIN!

REFRIGERATOR
- ☐ Creamy salad dressing
- ☐ Ground meat
- ☐ Fresh vegetables
- ☐ Cheese
- ☐ Cream cheese
- ☐ Chicken
- ☐ Ham
- ☐ Luncheon meat
- ☐ Alfalfa sprouts
- ☐ Apples
- ☐ Lemons

PANTRY
- ☐ Seasoned stuffing mix
- ☐ Cranberry sauce

- ☐ Dry white wine
- ☐ Noodles
- ☐ Canned salmon
- ☐ Corn muffin mix
- ☐ Canned soup
- ☐ Chili seasoning mix
- ☐ Canned kidney beans
- ☐ Couscous or rice
- ☐ Spaghetti sauce
- ☐ Canned tomatoes

FREEZER
- ☐ Fish fillets
- ☐ Vegetables
- ☐ Boil-in-bag rice
- ☐ Cooked shrimp

Photographs: Myron Beck. Food stylist: Janet Miller

ANY-TIME TURKEY

It's for real—a no-stuff, no-carve turkey, stuffing, and cranberry sauce dinner—

50 MINUTES

- 1 slightly beaten egg
- ¼ cup milk
- 1 cup herb-seasoned stuffing mix, crushed
- 1 pound ground raw turkey
- 2 tablespoons cooking oil
- 1 16-ounce can whole cranberry sauce
- ½ cup dry white wine
- 2 teaspoons instant chicken bouillon granules
- 2 cups hot cooked noodles

Combine egg and milk. Stir in stuffing. Add turkey; mix well. Shape mixture into eight 4x1-inch logs. Heat oil in 12-inch skillet. Brown meat logs; drain. Combine cranberry sauce, wine, and bouillon granules; pour over meat. Bring to boiling; reduce heat. Simmer, covered, for 15 minutes or till meat is done. Uncover; cook 5 minutes or till sauce is of desired consistency. Serve over hot cooked noodles. Makes 4 servings.

Nutrition information per serving: 650 cal., 37 g pro., 90 g carbo., 13 g fat, 165 mg chol., 783 mg sodium. U.S. RDA: 21% thiamine, 23% riboflavin, 46% niacin, 10% calcium, 21% iron, 39% phosphorus.

SIMPLE SALMON SALAD

Thaw the frozen vegetables and rice under running water for this quick salad—

30 MINUTES

- 1 10-ounce package frozen peas
- 1 10-ounce package frozen rice
- 4 ounces Swiss cheese, cubed
- ¼ teaspoon dried dillweed
- 1 7½-ounce can salmon, drained, skin and bones removed, and broken into chunks
- 2 cups spinach leaves
- ½ cup shredded carrot
- ½ cup creamy cucumber salad dressing

Place peas in a colander under cold running water for 2 minutes to thaw. Place rice pouch under warm running water till mixture can be broken up, about 5 minutes. Toss together rice, peas, cheese, and dillweed. Add salmon; toss lightly. Line 4 plates with spinach; place salmon mixture on top. Arrange carrot around edge. Pass dressing. Serves 4.

Nutrition information per serving: 427 cal., 26 g pro., 28 g carbo., 24 g fat, 61 mg chol., 836 mg sodium. U.S. RDA: 170% vit. A, 88% vit. C, 26% thiamine, 26% riboflavin, 33% niacin, 46% calcium, 28% iron, 43% phosphorus.

EASY CHEESY PIE

This meal-in-a-pie is a cinch to make, thanks to a spinach crust and muffin mix filling—

45 MINUTES

- 1 10-ounce package frozen chopped spinach
- 1 8-ounce package shredded cheddar cheese
- 4 eggs
- 1½ cups milk
- 1 8½-ounce package corn muffin mix
- ¼ teaspoon onion powder
- ¼ cup grated Parmesan cheese

Cook spinach according to package directions; drain well. Press spinach evenly in bottom of a greased 10-inch quiche dish. Sprinkle with cheese. Stir together eggs, milk, muffin mix, and onion powder; beat with rotary beater till well combined. Pour over mixture in quiche dish. Sprinkle with Parmesan cheese. Bake in a 350° oven for 30 to 35 minutes or till knife inserted near center comes out clean. Makes 6 servings.

Nutrition information per serving: 444 cal., 21 g pro., 35 g carbo., 25 g fat, 242 mg chol., 679 mg sodium. U.S. RDA: 90% vit. A, 16% vit. C, 16% thiamine, 30% riboflavin, 60% calcium, 17% iron, 56% phosphorus.

NO-FUSS CHILI CHICKEN

Relax! This family-pleasin' meal cooks on its own after 10 minutes of preparation—

65 MINUTES

- 1 large onion, sliced
- 1 tablespoon cooking oil
- 1 3-pound broiler-fryer chicken, cut up
- 1 11-ounce can tomato bisque soup
- 1 1¼-ounce package chili seasoning mix
- 1 9-ounce package frozen Italian cut green beans
- 1 8-ounce can red kidney beans
- 2 cups hot cooked couscous *or* rice

In skillet toss onion with oil. Place chicken, skin side down, over onion. Cover; cook over low heat 30 minutes. Drain fat. Combine soup, seasoning mix, and ⅔ cup *water*. Turn pieces over; add soup mixture. Cover; cook over low heat 15 minutes. Add green beans and *drained* kidney beans. Cover; cook 15 to 20 minutes more or till chicken is tender. Remove chicken and sauce to platter; serve with hot cooked couscous. Serves 6.

Nutrition information per serving: 376 cal., 34 g pro., 34 g carbo., 11 g fat, 131 mg chol., 671 mg sodium. U.S. RDA: 36% vit. A, 19% vit. C, 17% thiamine, 40% riboflavin, 51% niacin, 28% iron, 41% phosphorus.

JIFFY JAMBALAYA

Turn bottled spaghetti sauce into a jazzy New Orleans-style dinner—

30 MINUTES

- 1 16-ounce can tomatoes, cut up
- 1 15½-ounce jar chunky meatless spaghetti sauce
- 1 cup cubed fully cooked ham
- 1 green pepper, cut into strips
- ¼ teaspoon garlic powder
- 1 bay leaf

Several dashes bottled hot pepper sauce

- 1 8-ounce package frozen cooked shrimp
- 2 cups hot cooked orzo *or* rice

In saucepan combine *undrained* tomatoes, spaghetti sauce, ham, green pepper, garlic powder, bay leaf, hot pepper sauce, and dash *pepper*. Bring to boiling; reduce heat. Simmer, covered, 15 to 20 minutes. Add shrimp. Return to boiling; cook 1 minute or till shrimp are heated through. Remove bay leaf. Serve over hot cooked orzo. Serves 4.

Nutrition information per serving: 331 cal., 27 g pro., 44 g carbo., 5 g fat, 89 mg chol., 1,390 mg sodium. U.S. RDA: 24% vit. A, 100% vit. C, 26% thiamine, 24% niacin, 10% calcium, 20% iron, 22% phosphorus.

15-MINUTE OMELET

Quick! Gather all your ingredients and start your stopwatch for a fast-cookin' meal—

15 MINUTES

- 1 tablespoon cream cheese
- 2 slices luncheon meat
- 2 eggs
- 1 teaspoon butter *or* margarine
- 1 small tomato, chopped
- ¼ cup alfalfa sprouts
- 1 teaspoon sunflower nuts

Spread cream cheese on meat slices. Beat eggs and 2 tablespoons *water*. In a 10-inch skillet melt butter over medium-high heat till just beginning to brown; pour in egg. Push cooked egg with spatula toward center, tilting pan so uncooked egg touches pan surface. When egg is set and top is only slightly wet (about 15 seconds) place meat on one half of omelet. Sprinkle tomato, alfalfa sprouts, and nuts over meat. Fold omelet in half over filling. Turn out onto a plate. Serves 1.

Nutrition information per serving: 439 cal., 27 g pro., 9 g carbo., 32 g fat, 572 mg chol., 727 mg sodium. U.S. RDA: 56% vit. A, 35% vit. C, 37% thiamine, 28% riboflavin, 14% niacin, 30% iron, 39% phosphorus.

TORTILLA BOWL

In a 6-quart Dutch oven or deep-fat fryer heat about 2½ to 3 inches of *cooking oil* or *shortening* to 375°. Using a tortilla basket fryer, center one 8- or 10-inch *flour tortilla* on the bottom of the inner basket. Lightly place the outer basket over tortilla. Turn basket fryer over. Warm tortilla in oil for a few seconds before pushing the inner and outer baskets together. Deep-fry in hot oil for 30 seconds or till golden, rotating basket in oil so top portion of tortilla is cooked. Pour hot oil out of tortilla bowl before removing the basket fryer. Invert over paper towels to drain for a few seconds. Remove the outer basket. Using tongs, carefully lift tortilla bowl from basket. Repeat with another tortilla.

COUNTDOWN CURRIED LAMB PIE

Start your countdown an hour before serving. While the pie is baking, toss together a salad—

- 1 **pound ground lamb *or* ground beef**
- 1 **15-ounce can garbanzo beans, drained**
- 2 **tablespoons all-purpose flour**
- ½ **cup plain yogurt *or* dairy sour cream**
- ½ **cup milk**
- 1 **tablespoon dried minced onion**
- 2 **teaspoons curry powder**
- ½ **teaspoon salt**
- ½ **of a 15-ounce package folded refrigerated unbaked piecrusts (1 crust)**

Milk
Sesame seed
- 2 **tablespoons chopped peanuts**

Plain yogurt *or* dairy sour cream (optional)
Fresh fruit slices (optional)

For filling, in a 10-inch skillet cook ground lamb or beef till brown; drain off fat. Stir in garbanzo beans; set aside.

Meanwhile, stir flour into the ½ cup yogurt or sour cream. In a small mixing bowl stir together yogurt mixture, ½ cup milk, dried minced onion, curry powder, and salt. Stir the yogurt mixture into the meat mixture.

Following package directions, ease piecrust into a 9-inch pie plate, allowing pastry edges to extend over the sides. Fill with meat mixture. Fold the piecrust edges toward center to partially cover meat mixture.

Brush piecrust edges with additional milk and sprinkle edges with sesame seed. Bake in a 375° oven about 40 minutes or till crust is golden.

Let stand 5 minutes before serving. Sprinkle with peanuts. Dollop each serving with additional yogurt or sour cream and garnish with fruit slices, if desired. Makes 8 main-dish servings.

Nutrition information per serving: 395 cal., 15 g pro., 29 g carbo., 24 g fat, 36 mg chol., 326 mg sodium. U.S. RDA: 17% thiamine, 14% riboflavin, 18% niacin, 15% iron, 19% phosphorus.

Countdown Curried Lamb Pie

ZIPPY CHICKEN TACOS

- 8 **taco shells**
- 1 **16-ounce package loose-pack frozen mixed broccoli, cauliflower, and carrots**
- 1 **10-ounce can tomatoes and green chili peppers**
- ½ **teaspoon instant chicken bouillon granules**
- ¼ **teaspoon crushed red pepper**
- 2 **tablespoons cooking oil**
- 2 **cups frozen diced cooked chicken**
- 1 **4-ounce package shredded cheddar cheese**

Salsa
Frozen avocado dip, thawed (optional)

Zippy Chicken Tacos

Warm taco shells according to package directions. Run hot water over frozen vegetables in a colander till partially thawed; drain. Cut up any large vegetable pieces. Stir together *undrained* tomatoes, bouillon granules, and red pepper; set aside.

Preheat a wok over high heat; add cooking oil. Stir-fry vegetables in hot oil for 3 to 5 minutes or till tender. Remove and set aside. Add frozen chicken to the wok. Stir-fry for 2 to 3 minutes or till thawed. Push chicken to the side.

Stir tomato mixture; add to the center of the wok. Cook and stir till heated through. Return vegetables to the wok; stir gently to coat with sauce. Cover and cook for 1 minute more.

Spoon hot mixture into taco shells. Top with shredded cheese. Serve with salsa and avocado dip, if desired. Makes 8 tacos (4 servings).

Nutrition information per serving: 507 cal., 33 g pro., 32 g carbo., 27 g fat, 92 mg chol., 312 mg sodium. U.S. RDA: 103% vit. A, 90% vit. C, 11% thiamine, 22% riboflavin, 41% niacin, 36% calcium, 16% iron, and 36% phosphorus.

NO-PEEL POTATO CHOWDER

1 5½-ounce package dry
   scalloped potato mix
4 cups water
1 8-ounce package brown-and-
   serve sausage links
3 cups milk
2 cups loose-pack frozen mixed
   zucchini, carrot, cauliflower, lima
   beans, and Italian beans

In a 3-quart saucepan combine potatoes from the mix and water. Bring to boiling; reduce heat to medium. Cook, covered, about 15 minutes or till potatoes are nearly tender. Drain.

Meanwhile, brown sausage links according to package directions or omit browning. Slice sausage links into 1-inch pieces; set aside.

Stir sauce mix from the package, milk, vegetables, and sausage into the potato mixture in saucepan. Bring to boiling; reduce heat. Cook, uncovered, for 5 to 8 minutes or till slightly thickened and heated through, stirring occasionally. Makes 4 or 5 servings.

Nutrition information per serving: 460 cal., 18 g pro., 44 g carbo., 24 g fat, 59 mg chol., 1,023 mg sodium. U.S. RDA: 60% vit. A, 10% vit. C, 20% thiamine, 25% riboflavin, 18% niacin, 42% calcium, 10% iron, 36% phosphorus.

No-Peel Potato Chowder

Microwave Directions: The following three recipes are microwave variations. For the conventional cooking directions and nutrition information, see pages 37, 38, and 39.

ANY-TIME TURKEY

1 slightly beaten egg
¼ cup milk
1 cup herb-seasoned stuffing mix,
   crushed
1 pound ground raw turkey
1 16-ounce can whole cranberry
   sauce
2 tablespoons dry white wine
2 teaspoons instant chicken
   bouillon granules
2 cups hot cooked noodles

In a medium mixing bowl combine egg and milk; stir in stuffing mix. Add turkey; mix well. Shape into eight 4x1-inch logs. Arrange turkey logs in a 12x7½x2-inch microwave-safe baking dish. Cover with waxed paper. Micro-cook on 100% power (high) about 8 minutes or till done, turning logs over after 4 minutes. Drain.

For sauce, stir together cranberry sauce, white wine, and bouillon granules; pour over logs. Cook, uncovered, on high for 3 to 4 minutes or till heated through. Serve turkey logs and sauce over noodles. Makes 4 servings.

NO-FUSS CHILI CHICKEN

1   large onion, sliced
1   tablespoon water
1   3-pound broiler-fryer chicken,
    cut up
1   11-ounce can condensed tomato
    bisque soup
⅔   cup water
1   1¼-ounce package chili
    seasoning mix
1   9-ounce package frozen Italian
    green beans
1   8-ounce can red kidney beans,
    drained
2   cups hot cooked couscous

In a 12x7½x2-inch microwave-safe baking dish arrange onion slices in single layer. Add 1 tablespoon water. Cover with waxed paper and micro-cook on 100% power (high) about 3 minutes or till tender.

Arrange chicken pieces on top of the onion, with the skin side down and meatiest portions toward the outside of the dish. Cover with waxed paper. Cook for 13 minutes on high, giving the dish a half-turn and turning chicken pieces over after 7 minutes. Drain.

Combine condensed soup, ⅔ cup water, and chili seasoning mix. Stir in green beans and kidney beans; spoon over chicken. Cover with waxed paper. Cook on high for 11 to 13 minutes more or till the chicken and vegetables are tender, giving the baking dish a half-turn after 6 minutes. Serve over hot cooked couscous. Makes 6 servings.

JIFFY JAMBALAYA

Orzo, also called rosamarina, is a rice-like pasta—

1   16-ounce can tomatoes, cut up
1   15½-ounce jar chunky
    meatless spaghetti sauce
1   cup cubed fully cooked ham
1   green pepper, cut into strips
¼   teaspoon garlic powder
1   bay leaf
Several dashes bottled hot pepper
    sauce
1   8-ounce package frozen cooked
    shrimp
2   cups hot cooked orzo *or* rice

In a 2-quart microwave-safe casserole combine *undrained* tomatoes, spaghetti sauce, ham, green pepper, garlic powder, bay leaf, and hot pepper sauce. Micro-cook, covered, on 100% power (high) about 8 minutes or till boiling, stirring once.

Add frozen shrimp. Cook, covered, on high for 2½ to 3½ minutes or till heated through, stirring once. Remove bay leaf. Serve over hot cooked orzo or rice. Makes 4 servings.

CREATE A NEW RECIPE
A PAIR OF PRIMAVERAS
2 DISHES FROM THE SAME FIXINGS

By Joy Taylor

Eggs and butter; chicken and cheese; pasta and vegetables. There are hundreds of ways you can fix basic ingredients such as these; two ideas are featured right here. All of the ingredients are tossed together for *Primped-Up Primavera*. *Primavera Pie* features a pasta "crust" with a colorful filling. Try either dish, or create your own recipe using the same simple fixings.

WHAT YOU'LL NEED:

DAIRY PRODUCTS
- 4 tablespoons butter *or* margarine
- 3 tablespoons whipping cream
- ⅔ cup grated Parmesan cheese
- 3 eggs

PACKAGED GOODS
- 6 ounces linguine *or* capellini pasta (also called angel hair pasta)
- 1 teaspoon Italian seasoning, crushed

VEGETABLES
- 1 small sweet red *or* green pepper, cut into strips
- 1 medium onion, sliced and separated into rings
- 2 cups cooked and drained broccoli flowerets

POULTRY
- 1½ cups chopped cooked chicken *or* turkey

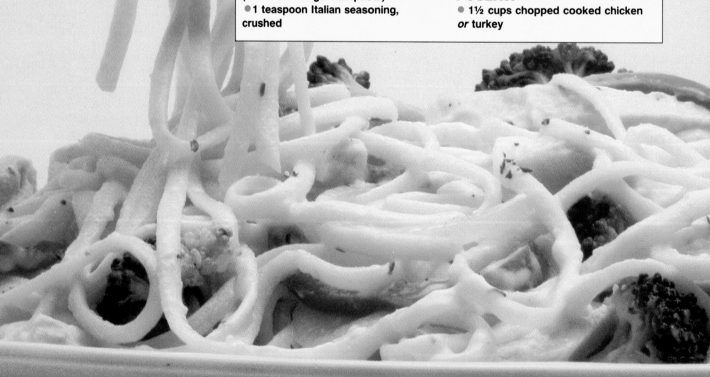

PRIMAVERA PIE

For a head start, shape the crust and chill it till you're ready to fill it.

Cook pasta according to package directions; drain well. Stir *2 tablespoons* of the butter or margarine into hot pasta; stir in *2* beaten eggs and *⅓ cup* of the Parmesan cheese. Form pasta mixture into a "crust" in a well-greased 9-inch pie plate. Set aside.

For filling, in a 10-inch skillet cook the sweet pepper and sliced onion in the remaining butter or margarine till vegetables are just tender. Stir in the broccoli,

chicken, *3 tablespoons* of the Parmesan cheese, and the Italian seasoning. Remove from heat. Combine cream and the remaining egg; stir into the vegetable mixture. Spoon vegetable mixture into the pasta crust. Cover pie with foil. Bake in a 350° oven for 25 minutes; uncover and sprinkle remaining Parmesan cheese over the filling. Bake 5 minutes more. Let pie stand 5 minutes before serving. Makes 6 servings.

PRIMPED-UP PRIMAVERA

The creamy sauce results when the eggs "cook" from the heat of the pasta.

Let eggs and butter or margarine stand at room temperature about 1 hour. (Chilled eggs and butter will cool down the cooked pasta.) Cook the pasta according to package directions; drain and return to saucepan.

Add *2 tablespoons* of the butter or margarine; cover pasta to keep warm.

Meanwhile, in a skillet cook the sweet pepper and onion in the remaining butter or margarine till the vegetables are just tender.

Stir in the broccoli, chicken, and Italian seasoning.

Beat together eggs and cream; pour over pasta in saucepan. Over very low heat (too-high heat may cause eggs to overcook), toss hot pasta till well coated

and eggs are slightly thickened and cooked. Add the vegetable mixture and *½ cup* of the Parmesan cheese; toss to mix. Serve immediately. Pass remaining cheese to sprinkle over each serving. Makes 6 servings.

Nutrition info per serving: 355 cal., 23 g pro., 25 g carbo., 18 g fat, 223 mg chol., 224 mg sodium. U.S. RDA: 45% vit. A, 106% vit. C, 15% thiamine, 22% riboflavin, 28% niacin, 19% calcium, 13% iron, 31% phosphorus.

Turn the page for more create-your-own ideas.

CREATE A NEW RECIPE

IMPROVISE! IMPROVISE! IMPROVISE!

Tired of the same old recipes week after week? Surprise and please your family—repackage their favorite foods. Start here:

RAID THE REFRIGERATOR
Milk, eggs, cheese, cooked vegetables

Option 1: Prepare a frittata instead of an omelet. Pour the beaten egg mixture into a greased skillet, and cook without stirring till almost set. Top the frittata with any cheese or cooked vegetable you'd put inside an omelet. Remove from heat, and let stand, covered, for 5 minutes to finish cooking the top of the eggs. Cut frittata into wedges to serve.

Option 2: Prepare a quiche in a 9-inch prebaked crust, using these ingredient proportions: 3 eggs to 1½ cups milk, 1 cup cooked vegetables, and 1½ cups shredded cheese. Bake in a 325° oven for 50 minutes or till knife inserted near center comes out clean.

Option 3: Serve poached eggs with a vegetable-cheese sauce.

MAKE MORE THAN MEAT LOAF
Ground meat, seasonings

Option 1: Shape your favorite meat loaf recipe into appetizer-size meatballs, then cook half at a time on the range top till done.

Option 2: For a taco salad, cook 1 pound ground meat with 1 teaspoon taco seasoning mix or chili powder. Serve over shredded lettuce along with chopped tomatoes, salsa, and sour cream.

Option 3: Stuff a big burger. Combine 2 pounds ground meat (beef, pork, or turkey), ½ teaspoon crushed dried herb, and ¼ teaspoon each salt and pepper. Halve mixture, and pat each portion into a 7-inch circle. Spoon cooked vegetables or chopped olives onto 1 circle. Pat circles together, sealing edges. Bake in a 350° oven or grill over medium coals. To serve, cut the crowd-sized burger into wedges.

CREATIVE GOURMET CHICKEN DISHES WITH STUFFING MIX
Chicken breasts, stuffing mix, vegetables

Option 1: Bone chicken breasts and pound each piece till ¼ inch thick. Wrap chicken around precooked vegetables; secure with wooden toothpicks. Bake in a 350° oven about 1 hour or till tender. Prepare stuffing according to package directions.

Option 2: Fix stuffing according to package directions; spoon into a casserole. Add chicken and chopped vegetables (carrots, celery, onions, and turnips). Bake, covered, at 350°.

Option 3: Coat chicken with crushed stuffing mix, drizzle with melted butter or margarine. Bake in a 375° oven about 50 minutes. Steam vegetables.

HINTS

Substitute ingredients or embellish a basic recipe to create a new recipe:

• Serve saucy meat mixtures over steamed vegetables rather than rice or noodles. This makes a colorful presentation and, depending on the vegetables, may be lower in calories.

• Substitute mild-flavored chicken or pork for veal. You may need to lengthen the cooking time.

• Turn 1 cup cream sauce into something special. To the thickened sauce, add 2 tablespoons wine, ½ teaspoon shredded lemon peel, 1 tablespoon snipped chives, *or* ½ teaspoon dried herb.

• Most herbs and spices are interchangeable, so experiment! Try tarragon in place of oregano; use fennel seed instead of cumin; ground cloves in place of allspice. The strength of herbs and spices varies, so add ¼ teaspoon at a time, tasting as you go and adding more as needed.

• Flavor ground meat mixtures by using bulk sausage in place of some of the ground beef, ham, pork, or turkey. Omit or cut the amount of salt and seasonings because sausages are well seasoned.

• Turn an Italian-flavored recipe into a Tex-Mex dish: use salsa instead of tomato sauce; monterey jack cheese in place of mozzarella; and beans instead of pasta.

• Turn a cream sauce into a creamy appetizer soup—just thin the mixture with milk, cream, or broth.

APRIL

The Idea Magazine For American Family

Better Homes and Gardens

April 1986 • $1.50

RAINY-DAY
CRAFTS
FOR
KIDS

Make-Ahead Dinners
Cook Up 5 Meals In 4 Hours!

THE IMPATIENT DECORATOR
**GETTING THE LOOK
YOU WANT WHEN
YOU WANT IT!**

PARENTING
**WHEN AGGRESSIVE
BEHAVIOR GETS
OUT OF HAND**

**NEW FACTORY-BUILT
HOUSES ARE
ON THE WAY!**

GREAT GREENS!
Salad Gardens
To Grow,
Spring Salads
To Make

LUNCH-HOUR PICNIC

PACK UP THIS TOTABLE NOONTIME FEAST FOR TWO OR MORE

By Lynn Hoppe

CHICKEN SALAD VÉRONIQUE

Make your outdoor getaway even merrier by inviting more people. Both recipes on this page are easy to double or triple—

- 1 **whole large chicken breast, cooked, skinned, boned, and cut into strips**
- 1 **medium orange, peeled and sectioned**
- ½ **cup seedless grapes, halved**
- 1 **tablespoon lemon juice**
- 1 **tablespoon honey**
- 2 **tablespoons salad oil**
- ½ **teaspoon sesame oil (optional)**
- 1 **cup chow mein noodles**

In a medium mixing bowl toss together chicken, orange sections, and grapes. In a screw-top jar combine lemon juice, honey, and dash *salt*. Add salad oil and, if desired, sesame oil; cover and shake well. Drizzle over chicken mixture. Toss to coat. Spoon into an airtight container. Cover and chill at least overnight or up to 2 days.

Up to 6 hours before serving, pack noodles in a plastic bag. Place chicken mixture in a cooler with a frozen ice pack. At mealtime, serve chicken mixture over noodles. Serves 2.

Nutrition information per serving: 490 cal., 33 g pro., 37 g carbo., 24 g fat, 360 mg sodium. U.S. RDA: 40% vit. C, 10% thiamine, 10% riboflavin, 70% niacin, 25% phosphorus.

ALMOND-CHEESE SPREAD

Don't forget the ice! To keep your picnic lunch safe and fresh, include an ice pack in a cooler with your chicken salad and cheese spread. Just be sure to put the ice pack in the freezer the night before the picnic so it's frozen solid when you need it—

- ½ **cup shredded process Gruyère cheese (2 ounces)**
- ⅓ **cup soft-style cream cheese**
- 2 **tablespoons milk**
- 2 **tablespoons chopped almonds, toasted**
- 1 **small loaf French bread**

Toasted pita wedges

In a small mixing bowl stir together cheeses till nearly smooth. Gradually stir in the milk. Stir in almonds. Spoon into an airtight container. Cover and chill at least overnight or up to 1 week.

Up to 6 hours before serving, pack the cheese spread in a cooler with a frozen ice pack. Pack the bread loaf and pita wedges in a clear plastic bag.

Slice French bread to serve. Spread bread slices and pita wedges with cheese spread. Makes ¾ cup.

Nutrition information per tablespoon: 83 cal., 3 g pro., 7 g carbo., 5 g fat, 102 mg sodium.

Photograph: Jim Hedrich
Food stylist: Janet Pittman

ALMOND-CHEESE SPREAD

Gruyère cheese gets credit for the sweet, nutlike flavor.

CHICKEN SALAD VÉRONIQUE

Oranges and grapes—sweet additions to chicken salad.

MAKE-AHEAD DINNERS
COOK UP 5 MEALS IN 4 HOURS

By Joy Taylor

SWEET AND SASSY CHICKEN

Simple! You can stash this chicken and fruit combination in your freezer with a minimum of effort.

COOKING STRATEGY

Four hours! One afternoon! That's all it takes to fix and freeze these five meals to serve this week or next month.

The key to no-hassle, multimeal cooking? Dovetailing! Follow our timetable to juggle five recipes without fretting.

☐ **1:00** Read through the five recipes.
● Assemble these utensils:
  Cutting board; measuring spoons
  Colander; can opener; tongs
  Rubber spatula; wooden spoon
  Chef's knife; paring knife; boning knife
  Shredder; kitchen shears; vegetable peeler
  Dry and liquid measuring cups
  Small and large mixing bowls
  4½-quart Dutch oven

GREEN AND WHITE LASAGNA

Here's a lasagna that's a whiz to make but tough to keep around—
you'll soon be tempted to thaw, bake, and serve it.

2-quart saucepan
10-inch skillet with lid
Baking sheet
Broiler pan and rack
12x7½x2-inch freezer-to-oven
 baking dish
Four freezer-to-oven individual au
 gratin dishes
1-quart freezer container
1½-quart freezer container

□ **1:10** Ready, set, cook!
● In the Dutch oven bring water to
 boiling. Cook noodles for Green
 and White Lasagna; drain.
● For lasagna filling, put package of
 frozen spinach in colander under
 hot running water to thaw.
● Cut up vegetable ingredients for
 the five recipes, and arrange portions on a sheet of waxed paper:

1 large onion, chopped and
 divided into two ½-cup portions
2 green onions, sliced
3 green onions, bias-sliced into
 1-inch pieces
1 green pepper, chopped
½ cup shredded carrot
1 carrot, chopped
½ cup sliced water chestnuts
2 sweet potatoes, cubed

LENTIL-BRATWURST STEW

Two dinners in one! Freeze half of this hearty stew and enjoy the remainder after preparing your freezerful of meals.

☐ **1:35** Prepare spinach filling and cheese filling for the lasagna.
● Assemble lasagna layers in the baking dish.
● Wrap, seal, label, and freeze the lasagna; or refrigerate it. The lasagna can chill for up to 24 hours; it could be your dinner tomorrow night.
● One recipe down!

● Rinse dishes so you can reuse them for the remaining recipes.

☐ **2:20** In the skillet cook turkey-tomato filling for the Curried Turkey Turnovers. (Simmer, covered, for 10 minutes; uncover, cook for 3 to 4 minutes more.)
● Spoon turkey filling into a large bowl to cool.

● Go ahead, sample the tasty turkey mixture!
● Skin, bone, and cut up the chicken breasts for the Sweet and Sassy Chicken.
● Let refrigerated pastry for the turnovers stand at room temperature. You'll assemble the meat-filled pastries in a few minutes.
● Wipe out skillet with paper towels.

CURRIED TURKEY TURNOVERS

These turkey-filled pastries go together fast because you start with ready-to-use refrigerated pastry.

☐ **2:55** In the skillet brown the cut-up chicken in hot oil for 3 to 4 minutes; transfer chicken to the 1-quart freezer container and let it cool slightly.

● Prepare soy-ginger sauce for Sweet and Sassy Chicken; transfer to the freezer container. Let recipe cool, uncovered, before placing it in the freezer.

☐ **3:15** Take a breather!

☐ **3:20** Spoon cooled turkey filling onto pastry and form into two turnovers. Wrap each turnover, separately, in foil; seal, label, and freeze.

● Two recipes down!

● Seal, label, and freeze the cooled Sweet and Sassy Chicken.

● Three recipes down!

☐ **3:35** In the Dutch oven assemble and simmer Lentil-Brat-wurst Stew.

● Slice the brats.

● Prepare the stuffing for the Hot-Stuff Chops.

● Preheat broiler for chops.

● You're almost done!

HOT-STUFF CHOPS

Both the taste and the convenience of this dish are hot stuff.
Individually frozen chops let your family dine alone or together.

☐ **3:55** Stuff pork chops and start to broil them. Broiling time totals about 15 minutes; turn the chops after 8 minutes.

● While chops broil, tidy up kitchen.

● Ladle *half* of the stew (about 6 cups) into the 1½-quart freezer container; let cool, uncovered.

● Keep remaining stew warm on the range. This is tonight's dinner!

☐ **4:35** Transfer the chops to freezer-to-table au gratin dishes. Top each with cheese sauce.

● Wrap, seal, label, and freeze chops. This makes four recipes stashed away in your freezer!

● Seal, label, and freeze *half* of the bratwurst stew.

☐ **5:00** You're done!

SIT DOWN! RELAX!

SHOPPING LIST

Check your larder to see what items you'll need to pick up before you start your week's worth of meals. You'll find the story and timetable for the recipes beginning on page 48—

Meat
2 whole medium chicken breasts (about 1½ pounds total)
12 ounces smoked bratwurst
1 pound ground raw turkey
4 pork loin rib chops, cut 1 inch thick

Dairy
2 cups milk
1 15-ounce carton ricotta cheese (1¾ cups)
1 8-ounce package shredded mozzarella cheese
½ cup grated Parmesan cheese (2 ounces)
1 7½- or 9-ounce container nacho cheese sauce
Plain yogurt *or* dairy sour cream (you'll need ½ to ¾ cup to dollop on turnovers)

Fresh Produce
1 large onion
5 green onions
1 medium green pepper
2 medium carrots
2 medium sweet potatoes (about 1 pound total)
1 cup seedless red *or* green grapes (about 5½ ounces)

Packaged and canned goods
1 24-ounce can tomato juice
1 12-ounce can beer
1 8-ounce can sliced water chestnuts
1 4-ounce can whole green chili peppers

1 2¼-ounce can sliced pitted ripe olives
1 7½-ounce can tomatoes
6 lasagna noodles
1½ cups dry lentils (about 10 ounces)
¼ cup raisins
¼ cup orange marmalade
Chutney (optional)
2 9-inch folded refrigerated unbaked piecrusts
1 6-ounce package corn bread stuffing mix
2 10-ounce packages frozen long grain and wild rice
1 10-ounce package frozen chopped spinach

Staples to have on hand
All-purpose flour
Bay leaf
Butter *or* margarine
Cooking oil
Cornstarch
Curry powder
Dried basil
Dried parsley flakes
Dried rosemary
Dried thyme
Eggs
Garlic powder
Ground cumin
Ground ginger
Ground nutmeg
Orange juice
Pepper
Salt
Soy sauce
Vinegar

HOT-STUFF CHOPS

Chill the rest of the cheese sauce to serve with tortilla chips another time. Top off this meal with homey cherry crisp—

1 **tablespoon butter *or* margarine**
¾ **cup corn bread stuffing mix**
2 **tablespoons orange juice *or* water**
4 **pork loin rib chops, cut 1 inch thick**
1 **4-ounce can whole green chili peppers, drained and seeded**
1 **7½- or 9-ounce container nacho cheese sauce**

In a small saucepan melt butter or margarine. Stir in stuffing mix and orange juice or water. Set aside.

Trim fat from chops. Make a pocket in each chop by cutting from the fat side almost to the bone edge. Place *one-fourth* of the chili peppers in *each* pocket. Spoon *one-fourth* of the stuffing mixture into *each* chop. Secure with wooden toothpicks.

Place chops on an unheated rack of a broiler pan. Broil chops 5 inches from heat for 8 minutes. Turn and broil 7 to 8 minutes or till no pink remains. Remove toothpicks. Cool slightly.

Place the chops in 4 individual au gratin dishes. Top *each* chop with *3 tablespoons* of the cheese sauce. Seal, label, and freeze.

To serve: Unwrap frozen chops. Cover the chops with foil and bake in a 375° oven for 60 to 65 minutes or until heated through. Makes 4 servings.

To serve without freezing: Prepare chops as above, *except do not broil.* Bake, covered, in a 350° oven for 45 minutes. Uncover and bake for 25 to 30 minutes more or till done. Top *each* chop with *3 tablespoons* of the cheese sauce. Bake for 3 to 5 minutes or till cheese is just melted. Makes 4 servings.

Nutrition information per serving: 498 cal., 44 g pro., 26 g carbo., 23 g fat, 137 mg chol., 735 mg sodium. U.S. RDA: 60% vit. C, 60% thiamine, 35% riboflavin, 47% niacin, 15% calcium, 15% iron, and 40% phosphorus.

SWEET AND SASSY CHICKEN

- 2 **whole medium chicken breasts (1½ pounds total), skinned, boned, and cut into 1-inch pieces**
- 1 **tablespoon cooking oil**
- ¼ **cup orange marmalade**
- 3 **green onions, bias-sliced into 1-inch pieces**
- 2 **tablespoons vinegar**
- 2 **tablespoons soy sauce**
- 1 **tablespoon cornstarch**
- ¼ **teaspoon ground ginger**
- 1 **cup seedless red *or* green grapes**
- ½ **cup sliced water chestnuts**
- 2 **10-ounce packages frozen long grain and wild rice**

In a 10-inch skillet cook chicken in hot cooking oil over medium-high heat for 3 to 4 minutes or till tender, turning to brown evenly. If necessary, add additional oil to prevent sticking. Spoon chicken into 1-quart freezer container; cool slightly.

In a small mixing bowl combine marmalade, green onions, vinegar, soy sauce, cornstarch, and ginger. Pour into skillet. Cook and stir over medium heat till thickened and bubbly. Stir in grapes and water chestnuts. Pour over chicken in container. Let stand, uncovered, to cool. Seal, label, and freeze.

Range-top reheating: Transfer the frozen mixture to a medium saucepan. Cover and place over medium-low heat for 15 to 20 minutes or till heated through, using a fork to break apart and stir the mixture occasionally.

Meanwhile, prepare the long grain and wild rice according to package directions. To serve, spoon chicken mixture over rice. Makes 4 servings.

Microwave reheating: Cut a slit in the center of each rice pouch. Place, slit side up, in the microwave oven. Microcook on 100% power (high) about 8 minutes or till heated through, rotating pouches 3 times. Cover and keep warm.

Transfer frozen chicken mixture to a 1½-quart microwave-safe casserole. Cover; cook on 70% power (medium-high) for 11 to 13 minutes or till heated through, breaking apart and stirring with a fork twice. Serve as above. Makes 4 servings.

To serve without freezing: Prepare long grain and wild rice according to package directions. For chicken mixture, reduce cornstarch to *1 teaspoon.* Do not remove browned chicken from skillet. Add marmalade mixture to skillet. Cook and stir till thickened and bubbly. Cook and stir for 1 minute more. Stir in grapes and water chestnuts. Heat through. Serve as above. Makes 4 servings.

Nutrition information per serving: 447 cal., 60 g pro., 59 g carbo., 10 g fat, 72 mg chol., 1,340 mg sodium. U.S. RDA: 15% vit. C, 27% thiamine, 11% riboflavin, 70% niacin, 19% iron, and 30% phosphorus.

GREEN AND WHITE LASAGNA

- 6 **lasagna noodles**
- ½ **cup chopped onion**
- 2 **tablespoons butter *or* margarine**
- 2 **tablespoons cornstarch**
- 1 **tablespoon dried parsley flakes**
- 1 **teaspoon dried basil, crushed**
- ¼ **teaspoon garlic powder**
- ⅛ **teaspoon ground nutmeg**
- 2 **cups milk**
- 1 **10-ounce package frozen chopped spinach, thawed and drained**
- 1 **2¼-ounce can sliced pitted ripe olives, drained**
- 1 **beaten egg**
- 1¾ **cups ricotta cheese**
- 1 **8-ounce package shredded mozzarella cheese**
- ½ **cup grated Parmesan cheese**

In a large kettle or Dutch oven cook lasagna noodles in a large amount of boiling salted water for 10 to 12 minutes or till tender; drain. Rinse in cold water; drain well.

Meanwhile, in a medium saucepan cook onion in hot butter or margarine till tender. Stir in cornstarch, parsley, basil, garlic powder, and nutmeg. Add milk all at once. Cook and stir till thickened and bubbly. Stir in spinach and olives. Set aside.

In a medium mixing bowl stir together the egg and ricotta cheese. Add mozzarella cheese and *half* of the Parmesan cheese; mix well. Set aside.

Arrange *three* of the noodles in the bottom of a greased 12x7½x2-inch baking dish. Top with *half* of the spinach mixture. Spoon on *half* of the ricotta cheese mixture. Repeat layers. Sprinkle with remaining Parmesan cheese.

To chill: Cover with foil. Place in the refrigerator for up to 24 hours. To serve, bake, covered, in a 350° oven for 30 minutes. Uncover; bake about 20 minutes more or till cheese is slightly golden and mixture is bubbly. Let stand for 10 minutes. Makes 9 servings.

To freeze: Wrap baking dish tightly in moisture- and vaporproof wrap. Label and freeze. To bake, remove wrap and cover dish with foil. Bake in a 350° oven for 1 hour. Uncover; bake about 30 minutes more or till cheese is slightly golden and mixture is bubbly. Let stand for 10 minutes. Makes 9 servings.

To serve immediately: Bake in a 350° oven about 40 minutes or till the cheese is slightly golden and the mixture is bubbly. Let stand for 10 minutes. Makes 9 servings.

Nutrition information per serving: 314 cal., 20 g pro., 20 g carbo., 17 g fat, 78 mg chol., 492 mg sodium. U.S. RDA: 52% vit. A, 12% vit. C, 12% thiamine, 23% riboflavin, 51% calcium, 10% iron, and 36% phosphorus.

LENTIL-BRATWURST STEW

4 cups water
3 cups tomato juice
1½ cups dry lentils, rinsed and
   drained
1 cup beer
1 medium carrot, chopped
½ cup chopped onion
1 bay leaf
1 teaspoon dried thyme, crushed
½ teaspoon dried rosemary,
   crushed
¼ teaspoon garlic powder
¼ teaspoon pepper
12 ounces smoked bratwurst, sliced
2 medium sweet potatoes, cut into
   ½-inch cubes (2 cups)

In a 4-quart Dutch oven combine water, tomato juice, lentils, beer, carrot, onion, bay leaf, thyme, rosemary, garlic powder, and pepper. Bring to boiling; reduce heat. Cover and simmer for 15 minutes. Stir in bratwurst and sweet potatoes. Return to boiling; reduce heat. Simmer, covered, for 10 minutes. Remove bay leaf.

Place *half* of the mixture (about 6 cups) in a 1½- or 2-quart freezer container. Cool. Seal, label, and freeze. To serve remaining mixture immediately, simmer for 10 to 15 minutes more or till lentils and sweet potatoes are tender. Makes 8 servings total.

Range-top reheating: Transfer frozen mixture from the freezer container to a 3-quart saucepan. Add ¼ cup *water.* Cover and cook over medium-low heat for 50 to 60 minutes or till heated through, stirring occasionally to break up chunks. Makes 4 servings.

Microwave reheating: Transfer the frozen mixture from the freezer container to a 2-quart microwave-safe casserole. Cover and cook on 100% power (high) for 13 to 15 minutes or till thawed, stirring twice to break up chunks. Cook for 6 to 8 minutes more or till heated through. Makes 4 servings.

Nutrition information per serving: 334 cal., 17 g pro., 40 g carbo., 12 g fat, 26 mg chol., 441 mg sodium. U.S. RDA: 106% vit. A, 42% vit. C, 29% thiamine, 13% riboflavin, 17% niacin, 25% iron, and 25% phosphorus.

CURRIED TURKEY TURNOVERS

Serve pea pods in a steamer basket as an easy side dish—

1 pound ground raw turkey
2 green onions, sliced (¼ cup)
1 7½-ounce can tomatoes, cut up
1 medium green pepper, chopped
½ cup shredded carrot
¼ cup raisins
1 teaspoon curry powder
½ teaspoon salt
½ teaspoon ground cumin
¼ teaspoon pepper
2 9-inch folded refrigerated
   unbaked piecrusts
All-purpose flour
1 beaten egg
Plain yogurt or dairy sour cream
Chutney (optional)

If turkey is frozen, let thaw overnight in the refrigerator. For filling, in a 10-inch skillet cook turkey and green onions till turkey is brown and onions are tender. Drain off any fat.

Stir in *undrained* tomatoes, green pepper, carrot, raisins, curry powder, salt, cumin, and pepper. Bring to boiling; reduce heat. Cover and simmer for 10 minutes. If necessary, uncover and cook over high heat for 3 to 4 minutes or till the liquid is evaporated. Spoon filling into a large mixing bowl. Cool.

Let the piecrusts stand at room temperature while the filling cools. To assemble turnovers, unfold piecrusts; sprinkle with flour according to package directions. Place the piecrusts, floured side down, on a baking sheet.

Spread *half* of the filling (about 1½ cups) over *half* of *each* crust, leaving a 1-inch edge along the outside. Moisten the edges of the piecrusts with *water.* Gently lift and fold the other half of the piecrust over the filling. Seal and flute edges. Wrap each turnover separately in heavy-duty foil; seal, label, and freeze.

To serve: Unwrap the frozen turnovers and place on a greased baking sheet. Brush with beaten egg. Cut slits in dough to let steam escape during baking. Bake in a 400° oven for 40 to 45 minutes or till the turnovers are golden brown and filling is heated through. Serve with plain yogurt or sour cream and chutney. Makes 6 servings.

To serve without freezing: Brush turnovers with beaten egg. Cut slits in the dough to let steam escape during baking. Bake in a 375° oven about 25 minutes or till turnovers are golden brown and filling is heated through. Serve as above. Makes 6 servings.

Nutrition information per serving: 488 cal., 22 g pro., 44 g carbo., 25 g fat, 96 mg chol., 703 mg sodium. U.S. RDA: 40% vit. A, 60% vit. C, 11% thiamine, 15% riboflavin, 23% niacin, 13% iron, and 25% phosphorus.

GREAT GREENS!

PUT 'EM TOGETHER
DRESS 'EM
ENJOY 'EM

By Terri Pauser Wolf

TIP-TOP SALAD TOPPERS: VINEGARS AND OILS

- Dress up even the simplest salads with specialty fruit-, nut-, and herb-flavored vinegars and oils that are a cinch to make.
- The "rule of thumb" for vinaigrette dressings is 1 cup of salad oil to ⅔ cup vinegar, plus seasonings. Adjust this ratio for a tarter or milder dressing.
- To show off your homemade or store-bought fancy vinegars and oils, feature just one in a vinaigrette.
- Combine strong-flavored vinegars with mild oils and vice versa. Try raspberry-flavored vinegar with olive oil on romaine, or dress up delicate Boston lettuce with hazelnut oil and white wine vinegar.

SALAD PIZZA Pizza and a salad—two favorite go-togethers become one in this ultimate salad pizza! Every bite of the warm crispy crust, garden greens, and melted mozzarella cheese will tantalize your taste buds. Best of all—it's a snap to make!

HOW TO STORE GREENS

Follow these quick steps for perfectly crisped greens. First, discard any bruised, discolored, tough, or wilted outer leaves. Then wash the greens in cold water. Lightly shake leaves to remove excess water and pat dry with paper towels, or use a salad spinner. Store greens in a plastic bag or an airtight container in the refrigerator until you are ready to use them. They'll stay crisp for three or four days. Sturdier greens such as iceberg may last a few days longer than delicate greens such as leaf lettuce or spinach.

See pages 58–60 for the salad, pizza, and more dressing recipes.

HIGH-RISE SALAD

Savor this tower of garden goodness! Each edible story is constructed from just-picked greens, fresh vegetables, and delicious salad fixings.

SALAD DRESSINGS

◀ LEMON-CHIVE DRESSING

In a small mixer bowl combine 1 *egg yolk,* 2 tablespoons *lemon juice,* and ¼ teaspoon *salt.* Beat with an electric mixer at medium speed till blended. Add ¼ cup *salad oil,* 1 teaspoon at a time, beating constantly. Continue to beat; slowly add ¾ cup *salad oil* in a thin, steady stream. Stir in 1 tablespoon snipped *chives* and ½ teaspoon grated *lemon peel.* Stir in 1 to 2 tablespoons *milk* till of desired consistency; chill. Makes 1 cup dressing (125 calories per tablespoon).

GREEN GOODNESS ▶

In a blender container combine ¼ cup chopped *spinach,* 1 *egg yolk,* 2 tablespoons *wine vinegar,* ¼ teaspoon *fennel seed,* and ¼ teaspoon *salt.* Cover; blend 10 seconds. With blender running, gradually add ½ cup *salad oil.* Stir in 1 to 2 tablespoons *milk;* chill. Makes 1 cup dressing (64 calories per tablespoon).

Easy Salad Fixing

For crisp, clean greens on the spur of the moment, use a *salad spinner* (A). Spin-dry the lettuce in one easy step while you and the kitchen stay dry. Keep mushrooms extra fresh by refrigerating them in a *mushroom keeper* (B). A *mushroom brush* (C) with very soft bristles gently cleans mushrooms and keeps them intact. Use only a small amount of water to dampen brush—mushrooms quickly absorb water.

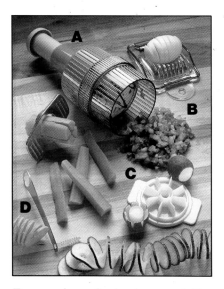

To coarsely or finely chop vegetables quickly and easily, use a *vegetable chopper* (A). Evenly slice hard-cooked eggs with no mess using an *egg slicer* (B). Try a *radish press* (C) to make attractive

roses in a jiff. Spiral-cut carrots or cucumbers with the *spiral slicer* (D). Cut into bite-size pieces for a salad. The *carrot stick maker* (E) turns out the orange munchies in a flash.

HERB VINEGAR

Capture garden-fresh herb flavors for year-round enjoyment by using them to flavor vinegars—

> 2 **cups tightly packed fresh tarragon** *or* **other herb leaves** *or* **sprigs (thyme, dill, mint,** *or* **basil)**
> 2 **cups white vinegar**
> **Fresh tarragon** *or* **other herb sprig (optional)**

Pack the 2 cups tarragon or herb sprigs into a hot, clean 1-quart jar. In a stainless steel or enamel saucepan heat vinegar till hot, *but not boiling.*

Pour the hot vinegar over herbs in jar. Cover loosely with a glass, plastic, or cork lid till mixture cools. (Vinegar corrodes metal lids.) Then, cover tightly with the lid. Let vinegar stand in a cool, dark place for 1 week before using.

To store, remove herbs from jar and transfer liquid to a clean 1-pint jar or bottle. Label. (Or, add another sprig of fresh herb to the jar for identification.) Cover tightly with a glass, plastic, or cork lid. Place in a cool, dark place. Store up to 3 months. Makes 2 cups.

Nutrition information per tablespoon: 2 cal., 0 g pro., 1 g carbo., 0 g fat, 0 mg chol., and 0 mg sodium.

Give your greens sass with quick homemade dressings. Make tangy *Herb Vinegar* (A) and mix it with olive oil; or cook up *Nut-Flavored Oil* (B) to combine with wine vinegar. Try any of these dressings over a crisp bowl of greens: *Creamy Dijon Dressing* (C), *Minted Lime Dressing* (D), or *Walnut-Garlic Vinaigrette* (E).

CREAMY DIJON DRESSING

Drizzle this dressing on top of spinach, watercress, or Swiss chard—

> 1 **8-ounce carton dairy sour cream**
> ⅓ **cup milk**
> 2 **tablespoons vinegar**
> 2 **tablespoons Dijon-style mustard**
> 1 **teaspoon fines herbes, crushed,** *or* **1 teaspoon snipped fresh tarragon, 1 teaspoon snipped fresh parsley,** *and* **1 teaspoon snipped fresh dill**

In a small mixing bowl stir together sour cream and milk. Add vinegar, Dijon-style mustard, and fines herbes or fresh tarragon, parsley, and dill. Stir the mixture till combined. Cover and chill in the refrigerator. Makes 1 cup.

Nutrition information per tablespoon: 36 cal., 1 g pro., 1 g carbo., 3 g fat, 7 mg chol., and 65 mg sodium.

WALNUT-GARLIC VINAIGRETTE

Attention, walnut lovers! For an even stronger walnut flavor, add more toasted walnuts to your salad before tossing with this dressing—

- ¼ **cup broken walnuts**
- 3 **cloves garlic**
- 1 **teaspoon paprika**
- ¼ **teaspoon salt**
- **Dash pepper**
- ½ **cup olive *or* salad oil**
- ¼ **cup vinegar**

In a small heavy skillet toast the walnut pieces over medium-low heat for 10 to 15 minutes or till golden, stirring occasionally; cool.

In a blender container or a food processor bowl combine the toasted walnuts, the garlic, paprika, salt, and pepper; cover and blend or process till the walnuts are finely ground.

With the blender or food processor running, add the olive or salad oil in a slow, steady stream, stopping to scrape the sides of the blender container or the food processor bowl as necessary. Add the vinegar. Cover and blend or process till the mixture is combined.

Transfer the mixture to a storage container. Cover and store in the refrigerator till ready to serve. Makes 1¼ cups dressing.

Nutrition information per tablespoon: 59 cal., 0 g pro., 1 g carbo., 6 g fat, 0 mg chol., and 27 mg sodium.

NUT-FLAVORED OIL

Pair this mild oil with a light-tasting vinegar for a well-rounded vinaigrette—

- 1½ **cups unblanched whole almonds, hazelnuts, *or* walnuts**
- 2½ **cups salad oil**
- **Whole almonds, hazelnuts, *or* walnuts (optional)**

Place the 1½ cups almonds, hazelnuts, or walnuts in a blender container or a food processor bowl. Cover and blend or process till the nuts are finely chopped.

With the blender or the food processor running on low speed, gradually add ½ *cup* of the salad oil through the opening in the lid. (If your blender does not have an opening in the lid, place the lid slightly ajar.)

Transfer the ground nut mixture to a 2-quart saucepan. Clip a candy or deep-fat-cooking thermometer on the side of the saucepan. Cook the mixture over low heat, stirring occasionally, till the thermometer registers 160°. Remove the saucepan from the heat and cool the mixture slightly.

In a 1-quart jar or bottle combine the nut mixture with the remaining salad oil. Cover the jar or bottle tightly and let stand in a cool place for 1 to 2 weeks before using.

To use the oil, line a colander with fine-woven cloth or a cup-shaped coffee filter. Place the colander over a bowl and pour the oil mixture through the cloth or coffee filter. Discard the nut paste in the cloth or coffee filter. Transfer the strained liquid to a 1½-pint jar or bottle. Add a few whole nuts to the jar or bottle, if desired, or label the jar or bottle for identification.

Store the oil, tightly covered, in the refrigerator up to 3 months. Makes about 2½ cups.

Nutrition information per tablespoon: 120 cal., 0 g pro., 0 g carbo., 14 g fat, 0 mg chol., and 0 mg sodium.

MINTED LIME DRESSING

Try serving this citrus-spiked dressing over a colorful assortment of cut-up fresh fruit—

- 1 **8-ounce carton plain yogurt**
- ½ **to 1 teaspoon finely shredded lime peel**
- 1 **tablespoon lime juice**
- 2 **teaspoons sugar**
- 2 **teaspoons finely snipped fresh mint *or* ½ teaspoon dried mint, crushed**
- ¼ **teaspoon salt**

In a small mixing bowl stir together the plain yogurt, shredded lime peel, lime juice, sugar, fresh mint or dried mint, and the salt.

Transfer the mixture to a storage container. Cover and store in the refrigerator till ready to serve. Makes about 1 cup dressing.

Nutrition information per tablespoon: 11 cal., 1 g pro., 2 g carbo., 0 g fat, 1 mg chol., and 43 mg sodium.

HIGH-RISE SALAD

The combinations are endless! Give your favorite greens and vegetables a try—

- ½ cup mayonnaise *or* salad dressing
- ½ cup dairy sour cream
- 2 tablespoons milk
- ½ teaspoon dried dillweed
- ¼ teaspoon garlic salt
- 1 small head radicchio *or* red cabbage
- 1½ cups torn curly endive
- 6 hard-cooked eggs, chopped
- 1 cup coarsely shredded carrots
- 1 cup sliced fresh mushrooms
- 3 cups torn spinach leaves
- ½ cup chopped red *or* green sweet pepper
- 1 cup broccoli flowerets, crisp-cooked, drained, and cooled
- 1 cup fresh alfalfa sprouts

For dressing, in a small mixing bowl combine mayonnaise or salad dressing, sour cream, milk, dillweed, and garlic salt; cover and chill.

In the bottom of a 4-quart straight-sided glass salad bowl arrange outer leaves of raddichio or red cabbage. Arrange remaining salad layers over the raddichio in this order: endive, eggs, carrots, mushrooms with the cut sides against sides of bowl, spinach, red or green pepper, and broccoli. Arrange alfalfa sprouts on top around the edge. Spoon dressing over center of salad. Cover and chill for 2 to 8 hours. Toss gently to serve. Makes 8 to 10 servings.

Nutrition information per serving: 219 cal., 7 g pro., 7 g carbo., 19 g fat, 221 mg chol., 227 mg sodium. U.S. RDA: 88% vit. A, 78% vit. C, 15% riboflavin, 11% iron, and 13% phosphorus.

SALAD PIZZA

Simply bake the frozen puff-pastry crust and broil the topping for a quick appetizer or late-night snacking pizza—

- ½ of a 17½-ounce package (1 sheet) frozen puff pastry
- 3 cups torn mixed greens (spinach, romaine, iceberg, Boston lettuce)
- ½ of a 14-ounce can (¾ cup) artichoke hearts, quartered
- 6 cherry tomatoes, halved
- ½ cup sliced pitted ripe olives
- 1 4-ounce carton (½ cup) herbed semisoft cheese spread *or* ½ cup soft-style cream cheese with chives and onion
- 2 teaspoons Dijon-style mustard
- 1 to 3 teaspoons milk
- 2 cups shredded mozzarella cheese (8 ounces)
- 1 medium avocado, halved, seeded, peeled, and sliced

For crust, thaw pastry according to package directions. On a lightly floured surface roll the pastry into a 12-inch square; cut into a 12-inch circle. Place on a large baking sheet or a 12-inch pizza pan; generously prick bottom. Bake in a 375° oven 15 to 18 minutes or till golden. (If using a clay pizza pan, bake for 22 minutes.) Cool.

In a large mixing bowl combine greens, artichoke hearts, tomatoes, and olives. In a small mixing bowl stir together cheese spread, mustard, and enough milk to make of drizzling consistency; drizzle over greens mixture. Toss to coat well.

Preheat broiler. Sprinkle *1½ cups* of the mozzarella cheese evenly over crust. Broil 3 inches from heat for 1 to 1½ minutes or till cheese is melted. Spoon the salad mixture evenly over cheese. Sprinkle remaining mozzarella on top. Broil 3 inches from heat for 1 to 2 minutes more or just till cheese starts to melt. Arrange avocado slices on top. Cut pizza into wedges. Serve at once. Makes 6 servings.

Nutrition information per serving: 320 cal., 14 g pro., 14 g carbo., 24 g fat, 36 mg chol., and 492 mg sodium. U.S. RDA: 48% vit. A, 30% vit. C, 14% riboflavin, 30% calcium, 10% iron, and 22% phosphorus.

SPICED CHOCOLATE PUDDING

If you're keeping tabs on calories, then aspartame is sweet revenge in the battle of the bulge. Five packets of aspartame sweetener have the sweetening power of 10 teaspoons of sugar. That's a difference of 32 calories per serving. To further cut calories, we used unsweetened cocoa powder and skim milk—

- 2 tablespoons cornstarch
- 2 tablespoons unsweetened cocoa powder
- ⅛ teaspoon ground cinnamon
- 2 cups skim milk
- 5 packets aspartame
- 1 teaspoon vanilla

In a heavy medium saucepan combine cornstarch, cocoa, and cinnamon. Stir in milk. Cook and stir over medium heat till bubbly. Cook and stir for 2 minutes more. Pour into a mixing bowl. Stir in aspartame and vanilla. Cover the surface with clear plastic wrap. Chill without stirring. To serve, spoon into dessert dishes. Makes 4 servings.

Nutrition information per serving: 70 cal., 5 g pro., 11 g carbo., 0 g fat, 3 mg chol., and 64 mg sodium. U.S. RDA: 13% riboflavin, 15% calcium, and 14% phosphorus.

The Idea Magazine for American Families

LANDSCAPING WITH HERBS

TIPS FROM CONNIE SUTHERLAND

May 1986 • $1.50

Better Homes and Gardens

IN THIS ISSUE
- PARENTING!
- HEALTH!
- CRAFTS!
- INVESTING!

TWO-PHASE REMODELING
How One Family Tackled The Job

50 NIFTY, FIX-FAST RECIPES
4 Ingredients Or Fewer For Each!

CONTAINER GARDENING
Crops In Pots

DESTINATION U.S.A.
20 Thrifty Family Vacations

What Every Woman **AND** Every Man Needs To Know To Get The **BEST** New Car Deal

• DECORATING •
THE RETURN TO ROMANCE
Charming, Simple, And Ever So Pretty!

PINEAPPLE!

Springtime Treat from the Tropics

By Terri Pauser Wolf

Add pizzazz to pine-apple salad—serve it in the shell! Then top it with a puff pastry cutout.

Pineapple is at its peak! Use the plump and oh-so-juicy fruit to make this company-special cake.

HOT FRUITED CHICKEN SALAD

Delight a guest with this warm pastry-topped salad that's just perfect for two—

- **2 frozen patty shells**
- **1½ teaspoons butter *or* margarine, melted**
- **1 small fresh pineapple**
- **½ cup chopped celery**
- **2 tablespoons butter *or* margarine**
- **2 teaspoons cornstarch**
- **½ cup orange juice**
- **½ teaspoon instant chicken bouillon granules**
- **1 cup diced cooked chicken**
- **¼ cup raisins**

Thaw patty shells at room temperature for 20 minutes. Cut a 3x5-inch pineapple shape out of paper. Roll out each shell to ⅛-inch thickness; cut a pineapple shape from each using the pattern. Using a small knife, make slash marks across but not through pastries. Brush cut-outs with the 1½ teaspoons melted butter; place on an ungreased baking sheet. Bake in a 400° oven for 15 to 20 minutes or till golden.

Halve pineapple length-wise, crown and all. Cut out pineapple meat, leaving ½-inch shells intact. Invert shells; drain on paper tow-els. Remove core; cut pineap-ple into ½-inch chunks to make 2 cups.

In a medium saucepan cook celery in the 2 table-spoons butter or margarine till tender. Stir in corn-starch. Add orange juice and bouillon granules. Cook and stir till thickened and bub-bly; cook and stir 2 minutes more. Stir in the 2 cups pine-apple chunks, chicken, and raisins. Heat through. Di-vide the mixture between the 2 pineapple shells. Place pastry atop each. Serves 2.

Nutrition information per serving: 664 cal., 25 g pro., 61 g carbo., 37 g fat, 101 mg chol., 572 mg sodium. U.S. RDA: 15% vit. A, 60% vit. C, 30% thiamine, 16% ribofla-vin, 39% niacin, 16% iron, 20% phosphorus.

FRESH PINEAPPLE CAKE

Tender, melt-in-your-mouth pleasure!

- **1 small fresh pineapple, peeled, cored, and cut into ½-inch pieces (about 2 cups)**
- **1 cup all-purpose flour**
- **¼ teaspoon baking soda**
- **¼ teaspoon salt**
- **2 eggs**
- **1 cup sugar**
- **2 tablespoons butter *or* margarine**
- **1 cup whipping cream**
- **2 tablespoons powdered sugar**
- **¼ cup pineapple-orange marmalade**

In a blender container or food processor bowl puree a *third* of the pineapple to make ½ cup puree; add wa-ter to measure ⅔ cup.

Grease and flour an 8-inch springform pan. Stir togeth-er flour, baking soda, and salt. In a mixer bowl beat eggs with an electric mixer on high speed for 4 minutes. Gradually add sugar; beat on medium speed for 4 to 5 minutes or till sugar nearly dissolves. Gradually add flour mixture; beat on low speed just till combined.

Heat pineapple puree and butter or margarine till but-ter melts; add to batter and mix just till combined. Turn into prepared pan. Bake in a 350° oven about 30 minutes or till a toothpick inserted near center comes out clean. Cool 10 minutes on a wire rack. Remove from pan; cool.

In a mixer bowl beat whip-ping cream and powdered sugar till soft peaks form. Cut cake horizontally into 2 layers. Place 1 cake layer on serving platter; spread with *half* of the whipped cream. Place *half* of the pineapple pieces atop; repeat. Heat marmalade and 1 table-spoon *water.* Cool slightly; drizzle over top. Garnish with *mint sprig.* Serves 12.

Nutrition information per serving: 233 cal., 3 g pro., 34 g carbo., 10 g fat, 78 mg chol., 107 mg sodium.

Photographs: William K. Sladcik. Food stylist: Fran Paulson

50 NIFTY FIX-FAST RECIPES

EACH USES 4 INGREDIENTS OR FEWER

Be a meal-time minute miser! These main dishes, side dishes, appetizers, and desserts have a minimum of ingredients. That means you save time from start to finish—in shopping, preparation, and cleanup.

By Lynn Hoppe

Photographs: Scott Little, Mike Dieter. Food Stylist: Janet Pittman

1. GORP 'N' SPICE CUPCAKES
cake mix, dried fruit, chocolate pieces, nuts

2. FAST FAJITAS
tortillas, beef, sour cream dip, salsa

3. USE-YOUR-NOODLE BROCCOLI
frozen broccoli, cream cheese, milk, pasta

4. DOUBLEHEADER PIZZA
frozen pizzas, sausage, olives, mozzarella cheese

5. CURRY-UP CHOW MEIN
canned stew, apple, curry, chow mein noodles

9. DANDY CANDY ICE CREAM
sweetened condensed milk, candy, whipping cream, cones

6. PRONTO CHICKEN AND GRAPES
chicken, marsala, butter, grapes

10. CHUCK-WAGON BEAN SALAD
macaroni wheels, three-bean salad, lettuce, mayonnaise

7. MAYO-PARMESAN BREAD
bread, Parmesan cheese, mayonnaise, chives

11. SURE-BET SURPRISE CUPS
chocolate pieces, truffles, sherbet, crème de cacao

8. PUSH-BUTTON PEACH SHAKE
peaches, frozen juice concentrate, dry milk, ice

12. SHANGHAI SKILLET
frozen pea pods, turkey luncheon meat, fried rice mix

13. MUCHO MOCHA MOUSSE
milk, instant coffee, pudding mix, dessert topping mix

17. CHEESE AND HAMDINGERS
broccoli in cheese sauce, English muffins, mustard, ham

14. SUNSHINE-SAUCED CAKE
oranges, canned vanilla pudding, orange liqueur, pound cake

18. 2-MINUTE TUNA-MAC SALAD
deli macaroni salad, tuna, radishes, lettuce

15. FROSTED BITES
frozen puff pastry, canned frosting, nuts

19. APPLE-OF-YOUR-EYE RICE
frozen rice, apple, raisins

16. PEPPERED TURKEY SALAD
turkey steaks, peppers, salad dressing, lettuce

20. COUNTRY FRENCH TOAST
bread, eggnog, oil, powdered sugar

21. MERRYMAKERS' MUSHROOMS
mushrooms, zucchini, green onion, Parmesan cheese

22. BAVARIAN BEEF SANDWICH
bread, beef, salad dressing, sweet-sour cabbage

23. MISSISSIPPI MUD SAUCE
sugar, cocoa powder, evaporated milk, peanut butter

24. SEASHELLS
tortillas, frozen vegetables, surimi, semicondensed soup

25. MARINATED VEGETABLES
frozen mixed vegetables, onion, salad dressing

26. SHORTCUT STRATA
seasoned croutons, cheddar cheese, eggs, cream

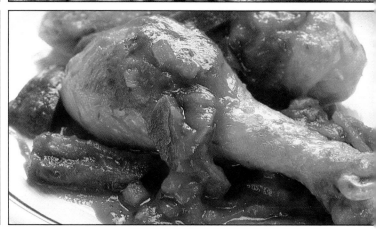

27. CLOCK-WATCHER CACCIATORE
chicken, green pepper, spaghetti sauce, Parmesan cheese

28. BLACK FOREST BROWNIES
refrigerated brownie dough, cherry pie filling, almonds

67

29. DAIQUIRI DESSERT
berries, rum, lemon juice, dessert topping

30. SALAMI REUBENS
salami, Swiss cheese, sauerkraut, buns

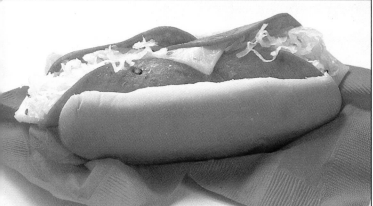

31. BISTRO BAGEL
bagel, butter, orange peel, cinnamon sugar

32. SHERRY TORTONI
marshmallows, sherry, whipping cream, almonds

33. PIZZA BUBBLE BREAD
cornmeal, refrigerated biscuits, spaghetti sauce, cheese

34. HERBIE'S HERBED POTATOES
potatoes, onion, basil, butter

35. HAM-IT-UP SAUCE
maple-flavored syrup, mustard, ham

36. EGGHEADS
eggs, turkey sausage, crackers, chili sauce

37. CHILI-FRANK BURRITOS
tortillas, chili-stuffed frankfurters, American cheese

38. PIQUANT CHUTNEY DIP
chutney, vinegar, dippers

39. CAULIFLOWER CHOWDER
frozen cauliflower, condensed soup, milk, Swiss cheese

40. CURLY NOODLE DINNER
ground beef, oriental noodles, canned tomatoes, canned corn

41. APRICOT PULL-APARTS
frozen bread dough, cake and pastry filling, butter, sugar

42. CONEY ISLAND SPUDS
ground beef, sloppy joe sauce, sour cream dip, potatoes

43. CROWNING GLORY VEGGIES
frozen mixed vegetables, egg whites, mayonnaise, cheese

44. MEXARONI AND CHEESE
canned tomatoes, green pepper, canned macaroni and cheese

45. RISE-AND-SHINE MUFFINS

packaged biscuit mix, instant oatmeal, egg, milk

48. FRUIT AND SPINACH SALAD

canned fruit cocktail, mayonnaise, spinach, raisins

46. CHICKEN SALAD IN MELON BOATS

deli coleslaw, chicken, berries, cantaloupe

49. VEGETABLE PITA POCKETS

pita bread, salad dressing, cooked vegetables, American cheese

47. SPANISH RICE PEPPERS

green peppers, rice, chili sauce, American cheese

50. CARAMEL-PECAN PINWHEELS

butter, ice cream topping, pecans, refrigerated breadsticks

50 NIFTY FIX-FAST RECIPES

MINUTE MENUS

MIX AND MATCH THE RECIPES FOR NIFTY FIX-QUICK MENUS. HERE ARE THREE OF THE MANY POSSIBILITIES.

◆

JIFFY DINNER

48. Fruit and Spinach
Salad
27. Clock-Watcher
Cacciatore
7. Mayo-Parmesan Bread
Ice cream with liqueur
Coffee or milk

◆

ON-CALL BRUNCH

26. Shortcut Strata
50. Caramel-Pecan
Pinwheels
Bacon
Coffee

◆

CELEBRATE!

38. Piquant Chutney Dip
Fresh fruit tray (grapes,
strawberries, pineapple, oranges)
15. Frosted Bites
Wine

GORP 'N' SPICE CUPCAKES

High-energy snacking!

- 1 **package 1-layer-size spice cake mix**
- ⅓ **cup water**
- ⅓ **cup mixed dried fruit bits**
- ⅓ **cup miniature semisweet chocolate pieces**
- ¼ **cup chopped pecans**

Line muffin cups with paper bake cups; set aside. Prepare cake mix according to the package directions, *except* use only ⅓ cup water. Stir in fruit bits. Fill each muffin cup ⅔ full. Sprinkle chocolate pieces and pecans over the tops. Bake in a 350° oven about 20 minutes or till done. Makes 12 cupcakes.

Nutrition information per cupcake: 163 cal., 2 g pro., 23 g carbo., 7 g fat, 20 mg chol., and 149 mg sodium.

FAST FAJITAS

Traditionally, fajitas (pronounced fah-HEE-tahs) are strips of grilled beef served in tortillas with salsa and other condiments. This easy version uses frozen sliced beef—

- 8 **6-inch flour tortillas**
- 1 **14-ounce package frozen very thinly sliced beef**
- ½ **cup sour cream dip with chives**
- ½ **cup salsa**

Wrap tortillas in foil; warm in a 350° oven for 5 minutes. Meanwhile, prepare beef according to package directions. Cut beef into bite-size strips.

For each fajita, arrange some beef strips down center of *each* tortilla to within 1 inch of edge. Spoon *1 tablespoon* sour cream dip and *1 tablespoon* salsa onto *each* tortilla. Roll up each tortilla. Makes 4 main-dish servings (2 tortillas each).

Nutrition information per serving: 424 cal., 33 g pro., 30 g carbo., 19 g fat, 104 mg chol., and 565 mg sodium. U.S. RDA: 18% thiamine, 22% riboflavin, 34% niacin, 26% iron, and 36% phosphorus.

USE-YOUR-NOODLE BROCCOLI

Substitute mixed vegetables, carrots, or cauliflower for the broccoli to serve with the creamy sauce and pasta—

- 1 **10-ounce package frozen cut broccoli**
- 1 **3-ounce package cream cheese with chives, cubed**
- ½ **cup milk**
- 5 **ounces mafalda *or* linguine**

For the sauce, in a 2-quart saucepan cook broccoli according to package directions; drain. Remove broccoli and set aside.

In the same saucepan combine cream cheese and milk. Heat and stir till smooth. Stir in broccoli. Season to taste with salt and pepper.

Meanwhile, prepare the mafalda (curly-edge wide noodles) or linguine according to package directions; drain. Arrange pasta on serving plates; pour sauce over. Makes 3 side-dish servings.

Nutrition information per serving: 321 cal., 12 g pro., 42 g carbo., 12 g fat, 37 mg chol., 115 mg sodium. U.S. RDA: 41% vit. A, 102% vit. C, 32% thiamine, 22% riboflavin, 17% niacin, 12% calcium, 13% iron, and 19% phosphorus.

DOUBLEHEADER PIZZA

Two pizzas are better than one! Serve two of them sandwich-style—

- 1 **13-ounce frozen cheese pizza**
- 1 **8-ounce package brown-and-serve sausage links, cut into ¼-inch-thick slices**
- ¼ **cup sliced pimiento-stuffed olives**
- 1 **4-ounce package shredded mozzarella cheese**
- 1 **13-ounce frozen cheese pizza**

Place 1 cheese pizza on a greased baking sheet. Arrange sausage slices and olives on top. Sprinkle *half* of cheese over all. Top with remaining cheese pizza, crust side up.

Cover the entire pizza with foil. Bake in a 375° oven for 30 minutes. Uncover and bake for 10 minutes more.

Sprinkle the remaining mozzarella cheese over pizza. Bake about 5 minutes more or till cheese is melted. Makes 6 main-dish servings.

Nutrition information per serving: 476 cal., 21 g pro., 45 g carbo., 23 g fat, 54 mg chol., 1,265 mg sodium. U.S. RDA: 13% vit. A, 12% vit. C, 28% riboflavin, 29% thiamine, 22% niacin, 32% calcium, 19% iron, 31% phosphorus.

CURRY-UP CHOW MEIN

For even more authentic Indian flavor, top each serving with chopped unsalted peanuts—

- 1 **15¼-ounce can chicken stew**
- 1 **medium apple, cored and chopped**
- 1 **teaspoon curry powder**
- **Chow mein noodles**

In a 1½-quart saucepan stir together chicken stew, apple, and curry powder. Cook over medium heat for 8 to 10 minutes or till heated through, stirring occasionally. Serve over chow mein noodles. Makes 2 main-dish servings.

Microwave directions: In a 1-quart microwave-safe casserole stir together chicken stew, apple, and curry powder. Micro-cook, covered, on 100% power (high) for 4 to 5 minutes or till heated through, stirring once. Serve as directed above.

Nutrition information per serving: 317 cal., 14 g pro., 39 g carbo., 13 g fat, 3 mg chol., 1,158 mg sodium. U.S. RDA: 142% vit. A, 13% vit. C, 17% niacin, and 14% phosphorus.

PRONTO CHICKEN AND GRAPES

Make this dish pronto plus by purchasing boneless chicken breasts—

- **2 whole medium chicken breasts (about 1½ pounds total)**
- **¼ cup marsala *or* cream sherry**
- **2 tablespoons butter *or* margarine**
- **½ cup seedless red *or* green grapes, halved**

Skin and bone chicken breasts, halving lengthwise. Place the chicken breast halves in a shallow baking dish. Pour marsala or cream sherry over chicken. Marinate for 20 to 30 minutes at room temperature, turning chicken once or twice. Drain chicken, reserving marinade. Pat chicken dry with paper towels. Sprinkle with salt and pepper.

In a large skillet melt butter or margarine. Add chicken. Cook over medium-high heat about 4 minutes on each side or till chicken is brown on both sides and tender. Transfer chicken to serving plates. Cover to keep warm.

For sauce, add the reserved marinade and grapes to the skillet. Cook and stir till the mixture boils. Boil, uncovered, about 30 seconds to reduce slightly. Pour over chicken. Makes 4 main-dish servings.

Nutrition information per serving: 200 cal., 25 g pro., 5 g carbo., 9 g fat, 83 mg chol., 240 mg sodium. U.S. RDA: 55% niacin and 19% phosphorus.

MAYO-PARMESAN BREAD

Surprise! No butter or margarine. Stir the Parmesan cheese right into the mayonnaise for a zippy topper—

- **¼ cup grated Parmesan cheese**
- **¼ cup mayonnaise *or* salad dressing**
- **1 tablespoon snipped chives *or* parsley (optional)**
- **French *or* Italian bread (cut ½ inch thick)**

In a small mixing bowl combine Parmesan cheese and mayonnaise or salad dressing. If desired, stir in snipped chives or parsley. Set aside.

Place 4 or 5 slices French or Italian bread on the rack of an unheated broiler pan. Broil 3 to 4 inches from heat about 1 minute or till toasted.

Spread some of the mayonnaise mixture on the untoasted side of each slice of bread. Broil, mayonnaise side up, 3 to 4 inches from heat for 2 to 3 minutes or till light brown. Makes 4 or 5 side-dish servings.

Nutrition information per serving: 229 cal., 6 g pro., 20 g carbo., 14 g fat, 14 mg chol., 398 mg sodium. U.S. RDA: 10% calcium.

DANDY CANDY ICE CREAM

Just stir, whip, and freeze—

- **1 14-ounce can sweetened condensed milk (1¼ cups)**
- **1 cup candy-coated milk chocolate pieces, chopped**
- **2 cups whipping cream**
- **Ice cream cones**
- **Candy-coated milk chocolate pieces, chopped (optional)**

In a medium mixing bowl combine sweetened condensed milk and candy-coated milk chocolate pieces.

In a large mixer bowl beat whipping cream with an electric mixer on medium speed till soft peaks form; fold into condensed milk mixture. Transfer to a 9x9x2-inch pan. Cover tightly with moisture- and vaporproof wrap. Freeze at least 6 hours or till firm.

Serve in ice cream cones or individual dessert dishes. Before serving, press additional chopped candy-coated milk chocolate pieces into scooped frozen mixture, if desired. Makes about 1½ quarts (12 servings).

Nutrition information per serving: 308 cal., 4 g pro., 29 g carbo., 20 g fat, 66 mg chol., 57 mg sodium. U.S. RDA: 14% vit. A, 11% riboflavin, 12% calcium, and 11% phosphorus.

PUSH-BUTTON PEACH SHAKE

Pour it into a disposable cup for a take-with-you breakfast—

- **1 8-ounce can peach slices**
- **½ of a 6-ounce can (⅓ cup) frozen pineapple-orange *or* orange juice concentrate**
- **⅓ cup nonfat dry milk powder**
- **4 *or* 5 ice cubes**
- **Mint leaves (optional)**

In a blender container combine *undrained* peach slices, frozen juice concentrate, and milk powder. Cover and blend till smooth. With the blender running, add ice cubes, one at a time, through opening in lid, blending well after each addition. Garnish each serving with mint leaves, if desired. Makes 2 (8-ounce) servings.

Nutrition information per serving: 184 cal., 8 g pro., 40 g carbo., 0 g fat, 3 mg chol., 101 mg sodium. U.S. RDA: 20% vit. A, 107% vit. C, 13% thiamine, 20% riboflavin, 23% calcium, and 22% phosphorus.

CHUCK-WAGON BEAN SALAD

Macaroni wheels add interest to this sweet-sour make-ahead salad—

- **1 cup wagon wheels *or* elbow macaroni**
- **1 15-ounce can three-bean salad**
- **⅓ cup mayonnaise *or* salad dressing**
- **Lettuce leaves**

Prepare wagon wheels or elbow macaroni according to package directions; drain. Rinse with cold water; drain. Drain three-bean salad, reserving *1 tablespoon* of the liquid.

In a medium mixing bowl combine wagon wheels and drained salad. Stir together reserved liquid and mayonnaise or salad dressing. Add to wagon wheels mixture. Toss to coat. Cover and chill several hours. Serve in a lettuce-lined bowl. Makes 4 side-dish servings.

Nutrition information per serving: 284 cal., 5 g pro., 33 g carbo., 15 g fat, 11 mg chol., 595 mg sodium. U.S. RDA: 14% thiamine and 22% iron.

SURE-BET SURPRISE CUPS

Choose your favorite sherbet flavor: lime, raspberry, pineapple, or orange—

- ¼ **cup semisweet chocolate pieces**
- 2 **1-inch white truffles**
- ½ **cup sherbet**
- 2 **tablespoons crème de cacao**

In a 1-quart heavy saucepan cook and stir chocolate pieces over low heat till melted. Place 1 paper bake cup in each of 2 muffin or custard cups. Spoon *half* of the melted chocolate into *each*. Using a narrow metal spatula, spread chocolate over the bottoms and up sides of the paper cups. Chill till firm.

Just before serving, carefully peel off paper bake cups. Place one 1-inch white truffle in *each* chocolate cup. Using a tablespoon, scoop the sherbet into thin petals. Arrange sherbet over and around the truffles in *each* chocolate cup. Pour *1 tablespoon* of crème de cacao over sherbet in *each* chocolate cup. Makes 2 servings.

Microwave directions: In a 1-cup glass measure micro-cook the chocolate pieces, uncovered, on 100% power (high) about 1 minute or till soft enough to stir smooth. Continue as directed.

Nutrition information per serving: 299 cal., 2 g pro., 47 g carbo., 11 g fat, 4 mg chol., and 66 mg sodium.

SHANGHAI SKILLET

Serve Shanghai Skillet over colorful vegetables. Just cook another package of pea pods using the package directions—

- 1 **6-ounce package frozen pea pods**
- 1 **8-ounce package turkey ham luncheon meat**
- 1 **6- or 6¼-ounce package regular stir-fried rice mix**

Place pea pods in a colander and rinse under warm running water to thaw and separate. Cut pea pods in half crosswise. Slice turkey ham luncheon meat into julienne strips.

In a 2-quart saucepan prepare rice mix according to package directions. Stir in *three-fourths* of the turkey ham and the pea pods. Cover and let stand for 5 minutes. Turn into a serving dish; top with remaining turkey ham. Makes 4 main-dish servings.

Nutrition information per serving: 232 cal., 17 g pro., 37 g carbo., 2 g fat, 35 mg chol., 887 mg sodium. U.S. RDA: 24% vit. C, 17% thiamine, 16% riboflavin, 24% niacin, 13% iron, and 30% phosphorus.

MUCHO MOCHA MOUSSE

A 10-minute dessert you can make a few hours ahead or serve right away—

- 1½ **cups milk**
- 2 **teaspoons instant coffee crystals**
- 1 **4-serving-size package *instant* chocolate pudding mix**
- 1 **1¼-ounce envelope whipped dessert topping mix**

In a large mixer bowl combine milk and coffee crystals. Let stand 5 minutes to dissolve crystals. Stir in pudding mix and dessert topping mix. Beat with an electric mixer on low speed about 30 seconds or till moistened. Beat on high speed about 4 minutes more or till fluffy. Spoon into individual dessert dishes. Serve immediately or chill till serving time. Makes 6 servings.

Nutrition information per serving: 141 cal., 3 g pro., 23 g carbo., 5 g fat, 9 mg chol., 114 mg sodium. U.S. RDA: 12% calcium.

SUNSHINE-SAUCED CAKE

A cinch to make, yet company special—

- 2 **oranges**
- 1 **4¼-ounce container vanilla pudding**
- 1 **tablespoon orange liqueur**
- 1 **10¾-ounce frozen loaf pound cake, thawed**

From oranges, finely shred enough peel to make *1 tablespoon*. Set aside. Remove and discard the remaining peel. Section oranges.

In a small mixing bowl stir together vanilla pudding and orange liqueur. Cut pound cake into 12 thin slices. Place 2 slices on *each* of 6 individual dessert plates. Top each serving with some orange sections, pudding mixture, and orange peel. Serves 6.

Nutrition information per serving: 184 cal., 3 g pro., 30 g carbo., 6 g fat, 59 mg chol., 126 mg sodium. U.S. RDA: 41% vit. C.

FROSTED BITES

For a chocolate-mint version, thin the chocolate frosting with white crème de menthe instead of water—

- ½ **of a 17½-ounce package frozen puff pastry (1 sheet)**
- 3 **to 4 teaspoons water**
- ½ **cup canned chocolate frosting**
- ¼ **cup finely chopped pistachio nuts *or* pecans**

Thaw puff pastry for 20 minutes at room temperature or overnight in the refrigerator. Unfold pastry. Cut on 3 fold lines; then cut each piece crosswise into 7 rectangles (21 total).

Arrange pastry rectangles on an ungreased baking sheet; prick several times with a fork. Bake in a 425° oven for 15 to 20 minutes or till light brown. Cool on a wire rack.

Meanwhile, stir water into chocolate frosting. Spoon frosting mixture over tops of warm pastries. Immediately sprinkle with chopped nuts. Cool thoroughly. Makes 21 pastries.

Nutrition information per pastry: 69 cal., 1 g pro., 8 g carbo., 4 g fat, 0 mg chol., and 50 mg sodium.

PEPPERED TURKEY SALAD

Stir-fry this colorful salad in oil and vinegar salad dressing—

- **2 boneless turkey breast tenderloin steaks (8 ounces total)**
- **2 red, green, *or* yellow sweet peppers**
- **½ cup oil and vinegar salad dressing**
- **2 cups torn lettuce**

Cut tenderloin steaks into ½-inch-wide strips. Cut peppers into strips. In a 10-inch skillet heat ¼ cup oil and vinegar salad dressing. Add turkey strips. Stir-fry over medium-high heat for 3 to 4 minutes or till tender. Cool slightly.

In a medium mixing bowl combine *undrained* turkey and peppers. Pour remaining *¼ cup* oil and vinegar salad dressing over turkey mixture; toss to coat. Cover and chill several hours or overnight. To serve, arrange over lettuce. Makes 2 main-dish servings.

Nutrition information per serving: 423 cal., 27 g pro., 9 g carbo., 32 g fat, 65 mg chol., 78 mg sodium. U.S. RDA: 59% vit. A, 284% vit. C, 10% thiamine, 15% riboflavin, 26% niacin, 19% iron, and 22% phosphorus.

2-MINUTE TUNA-MAC SALAD

Easy does it because your deli helps make it—

- **1 pint deli macaroni salad (2 cups)**
- **1 3¼-ounce can tuna, drained and flaked (water pack)**
- **½ cup sliced radishes**
- **Lettuce leaves**

In a medium mixing bowl combine macaroni salad, tuna, and radishes; toss gently to mix. Cover and chill till serving time. Serve on lettuce leaves. Makes 2 main-dish servings.

Nutrition information per serving: 323 cal., 20 g pro., 27 g carbo., 15 g fat, 54 mg chol., and 48 mg sodium. U.S. RDA: 43% vit. A, 44% vit. C, 11% thiamine, 42% niacin, 13% iron, and 17% phosphorus.

CHEESE AND HAMDINGERS

A meal-in-one, open-face sandwich—

- **1 10-ounce package frozen broccoli in cheese sauce**
- **2 English muffins, split and toasted**
- **Dijon-style mustard**
- **8 slices fully cooked ham (8 ounces)**

Prepare broccoli in cheese sauce according to package directions. Meanwhile, spread English muffins halves with mustard. Place muffin halves on 2 individual plates. Place 2 slices fully cooked ham on each muffin half. Spoon hot broccoli-cheese mixture over ham. Makes 2 main-dish servings.

Nutrition information per serving: 428 cal., 28 g pro., 40 g carbo., 17 g fat, 53 mg chol., 1,759 mg sodium. U.S. RDA: 27% vit. A, 95% vit. C, 64% thiamine, 34% riboflavin, 35% niacin, 19% calcium, 17% iron, 45% phosphorus.

APPLE-OF-YOUR-EYE RICE

Try this fruited rice with a pork chop dinner—

- **1 10-ounce package frozen long grain and wild rice**
- **1 medium apple, cored and coarsely chopped**
- **¼ cup raisins *or* chopped pecans**
- **2 tablespoons water**

Place rice pouch in a medium mixing bowl filled with hot *water.* Let stand about 10 minutes or till just thawed. Remove the pouch from water.

Remove rice from the pouch and place in a 2-quart saucepan. Stir in apple, raisins or pecans, and water. Cover and cook about 5 minutes or till rice is heated through and apples are crisp-tender, stirring occasionally. Makes 4 or 5 side-dish servings.

Nutrition information per serving: 132 cal., 16 g pro., 28 g carbo., 2 g fat, 0 mg chol., 380 mg sodium. U.S. RDA: 11% thiamine.

COUNTRY FRENCH TOAST

The built-in spices in canned or refrigerated eggnog make a delicious coating for French toast—

- **4 thick slices French *or* Italian bread**
- **½ cup dairy eggnog**
- **2 tablespoons cooking oil**
- **Sifted powdered sugar**

Dip both sides of French or Italian bread into eggnog. In a large skillet cook bread slices in hot cooking oil over medium heat about 2½ minutes or till golden. Turn bread; cook about 1½ minutes more or till golden. (Add more oil as needed.) Transfer to a serving plate. Sprinkle with sifted powdered sugar. Makes 2 main-dish servings.

Nutrition information per serving: 393 cal., 9 g pro., 54 g carbo., 16 g fat, 39 mg chol., 441 mg sodium. U.S. RDA: 20% thiamine, 17% riboflavin, 12% niacin, 11% calcium, 12% iron, and 13% phosphorus.

MERRYMAKERS' MUSHROOMS

For a large party, double the recipe and stagger the baking so your guests have stuffed mushrooms hot from the oven—

- **16 to 20 large fresh mushrooms**
- **1 small zucchini, shredded (¾ cup)**
- **2 tablespoons sliced green onion**
- **1 tablespoon water**
- **⅓ cup grated Parmesan cheese**

Remove stems from mushrooms; chop stems. Set mushroom caps aside. In a medium saucepan cook and stir mushroom stems, zucchini, and green onion in water over medium heat till tender. Drain. Stir Parmesan cheese into vegetable mixture.

Divide zucchini mixture among mushroom caps. Place mushrooms in a 13x9x2-inch baking dish. Bake in a 375° oven for 8 to 10 minutes or till mushroom caps are tender. Serve warm. Makes 16 to 20 appetizers.

Nutrition information per appetizer: 63 cal., 6 g pro., 5 g carbo., 3 g fat, 6 mg chol., 165 mg sodium. U.S. RDA: 13% vit. C, 22% riboflavin, 17% niacin, 13% calcium, and 16% phosphorus.

BAVARIAN BEEF SANDWICH

Sweet-sour cabbage zips up a roast beef sandwich for a fast and easy main-dish. Try one for lunch or dinner—

- 8 slices dark rye bread
- 8 ounces thinly sliced, cooked beef
- 8 teaspoons Thousand Island salad dressing
- 1 16-ounce jar sweet-sour cabbage, drained

On *each* of 4 slices dark rye bread layer *2 ounces* cooked beef. Drizzle *2 teaspoons* salad dressing over *each*. Top *each* with *one-fourth* of the sweet-sour cabbage. Top *each* with a slice of dark rye bread. Makes 4 main-dish servings.
Nutrition information per serving: 291 cal., 22 g pro., 31 g carbo., 10 g fat, 55 mg chol., 950 mg sodium. U.S. RDA: 18% vit. C, 14% thiamine, 15% riboflavin, 23% niacin, 22% iron, and 23% phosphorus.

MISSISSIPPI MUD SAUCE

Serve this peanut butter and chocolate sauce over ice cream or sliced pound cake for a super quick and rich dessert—

- ¾ cup sugar
- ⅓ cup unsweetened cocoa powder
- 1 5-ounce (⅔ cup) can evaporated milk
- ¼ cup chunky peanut butter

In a small saucepan stir together sugar and cocoa powder. Stir in evaporated milk. Cook and stir over medium-high heat till boiling. Remove from heat. Stir in peanut butter. Serve warm. Makes 1½ cups sauce.

Microwave directions: In a small microwave-safe mixing bowl stir together sugar and cocoa powder. Stir in evaporated milk. Micro-cook, uncovered, on 100% power (high) for 2 to 3 minutes or till boiling, stirring once. Stir in chunky peanut butter.
Nutrition information per 2 tablespoons: 96 cal., 21 g pro., 16 g carbo., 4 g fat, 0 mg chol., and 66 mg sodium.

SEASHELLS

A tortilla shell holds this creamy mock-crab and corn filling—

- 3 6-inch flour tortillas
- 1 10-ounce package frozen mixed Mexican-style vegetables
- 1 7½-ounce can semicondensed cream of mushroom soup
- 1 6-ounce package frozen salad-style crab-flavored fish, thawed

For tortilla shells, wrap tortillas in foil and heat in a 350° oven for 10 minutes. Fit each tortilla into a greased 10-ounce custard cup. Place on a baking sheet. Bake in a 350° oven for 12 to 15 minutes or till light brown. Transfer tortillas from custard cups to serving plates.
Meanwhile, prepare frozen mixed Mexican-style vegetables according to package directions. Stir in mushroom soup. Cut fish into 1-inch pieces. Gently stir fish into vegetable mixture. Heat through. Evenly divide among tortilla cups. Makes 3 main-dish servings.
Nutrition information per serving: 260 cal., 13 g pro., 36 g carbo., 8 g fat, 1 mg chol., 1,401 mg sodium. U.S. RDA: 25% vit. A, 35% vit. C, 12% thiamine, 11% niacin, and 12% phosphorus.

MARINATED VEGETABLES

A make-ahead salad saves precious minutes just before your guests arrive—

- 1 16-ounce package loose-pack frozen mixed broccoli, cauliflower, and carrots
- 1 small onion, thinly sliced and separated into rings
- ½ cup Italian salad dressing

In a medium saucepan cook frozen mixed broccoli, cauliflower, and carrots in a small amount of boiling salted water about 5 minutes or till crisp-tender; drain. Transfer to a medium mixing bowl. Add onion and salad dressing; toss to coat. Cover and chill for 2 to 24 hours, stirring once or twice. Makes 6 side-dish servings.
Nutrition information per serving: 150 cal., 2 g pro., 12 g carbo., 11 g fat, 13 mg chol., 311 mg sodium. U.S. RDA: 17% vit. A and 30% vit. C.

SHORTCUT STRATA

- 2 cups seasoned croutons
- 1 cup shredded cheddar, Swiss, *or* Monterey Jack cheese (4 ounces)
- 3 eggs
- 1½ cups light cream *or* milk

In an 8x1½-inch round baking dish arrange croutons in an even layer. Sprinkle cheese over croutons. In a small mixing bowl beat eggs. Stir in cream or milk; pour over croutons. Cover and chill for 3 to 24 hours.
Bake, uncovered, in a 350° oven for 20 to 25 minutes or till a knife inserted near the center comes out clean. Makes 4 main-dish servings.
Nutrition information per serving: 385 cal., 16 g pro., 17 g carbo., 26 g fat, 270 mg chol., 542 mg sodium. U.S. RDA: 18% vit. A, 21% riboflavin, 32% calcium, and 30% phosphorus.

CLOCK-WATCHER CACCIATORE

Cacciatore means cooked with tomatoes and herbs. This quick and easy version gets both from the convenient chunky-style spaghetti sauce—

8 chicken drumsticks *or* thighs (about 1¼ pounds)
1 green pepper, cut into ½-inch-wide strips
1 cup chunky meatless spaghetti sauce
Grated Parmesan cheese

In a medium nonstick skillet place chicken drumsticks or thighs, skin side down. Cook over medium heat about 15 minutes or till browned evenly, turning frequently. Drain off fat.

Add green pepper and spaghetti sauce to skillet. Cover and cook over low heat for 30 to 35 minutes or till chicken is tender. Transfer chicken to a serving platter. Stir mixture in skillet; pour over chicken. Pass the Parmesan cheese to sprinkle atop. Makes 4 main-dish servings.

Microwave directions: Arrange the chicken in a 12x7½x2-inch micro-wave-safe baking dish with meatiest portions toward outside of dish. Add green pepper. Cover with waxed paper. Micro-cook on 100% power (high) for 10 minutes, giving the dish a half-turn once. Drain off fat.

Spoon spaghetti sauce over all. Cook, covered, on high for 5 minutes more. Pass Parmesan cheese.

Nutrition information per serving: 219 cal., 27 g pro., 10 g carbo., 7 g fat, 82 mg chol., 502 mg sodium. U.S. RDA: 80% vit. C, 14% riboflavin, 26% niacin, 13% iron, and 21% phosphorus.

BLACK FOREST BROWNIES

So easy and so impressive—

1 roll refrigerated brownie cookie dough
1 21-ounce can cherry pie filling
¼ cup sliced almonds

Divide cookie dough between 2 greased 8x1½-inch round baking pans. Spread dough over the bottom of each pan. Bake in a 350° oven about 30 minutes or till done. Cool in pans on a wire rack for 10 minutes. Remove from pans. Cool thoroughly.

Reserve *½ cup* cherry pie filling; set aside. Place 1 brownie layer on a serving plate. Spoon remaining pie filling over layer. Place second brownie layer on top of the filling. Top with reserved pie filling. Sprinkle with sliced almonds. Makes 10 to 12 servings.

Nutrition information per serving: 281 cal., 2 g pro., 49 g carbo., 9 g fat, 0 mg chol., and 168 mg sodium.

DAIQUIRI DESSERT

A creamy strawberry dessert to spruce up any meal—

1 10-ounce package frozen strawberries, broken up
¼ cup light rum
2 tablespoons lemon juice
1 8-ounce container frozen whipped dessert topping, thawed

In a blender container or food processor bowl combine strawberries, light rum, and lemon juice. Cover and blend or process till thoroughly mixed. Transfer berry mixture to a medium mixing bowl. Fold in dessert topping. Spoon into 8 chilled glasses or sherbet dishes. Serve immediately. Makes 8 servings.

Nutrition information per serving: 122 cal., 1 g pro., 10 g carbo., 7 g fat, 0 mg chol., 8 mg sodium. U.S. RDA: 42% vit. C.

SALAMI REUBENS

To make an already spunky sandwich even spunkier, drizzle Italian salad dressing over salami after baking—

8 4- *or* 5-inch slices salami
4 slices Swiss *or* caraway cheese
1 cup sauerkraut, drained
4 frankfurter buns, split

On a flat surface arrange 2 slices salami so edges overlap. Repeat 3 times, using a total of 8 slices. Top *each* pair with *1 slice* cheese and ¼ *cup* sauerkraut. Fold edges of salami over cheese and sauerkraut. Place each bundle in a frankfurter bun. Wrap each bun in foil. Place on a baking sheet. Bake in a 375° oven about 15 minutes or till cheese is melted. Makes 4 main-dish servings.

Microwave directions: Prepare as directed above, *except* wrap each sandwich in a white paper towel. Micro-cook on 100% power (high) about 2 minutes or till cheese is melted.

Nutrition information per serving: 341 cal., 18 g pro., 25 g carbo., 19 g fat, 52 mg chol., 1,047 mg sodium. U.S. RDA: 21% vit. C, 12% thiamine, 17% riboflavin, 31% calcium, 11% iron, and 25% phosphorus.

BISTRO BAGEL

1 bagel, split
1 tablespoon butter *or* margarine, softened
¼ teaspoon finely shredded orange peel
1 teaspoon cinnamon sugar

Toast bagel under the broiler. Meanwhile, stir together butter or margarine and orange peel. Spread each bagel half with butter mixture. Sprinkle *each* with *½ teaspoon* cinnamon sugar. Return to broiler; broil till just bubbly. Makes 1 serving.

Nutrition information per serving: 269 cal., 6 g pro., 33 g carbo., 13 g fat, 31 mg chol., 312 mg sodium. U.S. RDA: 13% thiamine.

SHERRY TORTONI

An authentic tortoni, named for Tortona, Italy, is an ice cream made from heavy cream, often with almonds and maraschino cherries—

- **2 cups marshmallows**
- **¼ cup cream sherry**
- **1 cup whipping cream**
- **2 tablespoons chopped almonds, toasted**

In a small saucepan combine marshmallows and cream sherry. Cook over low heat till marshmallows melt, stirring occasionally. Remove from heat. Cool 10 minutes, stirring frequently.

In a chilled mixer bowl, beat whipping cream till soft peaks form. Fold marshmallow mixture into whipped cream. Fold in almonds. Spoon into 6 muffin cups lined with paper bake cups. Cover and freeze about 4 hours or till firm.

Remove desserts from muffin cups and store in moisture- and vaporproof containers in the freezer. Before serving, top with additional toasted sliced almonds. Makes 6 servings.

Microwave directions: In a 1-quart microwave-safe casserole combine marshmallows and sherry. Micro-cook, uncovered, on 100% power (high) for 1 to 2 minutes or till marshmallows are melted, stirring once. Continue as directed above.

Nutrition information per serving: 224 cal., 2 g pro., 15 g carbo., 17 g fat, 55 mg chol., 21 mg sodium. U.S. RDA: 12% vit. A.

PIZZA BUBBLE BREAD

For this bumpy, saucy pizza, start with a super easy crust made from refrigerated biscuits—

- **Cornmeal**
- **1 package (10) refrigerated biscuits**
- **½ cup spaghetti *or* pizza sauce**
- **1 cup shredded mozzarella cheese (4 ounces)**

Sprinkle a greased 12-inch pizza pan with cornmeal. Separate refrigerated biscuits. Snip *each* biscuit into 4 pieces. Place in a medium mixing bowl. Add spaghetti or pizza sauce; toss to coat. Arrange dough pieces in an 8-inch circle in the pizza pan. Sprinkle with mozzarella cheese. Bake in a 400° oven about 15 minutes or till golden. Makes 10 to 12 appetizer servings.

Nutrition information per serving: 126 cal., 5 g pro., 14 g carbo., 5 g fat, 7 mg chol., 431 mg sodium. U.S. RDA: 17% phosphorus.

HERBIE'S HERBED POTATOES

Choose your favorite herb—basil, oregano, or tarragon—

- **3 medium potatoes**
- **1 medium onion**
- **¼ teaspoon dried herb (basil, oregano, *or* tarragon), crushed**
- **1 tablespoon butter *or* margarine, melted**

Thinly slice potatoes and onion. In a 9-inch pie plate layer *half* of the potatoes and *half* of the onion. Sprinkle with herb. Drizzle with butter or margarine. Repeat the potato, onion, herb, and butter or margarine layers. Season with salt and pepper.

Cover and bake in a 425° oven for 20 minutes. Uncover and bake for 10 to 20 minutes more or till potatoes are tender. Makes 4 side-dish servings.

Nutrition information per serving: 142 cal., 3 g pro., 26 g carbo., 3 g fat, 8 mg chol., 36 mg sodium. U.S. RDA: 30% vit. C and 10% niacin.

HAM-IT-UP SAUCE

Try this maple-syrup and mustard sauce on chicken, too—

- **2 tablespoons maple-flavored syrup *or* maple syrup**
- **2 tablespoons brown mustard**
- **1 6-ounce package sliced fully cooked ham**

For glaze, in a small saucepan stir together maple-flavored syrup or maple syrup and brown mustard; heat through. Heat ham. Spoon glaze over ham. Makes 2 main-dish servings.

Microwave directions: In a 1-cup glass measure combine syrup and mustard. Micro-cook, uncovered, on 100% power (high) for 30 to 45 seconds or till heated through, stirring once. Serve as directed above.

Nutrition information per serving: 206 cal., 19 g pro., 20 g carbo., 6 g fat, 45 mg chol., 1,224 mg sodium. U.S. RDA: 20% vit. C, 43% thiamine, 10% riboflavin, 17% niacin, 10% iron, and 19% phosphorus.

EGGHEADS

- **1 pound frozen turkey sausage**
- **8 hard-cooked eggs**
- **2 eggs**
- **⅔ cup crushed rich round cheese crackers (about 16 crackers)**
- **Chili sauce**

Divide turkey sausage into 8 portions. Shape each portion into a 4-inch-round patty. Wrap *each* patty around 1 hard-cooked egg, covering egg completely.

In a small mixing bowl beat the 2 eggs. Roll each sausage-wrapped egg in the beaten egg, then roll in crushed rich round cheese crackers.

Arrange eggs in a shallow baking pan. Bake in a 375° oven for 25 to 30 minutes or till sausage is well done. Serve warm or cold with chili sauce. Makes 8 main-dish servings.

Nutrition information per serving: 229 cal., 18 g pro., 4 g carbo., 15 g fat, 383 mg chol., 456 mg sodium. U.S. RDA: 20% riboflavin, 13% niacin, 13% iron, and 21% phosphorus.

CHILI-FRANK BURRITOS

Wrap tortillas in foil and heat them in a 375° oven for 5 minutes so that they won't crack when rolled—

- 2 7-inch flour tortillas
- 2 slices American cheese *or* cheese spread
- 2 chili-stuffed frankfurters

On 1 side of *each* tortilla arrange 1 slice American cheese or cheese spread and 1 frankfurter. Fold in ends of tortillas; roll up tortillas around cheese and frankfurters. Wrap in foil. Bake in a 375° oven about 15 minutes or till warm. Makes 2 main-dish servings.

Nutrition information per serving: 392 cal., 17 g pro., 18 g carbo., 28 g fat, 67 mg chol., 1,335 mg sodium. U.S. RDA: 12% thiamine, 16% riboflavin, 13% niacin, 20% calcium, 10% iron, and 33% phosphorus.

PIQUANT CHUTNEY DIP

This sweet-sour dip with assorted dippers is a great snack for drop-in guests—

- 1 9-ounce jar chutney
- 1 tablespoon vinegar
- Shrimp, peeled, deveined, and cooked
- Green pepper strips
- Cooked chicken nuggets

Chop or snip any large pieces from chutney. In a small saucepan combine chutney and vinegar. Cook and stir till heated through. If necessary, add enough *water* to make of dipping consistency. Turn into a serving dish; place on a platter. Arrange shrimp, green pepper strips, or chicken nuggets around dip. Makes about ⅔ cup dip.

Microwave directions: In a 2-cup glass measure combine chutney and vinegar. Micro-cook, uncovered, on 100% power (high) for 1 to 2 minutes or till heated through. Serve as directed.

Nutrition information per tablespoon: 53 cal., 0 g pro., 13 g carbo., 0 g fat, 0 mg chol., and 43 mg sodium.

CAULIFLOWER CHOWDER

For variety, use 1 can cream of potato soup and 1 can green pea soup—

- 1 10-ounce package frozen cauliflower
- ½ cup water
- 2 10¾-ounce cans condensed cream of potato soup *or* two 11¼-ounce cans condensed green pea soup
- 2 cups milk
- 1 cup shredded Swiss cheese (4 ounces)

In a 3-quart saucepan combine cauliflower and water. Cover and cook about 5 minutes or till tender. *Do not drain.* Cut up large pieces. Mash all of the cauliflower slightly.

Stir in the condensed potato soup or green pea soup. Stir in milk and Swiss cheese. Cook and stir till cheese is melted and soup is heated through. Makes 6 side-dish servings.

Microwave directions: In a 2½- or 3½-quart microwave-safe casserole combine cauliflower and water. Micro-cook, covered, on 100% power (high) for 6 to 8 minutes or till cauliflower is tender. *Do not drain.* Cut up large pieces. Mash cauliflower slightly.

Add condensed potato soup or pea soup. Stir in milk and cheese. Cook, covered, on high for 8 to 10 minutes or till cheese is melted and soup is heated through, stirring twice.

Nutrition information per serving: 224 cal., 13 g pro., 21 g carbo., 10 g fat, 31 mg chol., 877 mg sodium. U.S. RDA: 10% vit. A, 34% vit. C, 15% riboflavin, 30% calcium, and 27% phosphorus.

CURLY NOODLE DINNER

- 1 pound ground beef
- 1 3-ounce package Oriental noodles with pork flavor
- 1 14½-ounce can stewed tomatoes
- 1 8-ounce can whole kernel corn

In a 10-inch skillet cook ground beef till brown; drain off fat. Stir in seasoning packet from the Oriental noodles, *undrained* tomatoes, and *undrained* corn.

Break up noodles; stir into the beef mixture. Bring to boiling; reduce heat. Cover and simmer about 10 minutes or till noodles are tender. Makes 4 or 5 main-dish servings.

Nutrition information per serving: 340 cal., 28 g pro., 27 g carbo., 13 g fat, 80 mg chol., 695 mg sodium. U.S. RDA: 19% vit. A, 25% vit. C, 16% thiamine, 18% riboflavin, 16% niacin, 24% iron, and 24% phosphorus.

APRICOT PULL-APARTS

Frozen bread dough means you can have this fancy fruit-filled loaf in no time—

- 1 16-ounce loaf frozen white bread dough, thawed
- 1 12-ounce can apricot *or* prune cake and pastry filling
- 3 tablespoons butter *or* margarine
- ⅓ cup sugar

Cut bread dough in half lengthwise; then cut crosswise into 8 pieces (16 pieces total). Flatten pieces of dough with fingers, stretching slightly to form 4-inch circles. Spoon about *1 tablespoon* of filling in center of *each* circle. Bring edges of dough together; pinch to seal.

Dip filled rolls in melted butter or margarine, then in sugar. Place, seam side down, in 2 layers in a greased 9x5x3-inch loaf pan. Cover and let rise in a warm place till almost double (about 1 hour).

Bake in a 350° oven for 35 to 40 minutes or till done, covering with foil the last 10 minutes of baking. Invert onto a serving plate. Remove the pan. Serve warm. Makes 1 loaf (16 servings).

Nutrition information per serving: 136 cal., 29 g pro., 24 g carbo., 4 g fat, 7 mg chol., and 159 mg sodium.

CONEY ISLAND SPUDS

A complete meal in a potato—

- **3 large baking potatoes**
- **¾ pound ground beef**
- **1 15¼-ounce can sloppy joe sauce**
- **1 cup sour cream dip with chives**
- **¼ cup water**

Scrub potatoes and prick skin. Bake in a 425° oven for 40 to 60 minutes; quarter lengthwise.

In a large skillet cook ground beef till brown; drain off fat. Stir in sloppy joe sauce. Bring to boiling; reduce heat. Cover and simmer for 5 minutes. Stir in ½ *cup* sour cream dip and water. Heat through. *Do not boil.*

Spoon meat mixture over potatoes. Top the potatoes with remaining sour cream dip. Makes 3 main-dish servings.

Microwave directions: Scrub the potatoes and prick skin. Arrange in a spoke pattern, leaving 1-inch space between. Micro-cook, uncovered, on 100% power (high) for 9 to 10 minutes or till slightly firm. Wrap in foil. Let stand for 5 minutes. Quarter lengthwise.

Crumble all of the ground beef into a 1½-quart microwave-safe casserole. Micro-cook, covered, on 100% power (high) for 3½ to 4 minutes or till brown, stirring once to break up. Drain off fat.

Stir in sloppy joe sauce. Cook, covered, on high about 4 minutes or till boiling, stirring once. Cook, uncovered, on 50% power (medium) for 2 minutes more. Stir in ½ *cup* sour cream dip and water. Cook, uncovered, on 100% power (high) for 1 to 1½ minutes more or till heated through. *Do not boil.* Continue as directed above.

Nutrition information per serving: 583 cal., 32 g pro., 56 g carbo., 27 g fat, 116 mg chol., and 933 mg sodium. U.S. RDA: 53% vit. A, 103% vit. C, 21% thiamine, 22% riboflavin, 47% niacin, 12% calcium, 35% iron, and 36% phosphorus.

CROWNING GLORY VEGGIES

The elegant soufflélike topper jazzes up any combination of frozen vegetables—

- **1 16-ounce package loose-pack frozen mixed carrot, cauliflower, green beans, zucchini, and butter beans**
- **3 egg whites**
- **¼ teaspoon salt**
- **½ cup mayonnaise *or* salad dressing**
- **¼ cup shredded cheddar cheese (1 ounce)**

In a medium saucepan cook mixed vegetables according to package directions. Drain. Divide vegetables among four 10-ounce custard cups.

In a small mixer bowl beat egg whites and salt with an electric mixer on medium speed till stiff peaks form (tips stand straight). Fold in mayonnaise or salad dressing.

Spoon mayonnaise mixture atop vegetables in custard cups. Sprinkle with cheddar cheese. Bake, uncovered, in a 350° oven for 12 to 15 minutes or till egg-white mixture is golden and vegetables are heated through. Makes 4 side-dish servings.

Nutrition information per serving: 350 cal., 9 g pro., 8 g carbo., 32 g fat, 32 mg chol., 558 mg sodium. U.S. RDA: 70% vit. C, 14% riboflavin, 12% calcium, and 12% phosphorus.

MEXARONI AND CHEESE

Add an extra kick with several dashes of bottled hot pepper sauce—

- **1 10-ounce can tomatoes and green chili peppers**
- **1 small green pepper, coarsely chopped**
- **1 14¾-ounce can macaroni and cheese**

In a medium skillet combine *undrained* tomatoes and green chili peppers and green pepper. Cook, covered, over medium heat about 5 minutes or till green pepper is crisp-tender. Stir in macaroni and cheese. Cook over medium heat for 3 to 5 minutes or till mixture is heated through, stirring occasionally. Makes 4 side-dish servings.

Microwave directions: In a 1-quart microwave-safe casserole combine tomatoes and green chili peppers and green pepper. Micro-cook, covered, on 100% power (high) 2 to 3 minutes or till pepper is crisp-tender. Stir in macaroni and cheese. Cook, covered, on high 3 to 5 minutes or till heated through, stirring once.

Nutrition information per serving: 122 cal., 5 g pro., 16 g carbo., 4 g fat, 11 mg chol., 394 mg sodium. U.S. RDA: 17% vit. A and 90% vit. C.

RISE-AND-SHINE MUFFINS

Have time to fix a bowl of cold cereal for breakfast? Then you'll have time to mix up these delicious oatmeal muffins. Just let them bake while you dress for work—

- **1 egg**
- **⅔ cup packaged biscuit mix**
- **1 envelope instant oatmeal with apples and cinnamon**
- **½ cup milk**

In a medium mixing bowl stir together egg, biscuit mix, instant oatmeal, and milk. Grease 6 muffin cups; fill muffin cups ⅔ full with batter. Bake in a 375° oven for 18 to 20 minutes or till golden. Serve warm. Makes 6 muffins.

Nutrition information per muffin: 105 cal., 3 g pro., 15 g carbo., 4 g fat, 49 mg chol., and 224 mg sodium.

CHICKEN SALAD IN MELON BOATS

Stop at your deli for creamy coleslaw. The slaw provides the dressing for this fruity chicken salad—

- 1 pint deli creamy coleslaw
- 2 5½-ounce cans chunk-style chicken, drained and broken up
- ½ cup halved strawberries *or* seedless grapes
- 1 medium cantaloupe

In a medium mixing bowl combine coleslaw, chicken, and strawberries or grapes. Toss gently to mix. Cover and chill in the freezer for 15 minutes.

Meanwhile, cut cantaloupe lengthwise into 4 pieces. Discard seeds. Fill each cantaloupe wedge with *one-fourth* of the chicken mixture. Makes 4 main-dish servings.

Nutrition information per serving: 243 cal., 19 g pro., 17 g carbo., 11 g fat, 55 mg chol., and 488 mg sodium. U.S. RDA: 90% vit. A, 143% vit. C, 30% niacin, 10% iron, and 13% phosphorus.

VEGETABLE PITA POCKETS

- 8 6-inch white *or* whole wheat pita bread rounds
- ½ cup creamy bacon salad dressing
- 32 pieces cooked broccoli flowerets, baby carrots, pea pods, asparagus cuts, *or* cauliflower flowerets
- 4 slices American cheese

Cut pita bread rounds into quarters. Spread inside each quarter with bacon salad dressing. Place 1 vegetable piece in each pita quarter.

Cut each cheese slice into 4 strips; halve each strip crosswise. Place 1 cheese piece in each pita quarter. Secure each bundle with a wooden toothpick, if necessary. Place on a baking sheet. Bake in a 375° oven about 5 minutes or till cheese starts to melt. Serve immediately. Makes 32 appetizers.

Nutrition information per appetizer: 263 cal., 10 g pro., 19 g carbo., 17 g fat, 26 mg chol., 534 mg sodium. U.S. RDA: 22% vit. A, 20% vit. C, 20% calcium, and 22% phosphorus.

SPANISH RICE PEPPERS

A green pepper stuffed with a savory rice filling—

- 2 medium green *or* red sweet peppers
- ½ cup long grain rice
- ⅓ cup chili sauce
- ¾ cup shredded sharp American cheese (3 ounce)

Cut peppers in half lengthwise. Remove membrane and seeds. Chop 1 pepper half; set aside. Cook the remaining pepper halves in boiling salted water for 5 minutes. Drain.

Meanwhile, in a small saucepan cook rice according to package directions, *except* add chopped green pepper. Stir chili sauce and ¼ cup cheese into the cooked rice. Divide the mixture between the 3 pepper halves.

Place filled peppers in an 8x8x2-inch baking dish. Cover with foil. Bake in a 350° oven for 15 to 20 minutes or till filling is heated through.

Sprinkle each pepper with ½ cup shredded sharp American cheese. Bake for 2 to 3 minutes more or till cheese is melted. Makes 3 side-dish servings.

Nutrition information per serving: 270 cal., 10 g pro., 44 g carbo., 7 g fat, 20 mg chol., 782 mg sodium. U.S. RDA: 148% vit. A, 360% vit. C, 19% thiamine, 13% riboflavin, 12% niacin, 16% calcium, 12% iron, 25% phosphorus.

FRUIT AND SPINACH SALAD

Here's a slick trick for washing spinach: place in a bowl of lukewarm water a few minutes, swirl, then lift from water—

- 1 17-ounce can fruit cocktail
- 4 cups torn spinach
- ¼ cup raisins
- ¼ cup mayonnaise *or* salad dressing

Drain fruit cocktail, reserving *1 tablespoon* of the liquid. In a large mixing bowl combine fruit cocktail, torn spinach, and raisins. Toss gently to mix.

For dressing, combine reserved liquid and mayonnaise or salad dressing.

Cover and chill spinach mixture and dressing for at least 1 hour. Before serving, add dressing to spinach mixture. Toss gently to coat. Makes 6 side-dish servings.

Nutrition information per serving: 129 cal., 2 g pro., 16 g carbo., 7 g fat, 5 mg chol., 82 mg sodium. U.S. RDA: 65% vit. A and 35% vit. C.

CARAMEL-PECAN PINWHEELS

Ooey-gooey caramel rolls that are so easy to make—

- ⅓ cup caramel ice cream topping
- 2 tablespoons melted butter *or* margarine
- ⅓ cup pecan halves
- 1 package (8) refrigerated breadsticks

In a 9x1½-inch round baking pan stir together caramel ice cream topping and melted butter or margarine; sprinkle with pecan halves.

Separate, but *do not uncoil*, refrigerated breadsticks. Arrange the dough coils atop caramel mixture. Bake, uncovered, in a 350° oven for 20 to 25 minutes or till golden. Let stand for 2 to 3 minutes. Loosen sides and invert rolls onto a serving platter. Serve warm. Makes 8 servings.

Nutrition information per serving: 201 cal., 4 g pro., 26 g carbo., 9 g fat, 8 mg chol., 292 mg sodium. U.S. RDA: 103% thiamine.

JUNE

HERBS!

One Fresh Herb Blend Flavors Four Zesty New Recipes

By Barbara Atkins

PICK-AN-HERB BLEND

Here's an incredibly versatile pestolike mixture. Use small amounts to season our recipes plus more—stews, cooked vegetables, and hot pasta—

- **3 cups snipped parsley**
- **1 cup mixed lightly packed fresh herb leaves: basil, fennel, oregano, *and/or* thyme**
- **2 tablespoons Dijon-style mustard**
- **2 cloves garlic, minced**
- **⅓ to ½ cup olive *or* cooking oil**
- **½ cup grated Parmesan cheese**

In a blender container or food processor bowl combine parsley, herb leaves, mustard, garlic, and ⅓ *cup* olive or cooking oil. Cover; blend or process till nearly smooth. If mixture is thick, add more oil, a teaspoon at a time, and continue blending or processing till mixture is the consistency of mayonnaise. Stir in Parmesan cheese. Cover; chill. Makes about 1 cup.

Note: If desired, divide into ⅓-*cup* portions; place in freezer containers. Seal, label, and freeze up to 6 months.

Nutrition information per tablespoon: 63 cal., 2 g pro., 1 g carbo., 6 g fat, 2 mg chol., 119 mg sodium. U.S. RDA: 22% vit. A, 34% vit. C.

continued

Photographs: Ron Crofoot   Food stylist: Judy Tills

HERB AND SQUASH CREAM SOUP

The ready-to-use herb blend flavors this first-course soup.

LAYERED TOMATO AND CHEESE SALAD

Top cheese strips and ripe tomatoes with herb dressing.

82

CHICKEN LOAF WITH HERB BLEND
Serve warm slices in a rich herb sauce for a light dinner.

CREAMY SEAFOOD CREPE CONES
Spread the herb blend over crepes; fill with enticing salad.

TURN FOR MORE ON HERBS.

TARRAGON
- very aromatic, full-flavored herb
- use sparingly in salads, sauces, seafood

SUMMER SAVORY
- pleasing fragrance
- spicy, peppery taste
- enhances vegetables, eggs, sauces

CHIVES
- mild-flavored member of onion family
- add to eggs, cheeses, vegetables, sauces

BASIL
- fragrant; sweet taste
- use with vegetables (especially tomatoes) and to make pesto

FENNEL
- pleasant sweet licorice-like flavor
- good for fish, breads, pastry, salads, pickles

OREGANO
- strong, heavy flavor with bitter undertones
- use in sauces, stews, egg dishes, vegetables

ROSEMARY
- sweet scent and bold flavor
- use sparingly with pork, lamb, vegetables

THYME
- strong and slightly sharp taste
- good in meats, soups, vegetables, dips

HERB ALMANAC
Nurture an Herb Patch

You can have the wonderful fragrance and flavor of fresh herbs at your fingertips if you save a spot in your garden—or on your windowsill—to grow them. Herbs thrive in most any well-drained soil, and demand little more than sun and water. After you relish the satisfaction of growing herbs, harvest and store them for year-round enjoyment.

HARVESTING

Pick your herbs just as the plant begins to bloom; the oil content in the leaves is greatest at this stage. The more oil in the leaf, the more flavor in the herb.

Rinse the herbs in cool water; discard any damaged leaves. For short-term storage, put the stems in water. Cover with a plastic bag, and store in the refrigerator several days. To keep herbs longer, dry or freeze them.

DRYING

To hang-dry herbs, tie the stems in bunches; hang upside down in a dry, warm place out of direct sunlight where air circulates freely. Let dry till the leaves are brittle, usually a few weeks. Then, pick off the leaves; discard the stems. Store in a tightly covered container.

Drying herbs in the microwave oven is not recommended. The herbs may catch on fire while in the oven cavity.

FREEZING

Chives and dill foliage freeze well. To freeze tarragon, parsley, or basil for more than 2 months, tie the herbs in bunches and blanch or steam about 1 minute. Cool; pat dry. Place the leaves in moisture- and vaporproof bags; seal, label, and freeze. Frozen herbs have a limp texture, so plan to use them in recipes that require cooking.

COOKING

Dried herbs have a more concentrated flavor than fresh. In fact, it takes about three times as much fresh herb to give you the same flavor intensity as that of its dried counterpart. If you're substituting dried herbs, use about *one-third* of the amount of fresh that the recipe suggests. A bonus for sodium watchers: Herbs can be a flavorful, sodium-free replacement for salt in cooking.

HERB AND SQUASH CREAM SOUP

For a light lunch, chill this pretty lime-green soup and serve with a sandwich—

- 2 small yellow summer squashes, coarsely chopped (2 cups)
- 1 14½-ounce can (1¾ cups) chicken broth
- 1 cup light cream *or* milk
- 2 to 3 tablespoons Pick-an-Herb Blend (see recipe, page 82)
- 4 teaspoons cornstarch
Snipped fresh basil (optional)

In a large saucepan combine squashes and broth. Bring to boiling. Reduce heat. Cover and simmer for 5 to 7 minutes or till tender. Remove from heat.

In a blender container combine cream or milk, Pick-an-Herb Blend, and cornstarch. Add squash mixture. Cover and blend till smooth. Return to the saucepan. Cook and stir over medium heat till thickened and bubbly. Cook and stir for 2 minutes more. To serve, ladle into soup bowls. Garnish with snipped basil, if desired. Makes 4 or 5 servings.

Nutrition information per serving: 189 cal., 5 g pro., 9 g carbo., 15 g fat, 41 mg chol., and 411 mg sodium. U.S. RDA: 28% vit. A, 49% vit. C, 11% riboflavin, 11% niacin, 12% calcium, and 12% phosphorus.

LAYERED TOMATO AND CHEESE SALAD

- ¼ cup Pick-an-Herb Blend (see recipe, page 82)
- 1 to 2 tablespoons vinegar
- 2 medium tomatoes (about ¾ pound), cut into ¼-inch slices
- 2 ounces mozzarella cheese, cut into strips (½ cup)
Fresh basil leaves (optional)

In a small mixing bowl stir together Pick-an-Herb Blend and vinegar. On a serving platter arrange tomato slices and cheese strips. Spoon herb mixture atop. Garnish with basil leaves, if desired. Serve immediately. Serves 4.

Nutrition information per serving: 119 cal., 6 g pro., 6 g carbo., 8 g fat, 11 mg chol., 188 mg sodium. U.S. RDA: 43% vit. A, 76% vit. C, 18% calcium, and 12% phosphorus.

CHICKEN LOAF WITH HERB BLEND

- 4 whole medium chicken breasts (about 3 pounds total), skinned, boned, and halved lengthwise
- 2 eggs
- ½ cup sliced green onion
- 2 tablespoons snipped fresh tarragon *or* 2 teaspoons dried tarragon, crushed
- 2 tablespoons brandy
- ½ teaspoon ground nutmeg
- 1 cup whipping cream
- ½ cup chopped hazelnuts (filberts)
- 1 recipe Pick-an-Herb Blend (see recipe, page 82)
Fresh tarragon leaves (optional)
Whole hazelnuts (optional)

On parchment paper or brown paper, trace around the top of a 9x5x3-inch loaf pan. Cut out rectangle and grease 1 side. Grease pan. Set aside.

Rinse chicken. Pat dry. In a food processor bowl process *one-third* of the chicken about 1 minute or till almost a smooth paste. Transfer to a large mixing bowl. Repeat with another one-third of the chicken.

In the food processor bowl combine remaining chicken, eggs, onion, tarragon, brandy, nutmeg, 1 teaspoon *salt*, and ½ teaspoon *pepper*. Process 1 minute. With processor running, add cream through feed tube. Process 20 seconds more or till mixed. Stir into chicken in bowl. Stir in chopped nuts.

Pour mixture into the prepared pan. Place prepared paper, greased side down, on top of the mixture. Set the pan in a baking pan. Pour hot water into the baking pan to a depth of 1 inch.

Bake in a 350° oven about 40 minutes or till set. Remove paper. Remove loaf pan from baking pan. Let stand for 15 minutes. Drain and reserve juices from loaf. Add water to make 1 cup.

For sauce, in a food processor bowl or blender container combine reserved juices and Pick-an-Herb Blend. Process or blend till creamy. Divide sauce among 8 rimmed dinner plates. Invert loaf and slice into eighths. Place one slice atop sauce on each plate. Garnish with tarragon and hazelnuts. Serves 8.

Nutrition information per serving: 450 cal., 34 g pro., 7 g carbo., 32 g fat, 187 mg chol., 536 mg sodium. U.S. RDA: 63% vit. A, 60% vit. C, 10% thiamine, 16% riboflavin, 61% niacin, 21% calcium, 20% iron, 34% phosphorus.

CREAMY SEAFOOD CREPE CONES

- 1 8-ounce package frozen salad-style crab-flavored fish, thawed
- 3 hard-cooked eggs, peeled and chopped
- ⅓ cup dairy sour cream
- ¼ cup sliced green onion
- ¼ teaspoon salt
- ⅛ teaspoon pepper
- 1 recipe Basic Crepes (see recipe, below)
- 1 recipe Pick-an-Herb Blend (see recipe, page 82)
Alfalfa sprouts
- 1 whole pimiento (optional)
Fresh basil leaves (optional)

Pat fish dry with paper towels. Chop any large pieces. In a small mixing bowl stir together fish, chopped eggs, sour cream, green onion, salt, and pepper. Cover and chill for 1 hour.

To assemble each cone, fold 1 crepe in half, forming a semicircle. Spread 1 side of the crepe with *1 teaspoon* of the Pick-an-Herb Blend. Place a few alfalfa sprouts in center of folded crepe. Spoon about *1 tablespoon* of the fish mixture over sprouts. Overlap sides of crepe, forming a cone. Secure filled cone with a toothpick.

Serve immediately with remaining herb blend. If desired, garnish with a pimiento flower and basil leaves. To make a pimiento flower, use a canapé cutter to cut a flower shape from the pimiento. Makes 9 side-dish servings (2 cones each) or 18 appetizer servings.

Basic Crepes: In a large mixer bowl combine 2 *eggs*, 1½ cups *milk*, 1 cup *all-purpose flour*, 1 tablespoon *cooking oil*, and ¼ teaspoon *salt*. Beat till mixed.

Heat a lightly greased 6-inch skillet. Remove from heat. Spoon in about *2 tablespoons* of the batter. Lift and tilt skillet to spread batter evenly. Return to heat till crepe is brown on 1 side only. Invert skillet over paper towel. Remove the crepe. Repeat to make 18 crepes. Grease skillet occasionally.

Nutrition information per crepe cone: 109 cal., 5 g pro., 8 g carbo., 6 g fat, 81 mg chol., 266 mg sodium. U.S. RDA: 11% vit. A and 15% vit. C.

By Terri Pauser Wolf

Regional Favorites that Put the Zing Back in Outdoor Cooking

PACIFIC NORTHWEST

Savor a Coastal Cookout

MARINATED SALMON STEAKS

Tender, flaky, fresh-from-the-ocean salmon stars in this menu.

GRILLED FRESH ASPARAGUS

Use a grill basket or foil to cook the spears.

CREAMY SORREL SAUCE

Fresh herbs abound in the Northwest; try sorrel or your own favorite.

Photographs: William K. Sladcik
Food stylist: Fran Paulson

86

GARDEN GREENS WITH HERBED BLUEBERRY VINAIGRETTE

Now's the time of year to savor fresh blueberries—in a fruity dressing over crisp salad greens.

HAZELNUT MUFFINS

Give yourself a head start—make these muffins the day before your cookout.

PACIFIC PEACH BUTTER

Turn plump, ripe peaches into a blue-ribbon fruit butter to spread on the muffins.

RASPBERRY-CURRANT ICE

It's cool and refreshing—just like a Pacific Coast breeze.

THE BEAUTY OF THIS 4-SERVING MENU? YOU CAN MAKE SO MUCH OF IT THE DAY BEFORE.

AMERICA'S BEST ★ COOKOUTS ★

MIDWEST
Serve Up a Heartland Picnic

STRAWBERRY-BANANA SHORTCAKE
A fit ending from shortcake country. Plan ahead—freeze the cake.

GRILLED CORN ON THE COB
What's a cookout without this all-American favorite? Grill it right in the husk.

IOWA PORK PLATTER
The number one pork-producing state shows its stuff at this cookout!

A MENU FOR 8 TO 10 PEOPLE.

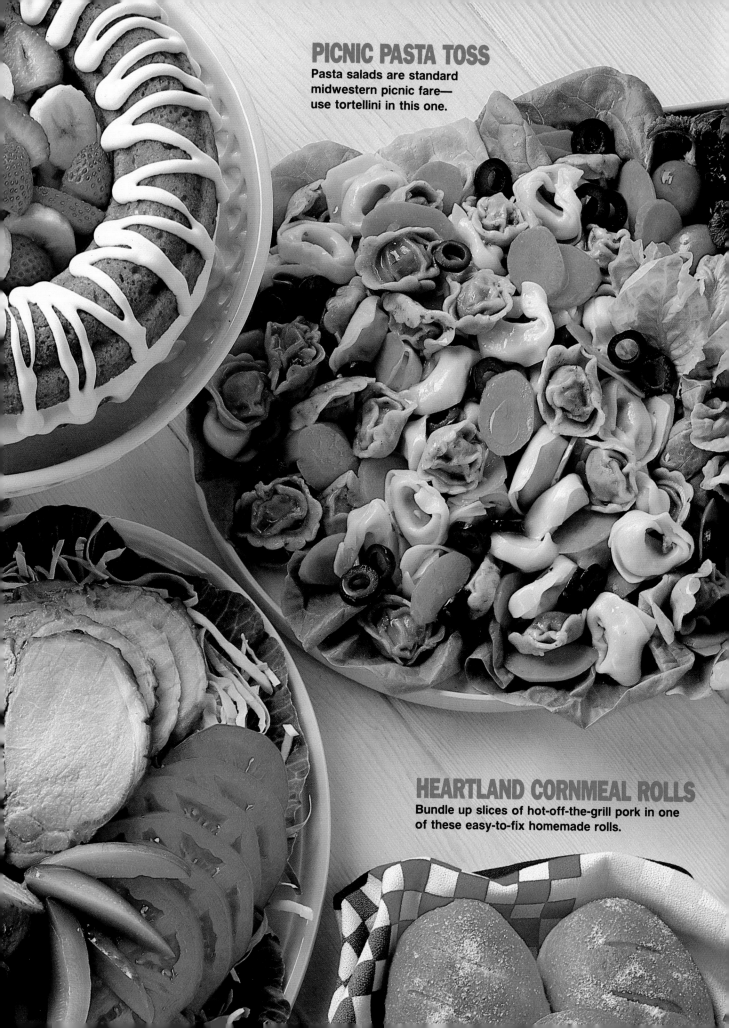

PICNIC PASTA TOSS
Pasta salads are standard
midwestern picnic fare—
use tortellini in this one.

HEARTLAND CORNMEAL ROLLS
Bundle up slices of hot-off-the-grill pork in one
of these easy-to-fix homemade rolls.

SOUTHWEST

Fire Up a Ranch-Style Barbecue

PACK-A-PUNCH CITRUS TEQUILA

Slowly sip this one—it packs a wallop!

TEXAS-STYLE BEEF BRISKET

Easy does it—slow-roasting is the key to a perfect mesquite-smoked brisket.

5-ALARM RED SAUCE

Slather on this perky sauce after the brisket is cooked to avoid charring.

FIESTA GRILLED PEPPERS

Colorful and simple to prepare, sweet peppers are great for grilling at any cookout.

A MENU FOR 8 TO 10 PEOPLE.

FRUIT PLATTER
Here's relief from the spicy foods—juicy fresh fruits.

PEPPED-UP PINTO BEANS
Pinto beans are a must, down Texas way! Keep a pot bubbling on the coals.

TORTILLA STRIPS
A zippy before-meal snack.

Tips for Great Grilling: To judge the temperature of coals for grilling, hold your hand, palm side down, above the coals at the height your food will cook. Start counting seconds, "one thousand one, one thousand two." If you need to withdraw your hand after two seconds, the coals are considered hot; after three seconds, medium-hot; after four seconds, medium; after five seconds, medium-slow; and after six seconds, slow.

Pacific Northwest

MARINATED SALMON STEAKS

- 4 fresh *or* frozen salmon steaks, cut 1 inch thick (about 2 pounds)
- ¼ cup cooking oil
- ¼ cup dry white wine
- 1 teaspoon finely shredded lime peel
- 2 tablespoons lime juice
- 1 tablespoon capers, drained
- 2 cloves garlic, minced
- ¼ teaspoon pepper

Thaw salmon, if frozen. Place in a shallow dish. For marinade, in a small mixing bowl combine cooking oil, white wine, lime peel, lime juice, capers, garlic, and pepper. Pour the marinade over salmon in dish. Turn salmon to coat with marinade. Cover the dish and marinate salmon in the refrigerator for 6 hours or overnight, turning the salmon occasionally.

Drain salmon, reserving the marinade. Pat excess moisture from salmon with paper towels. Grill salmon, on an uncovered grill, directly over *medium-hot* coals for 7 minutes. Turn and grill for 6 to 8 minutes more or till salmon flakes easily when tested with a fork, brushing salmon occasionally with reserved marinade. Makes 4 servings.

Nutrition information per serving: 412 cal., 33 g pro., 0 g carbo., 30 g fat, 102 mg chol., 77 mg sodium. U.S. RDA: 11% vit. A, 11% thiamine, 23% riboflavin, 26% calcium, 51% phosphorus.

GRILLED FRESH ASPARAGUS

- 1 pound asparagus
- 1 recipe Creamy Sorrel Sauce (see recipe, below) (optional)

To prepare asparagus, wash and scrape off scales. Snap off and discard the woody stems.

Open-grill directions: In a saucepan cook asparagus spears in a small amount of boiling water for 3 to 4 minutes. Drain. Place spears on grill rack over *medium-hot* coals. Grill about 3 minutes or till tender, turning once. Serve immediately with Creamy Sorrel Sauce, if desired. Makes 4 servings.

Cook-in-foil directions: Cut a 14-inch-square piece of heavy-duty foil. Place asparagus spears in center of foil. Sprinkle with 2 tablespoons *water.* Bring up the long edges of the foil and, leaving a little space for expansion of steam, seal tightly with a double fold. Fold up the short ends to seal.

Grill asparagus, on an uncovered grill, over *medium-hot* coals about 15 minutes or till tender, turning the packet once. Serve at once with the Creamy Sorrel Sauce, if desired.

Nutrition information per serving: 27 cal., 3 g pro., 5 g carbo., 0 g fat, 0 mg chol., and 2 mg sodium. U.S. RDA: 18% vit. A, 40% vit. C, 12% thiamine, and 12% riboflavin.

CREAMY SORREL SAUCE

Look for sorrel, a lemon-flavored herb, at your supermarket or local farmers' market. Or, grow some in your garden—

- ¼ cup plain yogurt
- ¼ cup mayonnaise *or* salad dressing
- ¼ cup finely snipped sorrel *or* fresh spinach
- 1 green onion, finely chopped

In a small mixing bowl stir together yogurt, mayonnaise or salad dressing, sorrel or spinach, and green onion. Cover and chill. Makes ¾ cup.

Nutrition information per tablespoon: 37 cal., 0 g pro., 1 g carbo., 4 g fat, 3 mg chol., and 31 mg sodium.

GARDEN GREENS WITH HERBED BLUEBERRY VINAIGRETTE

For a fresh-tasting summer salad, toss together this crunchy mix of greens: romaine, Boston, and spinach—

- 1 cup fresh *or* frozen and thawed blueberries,
- ½ cup white wine vinegar
- 3 to 4 teaspoons sugar
- ¼ teaspoon salt
- ¼ teaspoon pepper
- ⅓ cup salad oil
- 1 tablespoon finely snipped fresh basil *or* 1 teaspoon dried basil, crushed
- 4 cups torn mixed greens
- 1 apple, cored and sliced
- ½ cup sliced fresh mushrooms

For dressing, in a blender container or food processor bowl combine blueberries, vinegar, sugar, salt, and pepper. Cover and blend or process about 30 seconds or till blueberries are pureed. Sieve mixture. Discard the skins.

Transfer the blueberry mixture to a screw-top jar. Add salad oil and basil. Cover and shake well to mix. Chill in the refrigerator till serving time.

At serving time, arrange greens in a large salad bowl. Top with apple slices and mushrooms. Shake dressing and drizzle ½ cup over all. Toss gently to serve. Store remaining dressing in the refrigerator. Makes 4 servings.

Nutrition information per serving: 100 cal., 0 g pro., 10 g carbo., 6 g fat, 0 mg chol., and 51 mg sodium.

HAZELNUT MUFFINS

- 1¾ cups all-purpose flour
- 1 cup chopped hazelnuts (filberts) *or* pecans, toasted
- ¼ cup sugar
- 2 teaspoons baking powder
- ½ teaspoon salt
- 1 egg
- ¾ cup milk
- ⅓ cup cooking oil

In a large mixing bowl stir together flour, ⅔ cup of the chopped hazelnuts, sugar, baking powder, and salt. Make a well in the center. In a small mixing bowl beat egg slightly with a fork. Add milk and cooking oil. Add egg mixture all at once to dry ingredients, stirring just till moistened.

Grease muffin cups or line with paper bake cups. Fill ⅔ full. Sprinkle batter with remaining nuts. Bake in a 400° oven for 18 to 20 minutes or till golden. Makes 12 muffins.

Microwave directions: Prepare the muffin batter as directed above. Line a microwave-safe muffin dish or six 6-ounce custard cups with paper bake cups. Fill each cup ⅔ full. (You'll have half of the batter left over.) Sprinkle half of the remaining nuts over batter in the cups.

Place the muffin dish in a microwave oven (or arrange the custard cups in a circle in the microwave oven). Micro-cook, uncovered, on 100% power (high) for 2 to 2½ minutes or till a wooden toothpick inserted near the center comes out clean, giving the dish a half-turn (or rearranging the custard cups) after every minute. (The surface may still appear moist.) Remove muffins from the muffin dish or custard cups. Let stand on a wire rack. Repeat with remaining batter and nuts to make 6 more muffins.

Nutrition information per muffin: 214 cal., 4 g pro., 21 g carbo., 13 g fat, 25 mg chol., 154 mg sodium. U.S. RDA: 11% thiamine.

PACIFIC PEACH BUTTER

- 1 pound fresh peaches, peeled, pitted, and chopped, *or* one 12-ounce package frozen unsweetened peach slices, chopped
- ½ teaspoon finely shredded orange peel (set aside)
- ¼ cup orange juice
- ¾ cup sugar
- 2 tablespoons honey
- ⅛ teaspoon ground allspice

In a 2-quart saucepan combine fresh or frozen peaches and orange juice. Bring just to boiling. Reduce heat. Cover and cook peaches in juice for 5 to 10 minutes or till soft.

Place the *undrained* peach mixture in a blender container or food processor bowl. Cover and blend or process till the mixture is smooth. (You should have about 1½ cups puree.)

In a 3-quart saucepan combine peach puree, orange peel, sugar, honey, and allspice. Bring to a full boil. Reduce heat and boil gently, uncovered, about 15 minutes or till thickened, stirring often. Pour into a jar. Cover and store in the refrigerator. Makes 1¼ cups.

Nutrition information per teaspoon: 15 cal., 0 g pro., 4 g carbo., 0 g fat, 0 mg chol., and 0 mg sodium.

RASPBERRY-CURRANT ICE

No ice-cream maker? You can make this picnic-perfect ice in your freezer—

- 1 cup fresh currants *or* red grapes
- ¾ to 1 cup sugar
- 2 pints fresh *or* frozen raspberries
- 5 egg yolks
- 1 cup whipping cream
Mint leaves (optional)

In a small saucepan use a potato masher to lightly mash currants or grapes. Add sugar. Heat over medium-high heat to boiling, stirring frequently. Boil for 4 to 5 minutes or till mixture begins to thicken, stirring frequently. Sieve mixture, discarding seeds and skins. Return to the saucepan.

Place raspberries in a blender container or food processor bowl. Cover and blend or process till smooth. Sieve mixture. Discard seeds. Stir puree into currant mixture. Heat to simmering. Stir occasionally. Remove from heat.

In a small mixer bowl beat egg yolks with an electric mixer on high speed about 5 minutes or till thick and lemon colored. Reduce the mixer speed to low and gradually pour in warm fruit mixture. Beat till combined. Freeze as directed below. Serve ice in bowls and garnish with mint leaves, if desired. Makes 1 quart.

Ice-cream freezer directions: Place the fruit mixture in the freezer for 10 minutes to cool, stirring after 5 minutes. In a large mixer bowl beat whipping cream till soft peaks form. Fold into the cooled fruit mixture. Freeze in an ice-cream freezer according to the manufacturer's directions. Store, tightly covered, in the freezer.

Freezer directions: Turn the fruit mixture into a 9x9x2-inch pan. Cover and place in the freezer about 2 hours or till partially frozen. Chill a large mixer bowl.

When mixture is partially frozen, beat whipping cream in small mixer bowl till soft peaks form and set aside.

Break the raspberry mixture into chunks. Turn into the chilled large mixer bowl. Beat with an electric mixer on medium speed till nearly smooth. Fold in whipped cream. Return the mixture to the pan. Cover and place in the freezer overnight or till firm.

Microwave directions: In a 1½-quart microwave-safe casserole combine currants or grapes and sugar. Mash lightly with a potato masher. Micro-cook, uncovered, on 100% power (high) about 4 minutes or to a full boil, stirring twice. Sieve mixture. Discard seeds and skin. Return to the casserole.

Place raspberries in a blender container or food processor bowl. Cover and blend or process till smooth. Sieve mixture. Discard seeds. Add raspberry puree to currant mixture. Micro-cook, uncovered, on high for 5 to 6 minutes or till boiling, stirring twice.

In a small mixer bowl beat egg yolks with an electric mixer on high speed about 5 minutes or till thick and lemon colored. Reduce the mixer speed to low and gradually pour in warm fruit mixture. Beat till combined. Freeze as directed above.

Nutrition information per ½-cup serving: 256 cal., 3 g pro., 29 g carbo., 15 g fat, 211 mg chol., 17 mg sodium. U.S. RDA: 15% vit. A and 81% vit. C.

Midwest

IOWA PORK PLATTER

- 1 3-pound boneless pork loin roast, doubled and tied
- 1 12-ounce can (1½ cups) beer
- 2 tablespoons Worcestershire sauce
- 1 tablespoon dried minced onion
- 1 teaspoon dry mustard
- ½ teaspoon salt
- 2 tablespoons brown sugar
- ½ of a small cabbage or 2 medium zucchini (optional)
- 1 recipe Heartland Cornmeal Rolls (see recipe, right) (optional)
- Dill pickle spears (optional)
- Tomato slices (optional)
- 1 recipe Horseradish Sauce (see recipe, right) (optional)

Place pork roast in a plastic bag. Set in a large bowl. For marinade, in a small mixing bowl stir together beer, Worcestershire sauce, dried onion, mustard, and salt. Pour marinade over roast in bag. Close bag. Marinate roast in the refrigerator for 6 hours or overnight, turning occasionally.

In a covered grill arrange preheated coals around a drip pan. Test for *medium* heat (see tip, page 92).

Drain roast, reserving marinade. Insert a meat thermometer near center of roast. Stir brown sugar into reserved marinade. Place roast on grill over drip pan but not over coals. Lower grill hood. Grill for 1½ to 2 hours or till thermometer registers 170°, adding more coals* as necessary. Brush with marinade every 15 minutes.

To serve, if using cabbage, remove outer leaves. Set aside. Shred remaining cabbage or zucchini. Line serving platter with cabbage leaves and shredded cabbage or with zucchini. Thinly slice meat for sandwiches. Arrange meat on platter. Serve on Heartland Cornmeal Rolls with dill pickles, tomato slices, and Horseradish Sauce, if desired. Makes 10 to 12 servings.

Note: To maintain heat in a charcoal grill, add 10 to 12 new coals every 30 minutes when brushing meat.

Nutrition information per serving: 210 cal., 25 g pro., 1 g carbo., 11 g fat, 78 mg chol., 92 mg sodium. U.S. RDA: 34% thiamine, 16% riboflavin, 26% niacin, and 18% phosphorus.

HORSERADISH SAUCE

Perk up your piled-high pork sandwich with a heaping spoonful of this sauce—

- ⅓ cup dairy sour cream
- 2 tablespoons prepared horseradish
- ½ of a sweet red or green pepper (optional)
- Snipped chives (optional)

In a small mixing bowl stir together sour cream and horseradish. Cover and chill thoroughly. If desired, serve in pepper half and sprinkle with snipped chives. Makes about ½ cup.

Nutrition information per teaspoon: 8 cal., 0 g pro., 0 g carbo., 1 g fat, 2 mg chol., and 3 mg sodium.

GRILLED CORN ON THE COB

More mature corn may take 10 to 15 minutes longer to grill—

- 8 to 10 fresh ears of corn

Peel husks back just enough to remove silk. Return husks to their original position. In a sink or large kettle soak corn covered in water for 30 minutes. In an uncovered grill arrange preheated coals. Test for *medium-hot* heat (see tip, page 92).

Drain corn. Grill corn in husks directly over coals for 20 to 25 minutes or till kernels are tender, turning often. Makes 8 to 10 servings.

Nutrition information per ear: 70 cal., 3 g pro., 16 g carbo., 1 g fat, 0 mg chol., and 0 mg sodium.

HEARTLAND CORNMEAL ROLLS

Serve these tender, slightly sweet rolls with slices of any grilled meat—

- 3¼ to 3½ cups all-purpose flour
- 1 package active dry yeast
- 1 cup milk
- ¼ cup packed brown sugar
- ¼ cup butter or margarine
- ½ teaspoon salt
- 1 egg
- ½ cup cornmeal
- Cornmeal
- 1 slightly beaten egg white
- 1 tablespoon water

In a large mixer bowl combine *1½ cups* of the flour and yeast. In a small saucepan heat milk, brown sugar, butter or margarine, and salt just till warm (115° to 120°) and butter is almost melted, stirring constantly.

Add warm mixture to flour mixture. Add egg. Beat with an electric mixer on low speed for ½ minute, scraping bowl. Beat for 3 minutes on high speed. Add the ½ cup cornmeal. Beat on low speed till combined. Using a spoon, stir in as much remaining flour as you can.

Turn dough out onto a lightly floured surface. Knead in enough of the remaining flour to make a moderately stiff dough that is smooth and elastic (6 to 8 minutes total). Shape into a ball. Place in a greased bowl. Turn once to grease surface. Cover. Let rise in a warm place till double (about 1 hour).

Punch dough down. Turn out onto a lightly floured surface. Halve dough. Cut each half into 6 pieces, making 12 pieces total. Shape into balls. Cover. Let rest for 10 minutes. Shape each ball into a 4-inch oval. Grease, then sprinkle 2 or 3 baking sheets with cornmeal. Place rolls 2½ inches apart on sheets. Cover. Let rise in a warm place till nearly double (about 40 minutes).

Using a sharp knife, make 3 shallow cuts diagonally across the top of each oval. Combine egg white and water. Brush onto rolls. Sprinkle with additional cornmeal. Bake in a 375° oven about 20 minutes or till done. Make a day ahead and store tightly covered. (Or, seal, label, and freeze.) Makes 12.

Nutrition information per roll: 215 cal., 6 g pro., 35 g carbo., 6 g fat, 36 mg chol., 150 mg sodium. U.S. RDA: 17% thiamine, 13% riboflavin, 11% niacin, and 11% iron.

PICNIC PASTA TOSS

- 1 7-ounce package frozen *or* refrigerated cheese-filled egg tortellini
- 1 7-ounce package frozen spinach tortellini
- ⅔ cup sliced pitted ripe olives
- 1 large carrot, thinly bias sliced
- ¾ cup Italian salad dressing
- ½ teaspoon finely shredded orange peel
- 2 tablespoons orange juice
- Bibb lettuce leaves
- Radishes (optional)
- Brussels sprouts, cooked (optional)

In a large saucepan cook egg and spinach tortellini in a large amount of boiling unsalted water according to the package directions. Drain in a colander. Rinse with cold water. Drain.

In a large mixing bowl toss together tortellini, olives, and carrot. In a small mixing bowl combine salad dressing, orange peel, and orange juice. Pour over pasta mixture. Toss well. Cover and chill thoroughly.

Serve on a lettuce-lined platter with radishes and brussels sprouts, if desired. Makes 8 to 10 servings.

Nutrition information per serving: 245 cal., 8 g pro., 18 g carbo., 16 g fat, 74 mg chol., 283 mg sodium. U.S. RDA: 24% vit. A and 10% phosphorus.

STRAWBERRY-BANANA SHORTCAKE

No ring mold? Bake your shortcake in a 8x1½-inch round baking pan in a 425° oven for 20 to 22 minutes—

- 2 cups all-purpose flour
- ⅓ cup sugar
- 2 teaspoons baking powder
- 3 tablespoons butter *or* margarine
- 1 ripe medium banana
- 1 beaten egg
- ½ cup milk
- 1 8-ounce carton dairy sour cream
- 1 3-ounce package cream cheese, softened
- 2 tablespoons sugar
- 2 medium bananas
- 3 cups sliced strawberries
- 1 tablespoon milk

In a large mixing bowl combine flour, ⅓ cup sugar, and baking powder. Cut in butter or margarine till the mixture resembles coarse crumbs.

Mash 1 banana (you should have about ⅓ cup). In a medium mixing bowl combine egg, ½ cup milk, and mashed banana. Add all at once to dry ingredients. Stir just till moistened.

Spread dough in a greased 5½-cup ring mold. Bake in a 450° oven for 15 to 18 minutes or till done. Cool for 10 minutes on a wire rack. Remove from the pan. Cool thoroughly.

Cut cake horizontally into two layers. For filling, in a small mixing bowl combine sour cream, cream cheese, and 2 tablespoons sugar. Spread ⅔ *cup* of the filling over bottom shortcake layer. Replace cake top. Transfer cake to a platter. Cover remaining filling. Chill along with cake till serving time.

Before serving, slice the 2 bananas. In a small mixing bowl toss together strawberry and banana slices. Spoon into the center of the cake ring. Add 1 tablespoon milk to ¼ *cup* of the sour cream filling to thin. Drizzle over cake.

To serve, slice with a serrated knife. Top each serving with remaining sour cream filling. Makes 8 servings.

Nutrition information per serving: 371 cal., 7 g pro., 52 g carbo., 16 g fat, 72 mg chol., and 182 mg sodium.

Southwest

PEPPED-UP PINTO BEANS

After the brisket comes off the grill, keep this pot o' fire warm and ready for second helpings: place the cooked beans in a cast-iron pan on the grill—

- 2 cups dry pinto beans
- 6 cups water
- 4⅔ cups water
- 1 4-ounce can diced green chili peppers, drained
- 2 cloves garlic, minced
- 2 teaspoons chili powder
- 1 teaspoon salt
- 5 ounces jicama, peeled and cubed (1 cup)
- 1 6-ounce package shredded Monterey Jack cheese *or* Monterey Jack cheese with jalapeño peppers

Rinse beans. In a large saucepan or Dutch oven combine beans and 6 cups water. Cover and soak overnight. (Or, bring to boiling. Reduce heat and cover. Simmer 2 minutes. Remove from heat. Cover. Let stand 1 hour.) Drain beans.

In the same Dutch oven combine drained beans, 4⅔ cups water, chili peppers, garlic, chili powder, and salt. Bring to boiling. Reduce heat. Cover and simmer 1¾ hours or till tender.

Add jicama. Cook, uncovered, for 25 to 30 minutes more or till jicama is tender and beans are slightly mushy. Top with Monterey Jack cheese. Makes 8 to 10 servings.

Nutrition information per ½-cup serving: 264 cal., 17 g pro., 35 g carbo., 7 g fat, 19 mg chol., 393 mg sodium. U.S. RDA: 10% vit. A, 30% vit. C, 28% thiamine, 12% riboflavin, 23% calcium, 33% phosphorus, and 19% iron.

5-ALARM RED SAUCE

- 1 **cup catsup**
- 1 **large tomato, peeled, seeded, and chopped**
- 1 **green pepper, chopped**
- 2 **tablespoons chopped onion**
- 2 **tablespoons brown sugar**
- 2 **tablespoons Worcestershire sauce**
- 2 **tablespoons steak sauce**
- ½ **teaspoon garlic powder**
- ¼ **teaspoon ground nutmeg**
- ¼ **teaspoon ground cinnamon**
- ¼ **teaspoon ground cloves**
- ⅛ **teaspoon ground ginger**
- ⅛ **teaspoon pepper**

In a small saucepan stir together all ingredients. Bring to boiling. Reduce heat. Cover and simmer about 5 minutes or till green pepper is crisp-tender. Serve warm or at room temperature with Texas-Style Beef Brisket. Makes about 2½ cups.

Nutrition information per ¼-cup serving: 51 cal., 1 g pro., 12 g carbo., 0 g fat, 0 mg chol., 378 mg sodium. U.S. RDA: 11% vit. A and 43% vit. C.

FIESTA GRILLED PEPPERS

- 4 **or 5 assorted sweet green, yellow, and red peppers**
- 1 **to 2 tablespoons olive or cooking oil**

Quarter peppers. Remove seeds and membranes. Brush the skin side of each pepper with oil. Place peppers, skin side down, on the grill rack over *medium-hot* coals (see tip, page 92). Grill about 10 minutes or till peppers are crisp-tender and charred. Makes 8 to 10 servings.

Nutrition information per serving: 32 cal., 1 g pro., 4 g carbo., 2 g fat, 0 mg chol., and 10 mg sodium. U.S. RDA: 110% vit. C.

TEXAS-STYLE BEEF BRISKET

Celebrate summer the southwestern way. Serve a tender grilled brisket at your next picnic—

- 4 **to 6 cups mesquite wood chips**
- 2 **teaspoons seasoned salt**
- 1 **teaspoon paprika**
- 1 **teaspoon pepper**
- 1 **3- to 4-pound beef brisket**
- 1 **recipe Brushing Sauce (see recipe, below)**
- 1 **recipe 5-Alarm Red Sauce (see recipe, left)**

At least 1 hour before grilling, soak wood chips in enough water to cover.

In a small mixing bowl stir together seasoned salt, paprika, and pepper. Rub mixture over brisket.

Drain the wood chips. In a covered grill arrange preheated coals around a foil drip pan. Test for *medium-hot* coals above pan using the three-second test (see tip, page 92). Sprinkle the coals with some of the wood chips.

Place the brisket on the grill rack, fat side up, over the drip pan but not over the coals. Brush with Brushing Sauce. Lower the grill hood. Grill for 1½ to 2 hours or till brisket is tender, brushing with sauce every 20 minutes and adding more wood chips and coals* as necessary.

To serve, thinly slice the grilled brisket across the grain and arrange on a serving platter. Spoon some of the 5-Alarm Red Sauce over meat. Pass remaining sauce. Makes 8 to 10 servings.

*Note: To maintain heat in a charcoal grill, add about 8 new coals every 20 minutes when brisket is brushed.

Brushing Sauce: In a small mixing bowl stir together ½ cup *dry red wine;* 3 tablespoons *Worcestershire sauce;* 2 tablespoons *cooking oil;* 2 tablespoons *red wine or cider vinegar;* 2 cloves *garlic,* minced; 1 teaspoon *coriander seed,* crushed; 1 teaspoon *hot-style mustard;* and ⅛ teaspoon ground *red pepper.* Makes 1⅓ cups.

Nutrition information per serving: 438 cal., 26 g pro., 1 g carbo., 36 g fat, 107 mg chol., 1,486 mg sodium. U.S. RDA: 12% riboflavin, 19% iron, and 11% phosphorus.

TORTILLA STRIPS

A simple snack, this recipe makes enough crispy strips to feed 8 to 10 hungry guests—

- 10 **6-inch corn or flour tortillas**
- 2 **teaspoons salt**
- 1 **teaspoon ground cumin**
- ½ **to 1 teaspoon ground red pepper**

Cooking oil for deep frying

Cut tortillas into ½-inch strips. Set aside. Combine salt, cumin, and red pepper. Place in a shaker.

In a large saucepan or deep-fat fryer heat about 1½ inches (about 4 cups) cooking oil. Fry tortilla strips, a small amount at a time, in hot oil for ½ to 1½ minutes or till golden. Remove with a slotted spoon. Drain on paper towels.

Immediately shake some of the seasoning mixture over the hot strips. Repeat with remaining tortilla strips. Store tightly covered. Makes 8 cups.

Nutrition information per ½-cup serving: 40 cal., 1 g pro., 9 g carbo., 0 g fat, 0 mg chol., and 266 mg sodium.

PACK-A-PUNCH CITRUS TEQUILA

Keep a pitcher handy for thirst quenching during hot-summer-day cookouts—

Lemon or lime slices
- 4 **cups unsweetened pineapple juice**
- 1 **12-ounce can frozen lemonade concentrate**
- 1½ **cups tequila**
- 1 **cup orange liqueur**

For lemon or lime ice cubes, place lemon or lime slices in an ice-cube tray. Fill with water and freeze.

In a 2-quart pitcher stir together pineapple juice, lemonade concentrate, tequila, and orange liqueur. Cover and chill thoroughly. Just before serving add lemon and lime ice cubes. Makes 8 (8-ounce) servings.

Nutrition information per serving: 351 cal., 0 g pro., 62 g carbo., 0 g fat, 0 mg chol., and 3 mg sodium. U.S. RDA: 44% vit. C.

SUMMER ICES!

COOL!

PAPAYA ICE

A warm-weather pleasure that's lighter than ice cream, sherbetlike in texture.

PAPAYA ICE

 1 cup sugar
 2 fresh papayas (about 1 pound total), peeled, seeded, and cut up, *or* two 15-ounce cans mango slices, drained
 2 tablespoons lemon juice
Several drops yellow food coloring (optional)

In a 2-cup measure stir sugar into 1 cup warm *water* till dissolved. In a blender container or food processor bowl combine *half* of the sugar mixture, *half* of the fruit, and *half* of the lemon juice. Cover and blend or process till smooth. Remove. Repeat. Stir in food coloring, if desired.

Pour into a 9x5x3-inch loaf pan. Cover; freeze for 4 to 5 hours or till almost firm. Break into chunks. Transfer to a chilled large mixer bowl. Beat with an electric mixer on medium speed about 2 minutes or till fluffy. Return to cold pan. Cover; freeze 6 hours or till firm. Serves 8.

Nutrition information per serving: 127 cal., 0 g pro., 33 g carbo., 0 g fat, 0 mg chol., 3 mg sodium. U.S. RDA: 31% vit. A, 81% vit. C.

PHOTOGRAPH: WILLIAM K. SLADCIK. FOOD STYLIST: FRAN PAULSON

By Lynn Hoppe

Add to your summer fun with one of these frosty, fruity treats. As summer cool-downs, they're great. They start with two of the season's best—papayas and berries.

BERRY-ROSÉ SORBET

- 1½ cups fresh *or* frozen strawberries *or* raspberries
- 2 cups rosé wine
- ½ cup sugar
- ¼ teaspoon ground cinnamon
- 4 teaspoons cornstarch

Thaw frozen berries. In a blender container combine berries and wine. Blend till nearly smooth. If using raspberries, strain, if desired; discard seeds.

Bring wine mixture, sugar, and cinnamon to boiling, stirring to dissolve sugar. Reduce heat; boil gently for 2 minutes, stirring often. Stir 2 tablespoons *water* into cornstarch. Stir into the wine mixture. Cook and stir till thickened and bubbly. Cook and stir 2 minutes more. Cool for 1 hour. Pour into an 8x8x2-inch pan. Cover; freeze for 4 to 5 hours or till almost firm. Break into chunks. Turn into a chilled large mixer bowl. Beat with an electric mixer on medium speed till fluffy. Return to cold pan. Cover; freeze 6 hours or till firm. Makes 6 servings.

Nutrition information per serving: 167 cal., 0 g pro., 25 g carbo., 0 g fat, 0 mg chol., 6 mg sodium. U.S. RDA: 35% vit. C.

BERRY-ROSÉ SORBET
Wine and cinnamon add elegance to this refreshing summer dessert.

FEEDING THE FOLKS

3 COMPLETE MEALS FOR FAMILY REUNIONS

By Barbara Atkins

PICNIC LUNCH

L aughing, crying, hugging, kissing, reminiscing—and eating! That's the heart of family reunions!

A fun-filled picnic in the park is a classic way to gather generations. Make it fun for all with these easy-to-pack foods. They'll delight gramps and babes alike!

For a pleasin' brunch and dinner, read on.

MENU
FOR 20

EASY ANTIPASTO TRAY
▲
BUILD-YOUR-OWN
STEAK SANDWICHES
▲
SUMMER
VEGETABLE BAKE
▲
TRIPLE-BEAN
CASSEROLE
▲
GINGERED FRUIT SLAW
▲
GAZPACHO PASTA TOSS
▲
NO-CHOP
POTATO SALAD
▲
TOTABLE BERRY TARTS
▲
ON-THE-SPOT
SPICE CREAM

MAKING IT WORK
FOR 40 OR 60

ROASTS REPLACE STEAKS
● For the sandwiches, cook beef rump roasts. Then, slice and marinate the meat before serving.

EXTRA SALAD IS EASY
● There's no peeling or chopping when you use frozen hash brown potatoes to make potato salad. Just cook an extra bag or two of them and increase the dressing.

TARTS TURN COBBLER
● From the pastry, make stars instead of tarts. Pour the berry filling into a pan and top with the stars.

ICE CREAM IN THE PARK
● Gather up extra ice-cream makers—two to serve 40; three to serve 60. Bring all the ingredients to the picnic site and crank the ice cream right outdoors.

FOOD PHOTOGRAPHS: MYRON BECK. FOOD STYLIST: MABLE HOFFMAN

ON-THE-SPOT
SPICE CREAM

TOTABLE BERRY TARTS

TRIPLE-BEAN
CASSEROLE

BUILD-YOUR-OWN
STEAK SANDWICHES

SUMMER
VEGETABLE BAKE

EASY ANTIPASTO TRAY

GINGERED FRUIT SLAW

GAZPACHO PASTA TOSS

NO-CHOP POTATO SALAD

CRISPY CHEDDAR CRACKERS
A rich, cheesy snack that'll keep 'em reaching for more.

VEGETABLE-BARLEY SALAD
Toss together vegetables, barley, and a tangy dressing.

MAKE-AHEAD HAM 'N' EGG BAKE
A gussied-up version of scrambled eggs.

YOU CAN DO IT!

FEEDING THE FOLKS

BRUNCH

Celebrate your generations with a sunny midmorning feast. Keep hosting simple with this make-ahead menu.

MENU
FOR 15

CRISPY CHEDDAR
CRACKERS

▲

MAKE-AHEAD
HAM 'N' EGG BAKE

▲

VEGETABLE-BARLEY SALAD

▲

ON-CALL FRUIT COMPOTE

▲

SPICY BRAN SCONES

▲

MIX-AND-SERVE
APPLE PUNCH

ON-CALL FRUIT COMPOTE
Drizzle a sweet-tart yogurt topper over layers of fruit.

MIX-AND-SERVE APPLE PUNCH
Just two ingredients make one refreshing punch.

SPICY BRAN SCONES
So quick to make; simply spice up a baking mix.

MAKING IT WORK FOR 40

MAKE ROUND CRACKERS SQUARE
● To make a bunch of crackers fast, roll out the dough directly on the baking sheet. Then, use a fluted pastry wheel to cut the cheesy dough into attractive squares.

FINDING FRIG SPACE
● Clear out your refrigerator before your get-together to make room for the scrumptious brunch foods you'll be serving. If you still need extra space, see if a neighbor has an empty refrigerator shelf you can fill.

DOUBLE-BATCH EGGS
● You'll need two 2½-quart casserole dishes to hold the egg casserole. If you have only one, put half of the recipe in a 13x9x2-inch baking pan.

MIX A HEFTY SALAD
● Make the 40-serving-size barley salad the night before the brunch. Cook the barley in an 8-quart Dutch oven, then stir together the salad right in the same pan. Divide the mixture between two large serving bowls and place the bowls in the refrigerator to chill.

ONE READY, ONE WAITING COMPOTE
● Divide the fruit and topping for the doubled fruit compote between two serving dishes. Serve one of the dishes and keep the other chilled till the first one is gone.

ONE-PAN SCONES
● Make, freeze, and reheat the scones in pie plates.

PITCH-IN PUNCH
● Ask a cousin to bring the chilled punch ingredients. You can mix it up right on site.

CREAMY HERB DIP
Serve pattypan and yellow squash slices with this dip.

SAVORY PITA CRISPS
Bake seasoned pita pieces till crisp and crunchy.

GRILLED SPICED HENS
Rub hens with seasonings that mimic barbecue sauce.

DILLED CORN AND PEA PODS
Cook this colorful side dish at the last minute.

YOU CAN DO IT!

FEEDING THE FOLKS

DINNER

They're your family! Go all out and treat them to this elegant yet easy-to-make dinner.

MENU
FOR 10

SAVORY PITA CRISPS
▲
CREAMY HERB DIP
▲
GRILLED SPICED HENS
▲
DILLED CORN AND PEA PODS
▲
GREENS WITH PARSLEY DRESSING
▲
PECAN CORN MUFFINS
▲
SLICED MELON WITH
LIME-POPPY DRIZZLE
▲
CHOCOLATE-LADYFINGER LOAF

GREENS WITH PARSLEY DRESSING
Blend the creamy, piquant dressing in minutes.

PECAN CORN MUFFINS
Ground pecans make these muffins special.

CHOCOLATE-LADYFINGER LOAF
Convenient to make ahead; dazzling to present.

SLICED MELON WITH LIME-POPPY DRIZZLE
Pour this citrus dressing over your favorite melon.

MAKING IT WORK FOR 30

DIP AND CRISPS FOR ALL
● Fill two cabbage-leaf bowls with the herb dip, then surround each with plenty of pita crisps. Set the plates around the room so your relatives can nibble while they reminisce.

TIMESAVING BREAD
● Instead of baking 30 muffins, spread the batter in round baking pans. To serve, cut into wedges. Want to save even more time? Bake this nutty bread ahead. Then, freeze and reheat right in the pan.

GRILL TWO TURKEYS
● To serve a crowd, grill turkeys instead of Cornish hens. You'll need two covered grills, so plan to borrow one from a friend, relative, or neighbor. (Or, grill one turkey and roast the other in your oven.)

GLAZE THE TURKEYS
● Transform the spice rub for the hens into a glistening glaze by adding a jar of orange marmalade. Brush over the turkeys during the last few minutes of grilling.

TUNNEL CAKES FOR DESSERT
● To simplify making dessert, start with two white angel food cakes from your bakery. Hollow them out and fill with the decadent chocolate mixture from the ladyfinger loaf.

CUSTOMIZE A DELI MELON BOWL
● Order a carved melon shell filled with a colorful assortment of melon balls from your local deli. Make the drizzle ahead of time, then pour it over before serving for your own custom fruit bowl.

FEEDING THE FOLKS
HINTS FOR HOSTING A FAMILY HOMECOMING

THE PLAN Enlist a committee of relatives! Have them write the foods and cleanup chores on slips of paper. Let each family draw an assignment from a hat. Don't forget to draw for the families not represented at the planning session, then mail their slips.

● A rental store is a great resource for reunion gear. You can rent dishes, flatware, chairs, tables, barbecue grills, small refrigerators, and ice chests.

● Capitalize on colorful paper plates, cups, napkins, and plastic flatware. They add a festive touch to your gathering *and* shortcut cleanup.

THE FUN If your family is blessed with lots of young ones, plan ways to keep them busy. Put high-school-aged nieces and nephews in charge of arranging for activities. Who knows? The grown-ups very well might join in the fun of three-legged contests, water balloon tosses, and gunnysack races.

● Color-code your immediate family! Have them all wear green shirts. If a cousin wants to know which kids are yours, say, "The two in green shirts."

● They'll want your recipes! Remind relatives to bring copies of their recipes to hand out. You may want to compile a family recipe book afterward.

THE FOOD Invite nearby relatives over a day before the big event for a cookathon.

● When marking pans and utensils, keep in mind there'll be others with the same name—even initials—as you. Assign each family a certain color.

● Set mealtime; let everyone know it.

● Stock up on munchies and beverages to keep volley- and softball players energized before the main food event. See the chart below for amounts to buy.

● Let the deli save your day. Take advantage of their cheese trays, assorted bread baskets, fresh fruit plates, and salad bowls to round out your menu.

● Freeze jugs of water or fruit juice and use them as ice packs in coolers. Drink them when they thaw.

● Keep cold foods cold! Ask relatives who are bringing cold dishes to supply ice-filled coolers. That way, there'll be a place to store the food till serving time, even if your refrigerator is full.

● Keep hot foods hot! Wrap the dishes in foil or a towel and place in a plastic-foam cooler (without ice, of course!) to tote. On the table, use slow cookers, electric frypans, and warming trays to keep food hot throughout the meal.

THE CLEANUP Be prepared with plenty of large plastic garbage bags. Keep several cousins busy passing around the bags as people finish eating.

● If you aren't using disposable dishes and flatware, designate a place for dirty table service. Set aside one whole table or counter specifically for this.

HOW MUCH FOR HOW MANY

BEVERAGES

Orange juice—1 gallon	32 (4-ounce) servings
Lemonade—2 gallons	32 (8-ounce) servings
Iced tea—2 gallons	32 (8-ounce) servings
Beer—8-gallon keg	85 (12-ounce) servings
Coffee—1 pound (using 1½ tablespoons per serving)	56 (6-ounce) servings
Wine—1.5-liter bottle	10 (5-ounce) servings

SNACKS

Potato chips—16-ounce package	16 servings
Cheese curls—12-ounce package	24 servings
Pretzels—12-ounce package	12 servings
Corn or tortilla chips— 16-ounce package	16 servings
Sour cream dip— 8-ounce container	8 servings
Mixed nuts—56-ounce container	56 servings

EASY ANTIPASTO TRAY

Use a combination of pickled peppers and olives for visual appeal—

- 1 6½-ounce can tuna, drained and flaked
- 1 hard-cooked egg, chopped
- ¼ cup mayonnaise *or* salad dressing
- 1 teaspoon dried oregano, crushed
- 1 teaspoon lemon juice
- 2 4-ounce packages sliced Genoa salami *or* 15 slices turkey salami, halved
- 1 6-ounce block mozzarella cheese, cut into thirty 2-inch julienne strips

Red *or* green leaf lettuce leaves
- 1 10-ounce jar whole pickled yellow *or* green chili peppers *or* red sweet cherry peppers
- 1 6- *or* 6½-ounce can pitted ripe *or* pimiento-stuffed green olives, drained
- 1 6-ounce jar marinated artichoke hearts, drained and halved

In a small mixing bowl use a fork to mash together tuna, egg, mayonnaise or salad dressing, oregano, and lemon juice. Spread *1 rounded teaspoon* of tuna mixture over *each* salami piece. Place *one* cheese strip in the center. Roll up; secure with wooden toothpicks, if necessary. Cover; chill up to 24 hours.

To transport, line the bottom or top of a 12- or 13-inch pie carrier or the bottom of a 13x9x2-inch moisture- and vaporproof container with red or green lettuce leaves. Arrange salami rolls, peppers, olives, and artichoke hearts around. Cover tightly. Pack on ice or with several ice packs in a well-insulated cooler. Serve within 3 hours. Makes 20 appetizer servings.

For 40 servings: Double recipe for Easy Antipasto Tray; use 2 containers.

For 60 servings: Triple recipe for Easy Antipasto Tray; use 3 containers.

Nutrition information per appetizer roll and 3 tablespoons condiments: 105 cal., 7 g pro., 2 g carbo., 8 g fat, 33 mg chol., 274 mg sodium. U.S. RDA: 34% vit. C.

BUILD-YOUR-OWN STEAK SANDWICHES

Make this marinated meat up to 48 hours ahead so it's ready to tote—

- 4 1- to 1¼-pound beef flank steaks
- 1 cup olive *or* cooking oil
- ⅔ cup lemon juice
- 2 tablespoons snipped fresh rosemary *or* 2 teaspoons dried rosemary, crushed
- 5 cloves garlic, halved
- 2 teaspoons seasoned salt
- ½ teaspoon pepper
- 20 sandwich buns

Desired condiments (such as catsup, mustard, and mayonnaise)

With a sharp knife, score meat ¼ inch deep and at ½-inch intervals on both sides. Place meat in a 2-gallon plastic bag set in a 13x9x2-inch baking pan. For marinade, in a small mixing bowl combine oil, lemon juice, rosemary, garlic, seasoned salt, and pepper. Pour over meat. Close the bag. Place in the refrigerator for several hours or overnight, turning occasionally.

Remove meat from marinade, reserving marinade. Place *half* of the meat on the unheated rack of a broiler pan. Broil 3 inches from heat for 6 minutes. Brush with reserved marinade; turn and brush with marinade again. Broil 6 minutes more for medium rare or till meat is of desired doneness. Remove from rack. Repeat broiling with remaining meat. Cool slightly.

Carve meat diagonally across the grain into very thin slices. Wrap in foil or place in a 13x9x2-inch moisture- and vaporproof container and cover tightly. Chill thoroughly.

To transport, pack wrapped meat on ice or with several ice packs in a well-insulated cooler. Serve within 3 hours. To serve, let diners assemble their own sandwiches by placing meat on sandwich buns and adding desired condiments. Makes 20 servings.

For 40 servings: Place two 5-pound *boneless beef round rump roasts,* fat side up, on a rack in a large shallow roasting pan. Insert a meat thermometer. Roast in a 325° oven for 3 to 3½ hours or till thermometer registers 150° (medium rare) to 170° (well-done). Remove from oven and cool. Carve into very thin slices. Divide meat between two 13x9x2-inch moisture- and vaporproof containers.

For marinade, in a medium mixing bowl stir together *2 cups* cooking oil; *1⅓ cups* lemon juice; *¼ cup* snipped fresh rosemary *or 4 teaspoons* dried rosemary, crushed; *1 teaspoon garlic powder; 4 teaspoons* seasoned salt; and *1 teaspoon* pepper. Pour *half* of the marinade over the cooked meat in *each* container. Cover tightly. Chill overnight, turning meat occasionally. Transport as at left. Serve with *40* sandwich buns and condiments.

For 60 servings: Prepare Build-Your-Own Steak Sandwiches as directed for 40 servings above, *except* use *three* 5-pound boneless beef round rump roasts. Place *two* of the roasts, fat side up, on a rack in a 13x9x2-inch baking pan. Place remaining roast, fat side up, on a rack in a 9x9x2-inch baking pan. Insert a meat thermometer.

Roast in a 325° oven for 3 to 3½ hours or till the thermometer registers 150° to 170°. Remove from oven and cool. Carve into very thin slices. Divide meat between three 13x9x2-inch moisture- and vaporproof containers.

For marinade, in a large mixing bowl combine *3 cups* cooking oil; *2 cups* lemon juice; *⅓ cup* snipped fresh rosemary *or 2 tablespoons* dried rosemary, crushed; *1½ teaspoons garlic powder; 2 tablespoons* seasoned salt; and *1½ teaspoons* pepper. Pour *one-third* of the marinade over the cooked meat in *each* container. Cover and chill in the refrigerator overnight, turning occasionally. Transport as at left. Serve with *60* sandwich buns and condiments.

Nutrition information per sandwich: 263 cal., 22 g pro., 21 g carbo., 9 g fat, 60 mg chol., and 274 mg sodium. U.S. RDA: 13% thiamine, 14% riboflavin, 21% niacin, 19% iron, and 13% phosphorus.

SUMMER VEGETABLE BAKE

You needn't always bring extra servings as the reunion crowd grows; just bring a greater variety of recipes to appeal to different tastes. This sophisticated casserole is good for 10 to 20 servings—

- 1 **pound green beans, cut into 1-inch pieces (3 cups)**
- ½ **of a 12-ounce package (1½ cups) frozen chopped onion**
- 2 **10-ounce packages frozen chopped spinach *or* broccoli**
- 2 **tablespoons butter *or* margarine**
- ⅛ **teaspoon minced dried garlic**
- 2 **tablespoons all-purpose flour**
- ½ **teaspoon salt**
- ⅛ **teaspoon ground nutmeg**
- ⅛ **teaspoon pepper**
- 1¼ **cups milk**
- 1 **3-ounce package cream cheese, cut up**
- 1 **cup soft bread crumbs**
- ¼ **cup grated Parmesan cheese**
- 2 **tablespoons butter *or* margarine, melted**

In a large saucepan bring 2 cups *water* to boiling. Add beans and onion; cover and simmer for 10 minutes. Add spinach or broccoli; cook till thawed, stirring occasionally. Simmer, covered, for 5 minutes more. Drain well.

Meanwhile, for sauce, in a small saucepan combine 2 tablespoons butter or margarine and garlic. Heat till butter is melted. Stir in flour, salt, nutmeg, and pepper. Add milk all at once. Cook and stir till thickened and bubbly. Add in cream cheese, stirring till melted. Stir sauce into vegetable mixture. Turn into a 2-quart casserole. Bake, uncovered, in a 350° oven for 30 minutes.

In a mixing bowl toss together bread crumbs, Parmesan cheese, and 2 tablespoons melted butter or margarine. Sprinkle over casserole. Bake, uncovered, for 20 to 30 minutes more or till heated through.

To transport, cover hot casserole, wrap in foil, then wrap in a terry cloth towel. Place in foam cooler *without* ice. Serve within 3 hours. Serves 10.

For 20 servings: Prepare Summer Vegetable Bake as directed, *except* double all ingredients. Cook vegetables in a 4- or 5-quart Dutch oven. Prepare sauce in a large saucepan. Turn mixture into a 4-quart casserole. Bake for 60 to 65 minutes total or till heated through, adding topping after 30 minutes.

Nutrition information per ¾-cup serving: 153 cal., 6 g pro., 12 g carbo., 10 g fat, 28 mg chol., 303 mg sodium. U.S. RDA: 82% vit. A, 26% vit. C, 12% riboflavin, 17% calcium, 11% phosphorus.

GINGERED FRUIT SLAW

Put the cabbage and nuts on top to keep them crisp during overnight chilling—

- 2 **8-ounce cans pineapple tidbits (juice pack)**
- 1 **6-ounce package (1½ cups) mixed dried fruit bits**
- 2 **large carrots, shredded (1½ cups)**
- 1 **small head cabbage, shredded (5 cups)**
- ½ **cup chopped walnuts**
- 2 **tablespoons salad oil**
- 2 **tablespoons honey**
- 1 **tablespoon lemon juice**
- ¼ **to ½ teaspoon ground ginger**

Drain pineapple, reserving ⅓ cup of juice; set aside. In a 3-quart moisture- and vaporproof serving container layer pineapple, fruit bits, carrots, cabbage, and walnuts.

For dressing, in a screw-top jar combine reserved pineapple juice, salad oil, honey, lemon juice, and ginger. Cover and shake well. Pour over cabbage mixture. Cover and chill for several hours or overnight.

To transport, pack the container of cabbage mixture on ice or with several ice packs in a well-insulated cooler. Serve within 3 hours. Toss just before serving. Makes 20 servings.

For 40 servings: Double the ingredients and pack in a 6½-quart moisture- and vaporproof container.

For 60 servings: Triple the ingredients, placing *one-third* of the mixture in a 3-quart moisture- and vaporproof container and the remaining mixture in a 6½-quart moisture- and vaporproof container.

Nutrition information per ½-cup serving: 79 cal., 1 g pro., 13 g carbo., 3 g fat, 0 mg chol., 8 mg sodium. U.S. RDA: 49% vit. A, 21% vit. C.

TRIPLE-BEAN CASSEROLE

Lima, navy, and kidney beans make this juicy version of baked beans special—

- 4 **slices bacon**
- 1 **large onion, sliced**
- 1 **16-ounce can lima beans, drained**
- 1 **16-ounce can pork and beans in tomato sauce**
- 1 **15½-ounce can red kidney beans, drained**
- 1 **7½-ounce can tomatoes, cut up**
- ¼ **cup packed brown sugar**
- 1 **tablespoon Worcestershire sauce**
- ½ **teaspoon dry mustard**

In a medium skillet cook bacon till crisp. Remove bacon, reserving *2 tablespoons* drippings in skillet. Drain bacon on paper towels; crumble. Set aside.

Cook onion in reserved drippings till tender but not brown; drain. In a 2-quart casserole or bean pot combine crumbled bacon, onion, lima beans, *undrained* pork and beans, kidney beans, and *undrained* tomatoes. Stir in brown sugar, Worcestershire sauce, and dry mustard. Bake, covered, in a 375° oven for 40 minutes. Uncover and bake for 20 to 25 minutes more or till of desired consistency.

To transport, cover hot casserole, wrap in foil, then wrap in a terry cloth towel. Place in a foam cooler *without* ice. Serve within 3 hours. Serves 20.

For 40 servings: Make 2 recipes. Use two 2-quart casseroles or bean pots.

For 60 servings: Make 3 recipes and divide among three 2-quart casseroles or bean pots.

Crockery-cooker directions: Prepare Triple-Bean Casserole as directed above, *except* turn into an electric crockery cooker. (Turn 40-serving-size recipe into a 4-quart electric crockery cooker. Turn 60-serving-size recipe into two 3½- or 4-quart electric crockery cookers *or* one 5- or 6-quart electric crockery cooker.)

Cook, covered, on high-heat setting for 3 to 4 hours or till heated through. Uncover for the last hour of cooking. Transport cooker to picnic site. If electricity is available, plug cooker in and keep on a low setting. Otherwise, serve within 3 hours.

Nutrition information per ⅓-cup serving: 83 cal., 4 g pro., 14 g carbo., 1 g fat, 2 mg chol., 155 mg sodium.

GAZPACHO PASTA TOSS

A refreshing marinated salad that mimics the flavors of Spain's traditional chilled vegetable soup: gazpacho—

- 4 ounces rigatoni *or* mostaccioli (about 2 cups)
- 1 medium cucumber, thinly sliced (2 cups)
- 1 medium green pepper, coarsely chopped (1 cup)
- 2 tablespoons snipped parsley
- 3 tablespoons salad oil
- 2 tablespoons snipped fresh basil *or* 2 teaspoons dried basil, crushed
- 2 tablespoons lemon juice
- 1 tablespoon white wine vinegar
- ½ teaspoon salt
- 3 small tomatoes, cut into thin wedges

Lettuce leaves (optional)

In a large kettle cook pasta in a large amount of boiling salted water about 15 minutes or till tender. Drain. Rinse with cold water; drain well.

In a 2-quart moisture- and vapor-proof serving container toss together cooked pasta, cucumber, green pepper, and parsley.

For dressing, in a screw-top jar combine salad oil, basil, lemon juice, vinegar, and salt. Cover and shake well to mix. Pour dressing over pasta mixture. Toss gently till well coated. Cover and chill for several hours or overnight, stirring occasionally.

To transport, place tomatoes and lettuce in separate plastic bags or containers. Pack along with bowl containing salad on ice or with several ice packs in a well-insulated cooler. Serve within 3 hours. Before serving, add tomatoes to salad and toss gently. Then, place lettuce around the top edge of the bowl, if desired. Makes 20 servings.

For 40 servings: Double the ingredients. Divide between two 2-quart moisture- and vaporproof containers.

For 60 servings: Triple the ingredients. Place in a 6½-quart moisture- and vaporproof container.

Nutrition information per ⅓-cup serving: 46 cal., 1 g pro., 6 g carbo., 2 g fat, 0 mg chol., 56 mg sodium. U.S. RDA: 23% vit. C.

ON-THE-SPOT SPICE CREAM

If you like, crank the ice cream before leaving home instead of at the picnic. Transport by packing the freezer container in crushed ice and rock salt in a well-insulated cooler. Count transporting time as part of the ripening (mellowing) period. Serve within 4 hours—

- 1 quart (4 cups) light cream
- 2 cups packed brown sugar
- 4 teaspoons vanilla
- 1½ teaspoons ground cinnamon
- ¼ teaspoon ground allspice
- 1 quart (4 cups) whipping cream

In a large mixing bowl combine light cream, brown sugar, vanilla, cinnamon, and allspice. Stir till the sugar dissolves. Stir in whipping cream.

Pour the cream mixture into a 4- to 5-quart ice-cream freezer container. Freeze according to the manufacturer's directions, using crushed ice and rock salt. Makes about 4 quarts ice cream (20 servings).

For 40 servings: Make 2 ice cream recipes, using two 4- or 5-quart ice-cream freezers.

For 60 servings: Make 3 ice cream recipes; use three 4- or 5-quart ice-cream freezers.

Nutrition information per ¾-cup serving: 340 cal., 2 g pro., 24 g carbo., 27 g fat, 97 mg chol., 43 mg sodium. U.S. RDA: 21% vit. A.

NO-CHOP POTATO SALAD

Just like old-fashioned potato salad, only easier!

- 1 24-ounce package frozen hash brown potatoes with onion and peppers
- 3 stalks celery, thinly sliced (1½ cups)
- 1 8-ounce container sour cream dip with chives
- ⅔ cup mayonnaise *or* salad dressing
- 1 tablespoon sugar
- 1 tablespoon white wine vinegar
- 1 tablespoon prepared mustard
- ½ teaspoon salt
- 3 hard-cooked eggs, coarsely chopped

Lettuce leaves (optional)
Celery leaves (optional)
Pimiento strips (optional)

In a 3- or 4-quart saucepan cook potatoes with onion and peppers in a large amount of boiling water, covered, 6 to 8 minutes or till potatoes are tender; drain well. In a large bowl combine cooked potatoes and celery. Set aside.

For dressing, in a small bowl stir together sour cream dip, mayonnaise or salad dressing, sugar, vinegar, mustard, and salt. Add dressing to potato mixture; toss gently to coat. Gently fold in chopped eggs. Turn into a 2- or 2½-quart moisture- and vaporproof serving container. Cover and chill for several hours or overnight.

To transport, place lettuce, celery leaves, and pimiento, if desired, in separate plastic bags or containers. Pack along with bowl containing salad on ice or with several ice packs in a well-insulated cooler. Serve within 3 hours. Before serving, place lettuce around the top edge of the bowl and garnish with celery leaves and pimiento, if desired. Makes 20 servings.

For 40 servings: Double the ingredients. Divide the salad between two 2- or 2½-quart moisture- and vaporproof containers.

For 60 servings: Triple the ingredients. Place in a 6½-quart moisture- and vaporproof container.

Nutrition information per ⅓-cup serving: 121 cal., 2 g pro., 8 g carbo., 9 g fat, 51 mg chol., 137 mg sodium.

TOTABLE BERRY TARTS

2½ cups fresh *or* frozen berries (use blueberries, raspberries, *and/or* blackberries)
Plain pastry for 3 single-crust 9-inch pies
⅔ cup sugar
2 tablespoons cornstarch
½ cup water
½ teaspoon finely shredded lemon *or* orange peel
2 tablespoons crème de cassis *or* orange juice

Thaw berries, if frozen; *do not drain.* Meanwhile, on a lightly floured surface roll *half* of pastry dough ⅛ inch thick. Cut into ten 4-inch circles. Repeat with remaining dough. Gently fit circles into 2½-inch muffin cups; press and pleat dough to fit. Prick dough well with a fork. If desired, press tines of a fork around top edges of dough, forming decorative edges.

Bake in a 450° oven for 12 to 14 minutes or till golden. Cool. Loosen pastry from cups; return to cups.

For filling, in a medium saucepan stir together sugar and cornstarch. Stir in water. Add *undrained* berries and lemon or orange peel. Cook and stir over medium heat till thickened and bubbly. Cook and stir for 2 minutes more. Remove from heat. Stir in crème de cassis or orange juice.

Spoon the filling into baked pastry shells. Chill in the refrigerator for up to 48 hours. Garnish with additional fresh blueberries, raspberries, or blackberries. To transport, cover muffin pans. Makes 20 servings.

For 40 servings: Prepare Totable Berry Tarts as directed at left, *except* roll *half* of the pastry dough into a 13x9-inch rectangle about ⅛ inch thick. Using a 2-inch star-shaped cookie cutter (or other shaped cookie cutter), cut out 20 stars. Repeat with remaining dough for 40 stars total.

Transfer stars to 2 baking sheets. Prick stars well with a fork; sprinkle with *sugar* and ground *cinnamon.* Bake in a 450° oven for 8 to 10 minutes or till golden. Cool on a wire rack.

Prepare filling as directed at left, *except* use *11 cups* fresh berries *or three* 16-ounce packages frozen berries, *2⅔ cups* sugar, *½ cup* cornstarch, *2 cups* water, *½ cup* crème de cassis *or* orange juice, and *2 teaspoons* lemon *or* orange peel; use a 5-quart Dutch oven.

Spoon *half* of the filling into a 13x9x2-inch baking pan; spread evenly. Repeat with remaining filling and another pan. Arrange *20* pastry stars atop *each* pan of filling (see photo, below). Cover and chill in the refrigerator. Transport in the covered baking pan. For each serving, scoop out 1 star and the filling beneath.

For 60 servings: Prepare Totable Berry Tarts as directed at left, *except* use three 9-inch *folded frozen or refrigerated unbaked piecrusts.* Thaw frozen piecrusts. Using a 2-inch star-shaped cookie cutter (or other shaped cookie cutter), cut 20 stars out of each crust, rerolling scraps as necessary. Prick stars well with a fork; sprinkle with *sugar* and ground *cinnamon.* Bake in a 450° oven for 8 to 10 minutes or till golden. Cool on a wire rack.

Meanwhile, prepare filling as directed at left, *except* use *4 quarts* fresh berries *or four* 16-ounce packages plus ½ of a 16-ounce package frozen berries, *4 cups* sugar, *¾ cup* cornstarch, *3 cups* water, *¾ cup* crème de cassis *or* orange juice, and *1 tablespoon* finely shredded lemon *or* orange peel; use an 8-quart Dutch oven.

Spoon *one-third* of the filling into a 13x9x2-inch baking pan; spread evenly. Repeat twice more with remaining filling and 2 more pans. Arrange *20* of the pastry stars atop *each* pan of filling (see photo, left). Cover and chill. Transport in the covered pan. For each serving, scoop out 1 star and filling beneath it.

Microwave directions for 20 servings: Thaw frozen berries; *do not drain.* Prepare and bake pastry as directed for Totable Berry Tarts for 20 servings. For filling, in a 1½-quart microwave-safe casserole stir together sugar and cornstarch. Stir in the water. Add *undrained* berries and peel. Micro-cook, uncovered, on 100% power (high) for 5 to 6 minutes or till thickened and bubbly, stirring every minute. Cook on high for 1 minute more. Stir in crème de cassis or juice. Continue as directed.

Nutrition information per tart: 196 cal., 2 g pro., 24 g carbo., 10 g fat, 0 mg chol., 56 mg sodium.

MAKE-AHEAD HAM 'N' EGG BAKE

Scramble eggs the day before to save precious time when the clan arrives. It's even easy to serve 40 if you split up the preparation. Have one person make 15 servings, another 25—

  2 **16-ounce packages loose-pack frozen cut broccoli**
  2 **tablespoons butter *or* margarine**
 12 **beaten eggs**
  3 **tablespoons butter *or* margarine**
  3 **tablespoons all-purpose flour**
  ¼ **teaspoon white pepper**
  2 **cups milk**
  8 **ounces process Gruyère *or* Swiss cheese, cut up (2 cups)**
  1 **tablespoon prepared mustard**
  2 **4-ounce cans sliced mushrooms, drained**
  ¾ **pound fully cooked ham, cut into bite-size strips**

Cook broccoli according to the package directions; drain. Set aside.

In a 12-inch skillet melt 2 tablespoons butter or margarine over medium heat. Add the beaten eggs. Cook, without stirring, till mixture begins to set on the bottom and around the edges. Using a large spatula, scramble eggs by lifting and folding partially cooked eggs so uncooked portion flows underneath. Continue cooking over medium heat about 4 minutes or till eggs are cooked throughout, but are still glossy and moist. Immediately remove from heat.

For sauce, in a medium saucepan melt 3 tablespoons butter or margarine. Stir in flour and white pepper. Add milk all at once. Cook and stir till thickened and bubbly. Add Gruyère or Swiss cheese and mustard; stir till cheese melts.

Remove *2 cups* of the sauce; stir in broccoli and mushrooms. Place *half* of the broccoli mixture around the inside of an ungreased 1- or 1½-quart au gratin dish or 10x6x2-inch baking dish. Repeat with the remaining mixture and another dish.

Add remaining sauce and all of the ham to eggs in skillet; gently fold together till combined. Spoon *half* of the egg mixture into the center of *each* dish. Cover and chill for several hours or overnight. To serve, bake, covered, in a 350° oven for 30 to 40 minutes or till heated through. Makes 15 servings.

For 40 servings: Prepare 1 recipe of Make-Ahead Ham 'n' Egg Bake for 15 servings in 2 au gratin dishes as directed at left. For another 25 servings, fix Make-Ahead Ham 'n' Egg Bake as at left, *except* use *three* 16-ounce packages loose-pack frozen cut broccoli; *3 tablespoons* butter *or* margarine; *18* beaten eggs; *⅓ cup* butter *or* margarine; *⅓ cup* all-purpose flour; *¼ teaspoon* white pepper; *3 cups* milk; *12 ounces* process Gruyère *or* Swiss cheese, cut up (*3 cups*); *2 tablespoons* prepared mustard; *three* 4-ounce cans sliced mushrooms, drained; and *1¼ pounds* fully cooked ham, cut into bite-size strips.

Prepare the sauce in a 3- or 4-quart saucepan. Gently fold together cooked broccoli, eggs, sauce, mushrooms, and ham. Divide the mixture evenly between two 2½-quart casserole dishes *or* two 13x9x2-inch baking dishes. Cover and chill in the refrigerator for several hours or overnight. To serve, bake, covered, in a 350° oven till heated through, allowing 1¼ to 1½ hours for the 2½-quart casseroles or 50 to 60 minutes for the 13x9x2-inch baking dishes.

Microwave directions for 15 servings: In a 2-quart microwave-safe casserole stir together *one* 16-ounce package broccoli and 2 tablespoons *water*. Micro-cook, covered, on 100% power (high) for 7 to 8 minutes or till crisp-tender, stirring once. Drain well in a colander. Set aside. Repeat with remaining package of broccoli.

In a 12x7½x2-inch microwave-safe baking dish cook 2 tablespoons butter or margarine, uncovered, on high for 45 to 60 seconds or till melted. Add eggs. Cook, uncovered, on high for 6 to 8 minutes or till eggs are almost set, pushing cooked portions to the center of the dish several times during cooking. Set aside.

For sauce, in the 2-quart casserole cook 3 tablespoons butter or margarine, uncovered, on high for 45 to 60 seconds or till melted. Stir in flour and pepper. Add milk all at once. Cook, uncovered, on high for 6 to 7 minutes or till thickened and bubbly, stirring every minute. Add Gruyère or Swiss cheese and mustard. Stir till melted.

Remove *2 cups* of sauce; stir in broccoli and mushrooms. Place *half* of the broccoli mixture around the inside

of an ungreased 1- or 1½-quart au gratin dish or 10x6x2-inch baking dish. Repeat with remaining broccoli mixture and another dish.

Gently fold eggs and all of the ham into remaining sauce in the casserole. Spoon *half* of the egg mixture into the center of *each* dish. Cover and chill for several hours or overnight. To serve, reheat in a conventional oven as directed for Make-Ahead Ham 'n' Egg Bake for 15 servings.

Nutrition information per ¾-cup serving: 232 cal., 17 g pro., 7 g carbo., 15 g fat, 261 mg chol., 503 mg sodium. U.S. RDA: 31% vit. A, 44% vit. C, 17% thiamine, 21% riboflavin, 24% calcium, 10% iron, 28% phosphorus.

ON-CALL FRUIT COMPOTE

 2¼ **cups milk**
  1 **8-ounce carton plain yogurt**
  1 **4-serving-size package *instant* pineapple cream pudding mix**
  3 **17-ounce cans unpeeled apricot halves, drained**
  3 **cups seedless red *or* green grapes, halved (about 1 pound)**

For sauce, in a medium mixing bowl stir together milk, yogurt, and pudding mix. Beat according to package directions. Cover surface with clear plastic wrap; chill till serving time. Beat with a wire whip occasionally during chilling.

Cut apricot halves in half; reserve 2 pieces for garnish. In a 3-quart serving bowl layer *half* of the grapes, remaining apricot pieces, and remaining grapes. Cover; chill till serving time.

To serve, drizzle sauce over fruit. Garnish with reserved apricot pieces and 2 grape halves. Makes 15 servings.

For 40 servings: Prepare On-Call Fruit Compote as directed above, *except* use 6¾ cups milk, *three* 8-ounce cartons plain yogurt, *three* 4-serving-size packages *instant* pineapple cream pudding mix, *five* 30-ounce cans peeled whole apricots, and 7½ cups seedless red *or* green grapes, halved. Prepare sauce in a 4-quart mixing bowl. Layer *half* of the fruit as above in *each* of 2 large serving bowls. Top each with *half* of the sauce. Garnish as above.

Nutrition information per ½-cup fruit and 3 tablespoons sauce: 103 cal., 3 g pro., 21 g carbo., 2 g fat, 6 mg chol., 73 mg sodium. U.S. RDA: 37% vit. A.

CRISPY CHEDDAR CRACKERS

Nonstick spray coating
¾ cup all-purpose flour
¼ cup ground walnuts*
½ teaspoon paprika
¼ teaspoon onion powder
3 tablespoons butter *or* margarine, softened
1 cup shredded cheddar cheese (4 ounces), at room temperature (*not* preshredded cheese)
1 to 2 tablespoons cold water

Spray a baking sheet with nonstick spray coating. Set aside. In a medium mixing bowl stir together flour, walnuts, paprika, and onion powder. Cut in butter or margarine till the mixture resembles coarse crumbs. Stir in cheese. Sprinkle *1 teaspoon* of water over part of the mixture; gently toss with a fork. Repeat till all is moistened.

Form dough into a ball; flatten slightly. Roll ⅛ inch thick. Cut dough with a 2-inch-round cookie cutter, re-rolling trimmings. Transfer to the prepared baking sheet.

Bake in a 350° oven about 12 minutes or till golden. Remove; cool on a wire rack. Cover; store in a cool place. Makes 55 crackers or 15 servings.

For 120 crackers or 40 servings: Prepare Crispy Cheddar Crackers as directed above, *except* use a 4-quart mixing bowl and increase ingredients to *2 cups* all-purpose flour, ⅔ *cup* ground walnuts, *1¼ teaspoons* paprika, *½ teaspoon* onion powder, *½ cup* butter or margarine, *2½ cups* shredded cheddar cheese (10 ounces), and *6 to 7 tablespoons* cold water. Sprinkle water over the dough *1 tablespoon* at a time (instead of 1 teaspoon).

Divide the dough into *fourths*. On a baking sheet sprayed with nonstick spray coating, roll *each* fourth of the dough into a 12½x10½-inch rectangle. Using a pastry cutter, cut dough into

thirty 2-inch squares (see photo, above). Bake as directed at left. Cool the baking sheet before rolling out the next portion of dough.

*Note: For ground walnuts, place *walnut pieces* in a blender container or food processor bowl. Blend or process till finely ground. (Use the same measure of walnut pieces as you need of ground walnuts.)

Nutrition information per cracker: 22 cal., 1 g pro., 1 g carbo., 2 g fat, 4 mg chol., 19 mg sodium.

VEGETABLE-BARLEY SALAD

Use barley to make this refreshing version of tabbouleh, a traditional Middle Eastern salad—

4½ cups water
1⅔ cups quick-cooking barley
1 teaspoon instant chicken bouillon granules
1 large cucumber, finely chopped (2 cups)
1 medium red *or* green sweet pepper, chopped (¾ cup)
¼ cup sliced green onion
3 tablespoons snipped fresh coriander *or* parsley
2 tablespoons snipped fresh mint *or* 2 teaspoons dried mint, crushed
⅓ cup salad oil
½ teaspoon finely shredded lemon peel
⅓ cup lemon juice
¼ teaspoon salt
¼ teaspoon pepper
Leaf lettuce leaves (optional)
Fresh mint sprigs (optional)

In a large saucepan bring water to boiling. Add barley and bouillon granules. Return to boiling; reduce heat. Simmer, covered, for 10 to 12 minutes or till tender. Drain and rinse with cold water. Drain well.

In a large mixing bowl stir together drained barley, cucumber, red or green sweet pepper, green onion, coriander or parsley, and mint.

For dressing, in a screw-top jar combine salad oil, lemon peel, lemon juice, salt, and pepper. Cover and shake well to mix. Pour over barley mixture; toss gently to coat. Season to taste with additional salt and pepper. Cover and chill in the refrigerator for several hours or overnight.

Before serving, line a salad bowl with lettuce leaves, if desired. Turn the barley mixture into the bowl. Garnish with fresh mint sprigs, if desired. Makes 15 servings.

For 40 servings: Prepare Vegetable-Barley Salad as directed above, *except* use *12 cups* water; *4¼ cups* quick-cooking barley; *1 tablespoon* instant chicken bouillon granules; *3 medium* cucumbers, finely chopped (*5 cups*); *2½ medium* red *or* green sweet peppers, chopped (*2 cups*); ⅔ *cup* sliced green onion; ½ *cup* snipped fresh coriander *or* parsley; ⅓ *cup* snipped fresh mint *or* 2 *tablespoons* dried mint, crushed; ¾ *cup* salad oil; *1¼ teaspoons* finely shredded lemon peel; ¾ *cup* lemon juice; ½ *teaspoon* salt; and ½ *teaspoon* pepper.

Add ⅓ cup *chicken broth or water* with oil-lemon juice mixture. Cook barley in an 8-quart Dutch oven or kettle. Store salad in 2 large serving bowls.

Nutrition information per ½-cup serving: 127 cal., 2 g pro., 19 g carbo., 5 g fat, 0 mg chol., 62 mg sodium. U.S. RDA: 10% vit. A, 31% vit. C.

SPICY BRAN SCONES

Try this easy bread with honey butter—

- 1 **cup whole bran cereal**
- ½ **cup buttermilk** *or* **sour milk**
- 1 **beaten egg**
- 1 **egg white**
- 3 **tablespoons butter** *or* **margarine, melted**
- 3 **cups packaged biscuit mix**
- ⅓ **cup sugar**
- 1 **teaspoon apple pie spice**
- 1 **egg yolk**
- 1 **tablespoon milk**
- 1 **tablespoon sugar**
- ½ **teaspoon apple pie spice**

In a medium mixing bowl combine cereal and buttermilk or sour milk; let stand for 3 minutes or till milk is absorbed. Stir in egg, egg white, and butter or margarine. Set aside.

In a large mixing bowl stir together biscuit mix, ⅓ cup sugar, and 1 teaspoon apple pie spice. Make a well in the center. Add bran-egg mixture; mix just till dough clings together.

Turn dough out onto a floured surface and knead gently 10 to 15 strokes or till smooth and well mixed. Divide dough in half. On a large ungreased baking sheet, with lightly floured fingers, pat each half of the dough into a 6½-inch circle.

Stir together egg yolk and milk. Brush over tops of circles. Combine the 1 tablespoon sugar and ½ teaspoon apple pie spice; sprinkle over circles. Cut each circle into 8 wedges. With a spatula, pull each wedge out of the circle slightly, leaving about ¼-inch space between the wedges (see photo, below).

Bake in a 425° oven for 12 to 14 minutes or till scones are golden brown. Serve warm. (Or, cool, seal, label, and freeze. Reheat on a baking sheet in a 325° oven for 10 to 12 minutes or till warm.) Makes 16 scones.

For 40 scones: Prepare 1 recipe of Spicy Bran Scones as directed to make 16 scones. To make an additional 24 scones, prepare dough using *1½ cups* whole bran cereal, *¾ cup* buttermilk *or* sour milk, *2 eggs*, *¼ cup* melted butter *or* margarine, *4½ cups* packaged biscuit mix, *½ cup* sugar, and *1½ teaspoons* apple pie spice.

Divide dough into thirds. Using 2 ungreased baking sheets, with lightly floured fingers, pat each *third* of dough into a 6½-inch circle. Combine *1* beaten egg and *1 tablespoon* milk. Brush over circles. Combine *2 tablespoons* sugar and *¾ teaspoon* apple pie spice; sprinkle over circles. Cut and bake scones as directed at left and above.

Nutrition information per scone: 158 cal., 3 g pro., 24 g carbo., 6 g fat, 52 mg chol., 370 mg sodium. U.S. RDA: 11% thiamine, 12% phosphorus.

MIX-AND-SERVE APPLE PUNCH

A fancy, fruity combination that's just right for a special occasion—

- 3 **750-milliliter bottles sparkling apple cider, chilled**
- 3 **12-ounce cans (4½ cups) apricot nectar, chilled**

In a 4-quart punch bowl combine apple cider and apricot nectar. Stir gently. Serve over ice. Makes 15 (7½-ounce) servings.

For 40 (7-ounce) servings: Prepare Mix-and-Serve Apple Punch as above, *except* use *eight* 750-milliliter bottles sparkling apple cider, chilled, and *two* 46-ounce cans apricot nectar, chilled. In a 6-quart punch bowl combine *4 bottles* sparkling apple cider and *1 can* apricot nectar. Stir gently. Repeat with the remaining ingredients in another 6-quart punch bowl. Serve as directed above.

Nutrition information per serving: 111 cal., 0 g pro., 28 g carbo., 0 g fat, 0 mg chol., 7 mg sodium.

CREAMY HERB DIP

Add color to your dinner table! Underline the platter for the dip and dippers with additional red cabbage leaves and place it all on a wicker tray—

- 1 **8-ounce package cream cheese, softened**
- 2 **teaspoons snipped chives** *or* **dried snipped chives**
- 1½ **teaspoons snipped fresh thyme** *or* **½ teaspoon dried thyme, crushed**
- ¼ **teaspoon garlic powder**
- ¼ **teaspoon pepper**
- **Milk** *or* **buttermilk**
- 4 **red** *or* **green cabbage leaves**
- **Fresh thyme sprig (optional)**
- **Yellow summer** *and* **pattypan squash slices (about 2½ cups total)**

For dip, in a small mixer bowl beat cream cheese with an electric mixer on medium speed for 30 seconds. Add chives, thyme, garlic powder, and pepper; beat well. Beat in enough milk (about ¼ cup) or buttermilk (about ⅓ cup) to make of dipping consistency. Cover and chill for several hours or overnight.

To serve, make a cabbage bowl by fitting cabbage leaves tightly inside each other. Place on a serving platter. If necessary, stir a little additional milk or buttermilk into the chilled dip to return it to dipping consistency. Spoon dip into the prepared cabbage bowl. Garnish with a thyme sprig, if desired. Serve with squash slices. Makes 1¼ cups dip or 10 servings.

For 3 cups dip or 30 servings: Prepare Creamy Herb Dip as directed above, *except* use *two* 8-ounce packages and *one* 3-ounce package cream cheese, softened; *5 teaspoons* snipped fresh *or* dried chives; *4 teaspoons* snipped fresh thyme *or* *1½ teaspoons* dried thyme, crushed; *½ teaspoon* garlic powder; and *½ teaspoon* pepper.

Beat in enough milk (about ½ cup) or buttermilk (about ¾ cup) to make of dipping consistency. Use *8* red *or* green cabbage leaves for 2 cabbage bowls. Serve with about *7½ cups* total yellow summer and pattypan squash slices.

Nutrition information per 2 tablespoons dip and ¼ cup vegetables: 91 cal., 2 g pro., 3 g carbo., 8 g fat, 26 mg chol., 72 mg sodium.

SAVORY PITA CRISPS

Here's a twist on tortilla chips: crunchy delights made from pitas. Arrange them on a plate or serve them in a basket—

- 3 **large pita bread rounds** *or* **six 7-inch flour tortillas**
- ¼ **cup butter** *or* **margarine, melted**
- ¼ **cup snipped fresh parsley** *or* **1 tablespoon dried parsley flakes**
- 1 **teaspoon dried oregano, crushed**
- ⅛ **teaspoon garlic powder**
- ⅛ **teaspoon onion powder**
- ¼ **cup grated Parmesan** *or* **Romano cheese**

If using pita bread, separate each into halves to form 2 round single layers.

In a small mixing bowl stir together butter or margarine, parsley, oregano, garlic powder, and onion powder. Brush a *scant tablespoon* of the mixture on the rough side of *each* pita half or on 1 side of *each* tortilla. Sprinkle *2 teaspoons* of cheese atop *each* pita round or tortilla. Cut *each* into 6 wedges.

Arrange wedges in a single layer on ungreased baking sheets. Bake in a 350° oven for 12 to 15 minutes or till crisp and golden brown. Serve warm or at room temperature. Makes 36 crisps or 10 servings.

For 30 servings: Triple the ingredients. Continue as directed above.

Nutrition information per crisp: 34 cal., 1 g pro., 4 g carbo., 2 g fat, 4 mg chol., 26 mg sodium.

GRILLED SPICED HENS

You can't beat this for convenience! Brush the hens with the spice mixture several hours before cooking; cover. Keep in your refrigerator till barbecue time—

- 5 **1- to 1½-pound Cornish game hens, thawed**
- 2 **tablespoons paprika**
- 2 **tablespoons chili powder**
- 4 **teaspoons garlic powder**
- 2 **teaspoons onion powder**
- 1 **teaspoon celery salt**
- ½ **teaspoon salt**
- ½ **teaspoon dry mustard**
- ½ **teaspoon ground red pepper**
- ⅓ **cup cooking oil**

Using a long, heavy knife or kitchen shears, halve hens lengthwise by cutting through the breastbone, just off-center. Then, cut through the center of the backbone. (Or, have your butcher halve the hens for you.) Rinse hen halves; pat dry with paper towels.

In a small mixing bowl combine paprika, chili powder, garlic powder, onion powder, celery salt, salt, dry mustard, and red pepper. Add oil; mix well. Brush mixture onto hen halves.

Grill hen halves, bone side up, on an uncovered grill, directly over *medium** coals for 20 minutes. Turn and grill for 10 to 20 minutes more or till tender enough to be easily pierced with a fork. Makes 10 servings.

For 30 servings: Substitute two 12- to 14-pound *turkeys* for the hens. Rinse turkeys; pat dry with paper towels. Skewer neck skin to the back of the bird. Tie legs to the tail with cord. Twist wing tips under back.

In each of 2 covered grills, arrange preheated coals around a drip pan; test for *medium-low** heat above each pan at the height the turkeys will be cooked. Place 1 of the turkeys on each grill rack, breast side up, over the drip pan, but not over the coals. Lower grill hood. Grill for 3 to 4 hours or till a meat thermometer inserted in center of inside thigh muscle registers 180° to 185°.

Meanwhile, for spice glaze, in a small saucepan combine paprika, chili powder, garlic powder, onion powder, celery salt, salt, dry mustard, red pepper, and cooking oil. Cook and stir over low heat for 5 minutes. Add one 10-ounce jar *orange marmalade;* cook and stir over low heat till marmalade is

melted. Brush glaze over the turkeys the last 5 minutes of grilling (see photo, above). Let turkeys stand for 20 minutes before carving.

Hen roasting directions for 10 servings: Prepare hens as directed for 10 servings, *except* place hen halves, cut side down, on racks in 2 shallow roasting pans. Cover loosely with foil. Roast in a 375° oven for 30 minutes. Uncover hens. Roast for 45 to 55 minutes more or till tender. Makes 10 servings.

Turkey roasting directions for 30 servings: Prepare turkeys as directed for 30 servings, *except* place turkeys, breast side up, on racks in 2 shallow roasting pans. Insert a meat thermometer in the center of the inside thigh muscle of each turkey, making sure the bulb does not touch the bone.

Cover turkeys loosely with foil. Roast in a 325° oven for 4½ to 5½ hours or till the thermometers register 180° to 185°. Cut the cords between legs after 2½ hours. Prepare spice glaze. Uncover turkeys and brush with spice glaze; roast for 5 minutes more. Let stand for 20 minutes before carving.

*Note: See page 92 for directions on testing the temperature of the coals.

Nutrition information per hen half: 171 cal., 29 g pro., 1 g carbo., 5 g fat, 87 mg chol., 170 mg sodium. U.S. RDA: 61% niacin, 24% phosphorus.

DILLED CORN AND PEA PODS

Use this colorful vegetable medley as a bed for the Grilled Spiced Hens. Garnish with fresh dillweed sprigs—

3 **cups fresh pea pods (12 ounces) *or* two 6-ounce packages frozen pea pods**
1 **16-ounce package frozen whole kernel corn**
1 **cup water**
1 **medium red sweet pepper, cut into bite-size strips**
2 **tablespoons butter *or* margarine**
1½ **teaspoons snipped fresh dill *or* ½ teaspoon dried dillweed**
¼ **teaspoon salt**
⅛ **teaspoon pepper**

If using fresh pea pods, remove tips and strings. If desired, cut pea pods crosswise into thirds. Set aside.

In a large saucepan combine corn and water. Bring to boiling; reduce heat. Simmer, covered, for 4 minutes. Add pea pods and red pepper strips. Return to boiling. Simmer, covered, about 2 minutes more or till vegetables are crisp-tender. Drain well.

Add butter or margarine, dill, salt, and pepper. Stir till butter is melted. Makes 10 servings.

For 30 servings: Prepare Dilled Corn and Pea Pods as directed above, *except* triple all ingredients. Combine corn and water in a 5- or 6-quart Dutch oven. Bring to boiling. Add red pepper strips; reduce heat. Simmer, covered, for 4 minutes. Add pea pods; heat through. Drain well. Continue as directed above.

Microwave directions for 10 servings: Prepare pea pods as directed for 10 servings; set aside. Omit the 1 cup water. In a 2-quart microwave-safe casserole combine corn and 2 tablespoons *water*. Micro-cook, covered, on 100% power (high) for 6 minutes. Uncover and stir. Add pea pods and red pepper strips. Cook, covered, for 7 to 9 minutes more or till vegetables are crisp-tender, stirring once. Drain well.

Add butter or margarine, dill, salt, and pepper. Stir till butter or margarine is melted.

Nutrition information per ½-cup serving: 74 cal., 2 g pro., 13 g carbo., 2 g fat, 6 mg chol., 82 mg sodium. U.S. RDA: 23% vit. A, 68% vit. C.

GREENS WITH PARSLEY DRESSING

Choose greens and vegetables to create a colorful salad. For the photograph on pages 104–105, we used green leaf lettuce, raddichio, and yellow sweet pepper strips—

⅓ **cup loosely packed parsley sprigs**
¼ **cup mayonnaise *or* salad dressing**
¼ **cup dairy sour cream**
2 **tablespoons snipped chives**
2 **teaspoons lemon juice**
2 **teaspoons Dijon-style mustard**
6 **cups torn mixed greens**
3 **cups assorted chopped *or* sliced vegetables (such as yellow *or* green sweet peppers, radishes, tomatoes, *and* mushrooms)**

For dressing, in a blender container or food processor bowl combine parsley, mayonnaise or salad dressing, sour cream, chives, lemon juice, and mustard. Cover and blend or process till smooth. Transfer to a screw-top jar. Cover tightly and chill up to 24 hours.

In a large salad bowl toss together greens and vegetables. Cover and chill for up to several hours. To serve, pour dressing over greens mixture and toss gently to coat. Makes 10 servings.

For 30 servings: Triple the ingredients. Use 2 or 3 large salad bowls (or refill 1 bowl as needed).

Nutrition information per 1-cup serving: 69 cal., 1 g pro., 3 g carbo., 6 g fat, 6 mg chol., 77 mg sodium. U.S. RDA: 27% vit. A, 50% vit. C.

PECAN CORN MUFFINS

⅔ **cup all-purpose flour**
⅔ **cup yellow cornmeal**
⅔ **cup ground pecans**
½ **cup sugar**
¾ **teaspoon baking powder**
½ **teaspoon baking soda**
2 **beaten eggs**
½ **cup buttermilk *or* sour milk***
⅓ **cup butter *or* margarine, melted**
⅓ **cup chopped pecans (optional)**

Grease muffin cups or line with paper bake cups; set aside. In a medium mixing bowl stir together flour, cornmeal, ground pecans, sugar, baking powder, and baking soda. Make a well in center.

In a small mixing bowl combine eggs, buttermilk, and butter or margarine. Add all at once to flour mixture. Stir just till moistened. (Batter should be lumpy.) Gently fold in chopped pecans, if desired. Fill muffin cups ¾ full.

Bake in a 375° oven for 18 to 20 minutes or till golden. Remove and serve warm. (Or, cool on a wire rack. Reheat as directed.) Makes 12 muffins.

To reheat: Place cooled muffins on foil. Sprinkle with a little water; seal. Warm in a 325° oven about 10 minutes or till heated through. (Or, place 6 muffins at a time on a microwave-safe plate. Cover with a microwave-safe paper towel. Micro-cook on 100% power (high) for 1 to 2 minutes or till heated through, giving the plate a half-turn after 40 seconds.)

For 30 servings: Prepare Pecan Corn Muffins as directed above, *except* triple all ingredients and omit muffin cups. Grease and flour three 8x1½-inch *or* 9x1½-inch round baking pans. Divide batter evenly among the 3 pans.

Bake in a 400° oven for 20 to 25 minutes or till golden. Cut bread in each pan into 12 wedges (see photo, below). Serve warm. (Or, cool completely in pan on a wire rack. Cover pan with foil and freeze in pan.)

To reheat: Place the wrapped pan in a 325° oven about 25 minutes or till heated through.

*Note: For ½ cup sour milk, in a 1-cup measure combine 1½ teaspoons *lemon juice or vinegar* plus enough *whole milk* to make ½ cup. Let stand for 5 minutes.

Nutrition information per muffin: 188 cal., 3 g pro., 20 g carbo., 11 g fat, 60 mg chol., 139 mg sodium.

SLICED MELON WITH LIME-POPPY DRIZZLE

- 3 tablespoons salad oil
- 2 teaspoons honey
- ¼ teaspoon finely shredded lime peel
- 2 teaspoons lime juice
- ¼ teaspoon poppy seed
- ½ of a small cantaloupe, seeded
- ½ of a small honeydew melon, seeded
- ¼ of a small watermelon

For dressing, in a screw-top jar combine salad oil, honey, lime peel, lime juice, and poppy seed. Cover and shake. Chill.

Cut the cantaloupe and honeydew melon into 1-inch-thick slices. With the longest cut side down on a cutting board, cut the watermelon into 1-inch-thick slices. Cut each slice into 4 pie-shaped wedges. Arrange melon on a large serving platter. Cover and chill. To serve, shake dressing well. Drizzle over melon. Makes 10 servings.

For 30 servings: Triple the ingredients and use 2 or 3 serving platters. (Or, refill 1 platter.)

Nutrition information per honeydew or cantaloupe slice and 2 watermelon wedges with dressing: 70 cal., 1 g pro., 8 g carbo., 4 g fat, 0 mg chol., 6 mg sodium. U.S. RDA: 20% vit. A and 36% vit. C.

CHOCOLATE-LADYFINGER LOAF

- ¼ cup sugar
- 1 envelope unflavored gelatin
- 2 slightly beaten egg yolks
- 1 cup milk
- 6 squares (6 ounces) semisweet chocolate
- 2 egg whites
- 2 tablespoons sugar
- 1 cup whipping cream
- 1 3-ounce package (12) ladyfingers, split
- Whipped cream (optional)
- Whole *and* sliced strawberries (optional)

In a medium saucepan combine ¼ cup sugar and gelatin. In a small mixing bowl combine egg yolks and milk; stir into gelatin mixture. Cook and stir over low heat till sugar and gelatin dissolve.

Add chocolate and continue cooking, stirring constantly till chocolate is melted. With a wire whip or rotary beater, beat mixture till chocolate is well mixed. Chill to consistency of corn syrup, stirring occasionally.

Remove from refrigerator (gelatin mixture will continue to set). In a large mixer bowl immediately begin beating egg whites with an electric mixer on high speed till soft peaks form (tips curl). Gradually add 2 tablespoons sugar, beating till stiff peaks form (tips stand straight).

When gelatin mixture is partially set (the consistency of unbeaten egg whites) fold in stiff-beaten egg whites.

In a large mixer bowl beat 1 cup whipping cream with an electric mixer on low speed till soft peaks form. Fold into gelatin mixture. Chill till mixture mounds when spooned.

Line the bottom of a 9x5x3-inch loaf pan with waxed paper. Place ladyfingers in the pan, round sides against the pan sides. Lay any remaining ladyfingers diagonally across the bottom of the pan. Turn gelatin mixture into the pan; spread evenly. Cover and chill for several hours or till firm.

To serve, invert cake onto a serving platter. Garnish with additional whipped cream and whole and sliced strawberries, if desired. Slice dessert, then spoon additional sliced strawberries over each serving. Serves 10.

For 30 servings: Prepare Chocolate-Ladyfinger Loaf as directed at left, *except* omit ladyfingers and use two 9-inch *angel food cakes.* Prepare gelatin-whipped-cream mixture.

While gelatin chills, hollow angel food cakes by cutting a ½-inch slice off top of each inverted cake; set slice aside. Hold a sharp, narrow knife parallel to sides of cake and make 2 circular cuts—one 1 inch from the center hole and the other 1 inch from outer edge. Use a spoon to carefully remove the cake between the cuts, leaving the bottom about 1 inch thick. Repeat with the second cake.

After chilling the gelatin-whipped-cream mixture till it mounds when spooned, spoon *half* of the mixture into 1 of the hollowed-out cakes; spread evenly. Replace the ½-inch top slice. Repeat with the remaining gelatin mixture and cake.

Frost tops and sides of both cakes with one 8-ounce container *frozen whipped dessert topping,* thawed. Cover and chill cakes for several hours or overnight. To serve, slice with a serrated or electric knife (see photo, below). Garnish with a whole strawberry sliced in thirds to, but not through, the top. Spoon sliced strawberries atop.

Nutrition information per ladyfinger loaf serving: 262 cal., 4 g pro., 25 g carbo., 18 g fat, 121 mg chol., 129 mg sodium. U.S. RDA: 10% vit. A, 10% phosphorus.

The Idea Magazine For American Families

Better Homes
and Gardens

August 1986
$1.50

GARDEN-FRESH
CUISINE Page 80
Light And Elegant Recipes
For Summer Fruits
And Vegetables

FIGHTING
ABOUT MONEY
Why You Do It
And How To Stop It

PRESCHOOL
EDUCATION
Too Much Too Soon?

3 SUPER
NEW HOUSES
With Today's
Most-Wanted Features

TALKING BACK
TO YOUR DOCTOR

DECORATING
MARVELOUS
MAKEOVERS
See Befores
And Afters

**GINGERSNAP
BERRY PIE**
Only 186 Calories
A Serving!

LAMB-BURGER PITAS

You'll find a cheesy surprise in the middle of this burger.

BURRITO BURGERS

A burger filled with beans and chili peppers.

BURGERS!

3 NEW VERSIONS OF AMERICA'S FAVORITE BARBECUE

By Barbara Atkins

HOT GRILLING TIPS

● The best burger chefs start with *medium-hot* coals. To test, hold your hand over the coals at the height burgers will be cooked. If you count three seconds before the heat drives your hand away, the coals are the right temperature.

● Some like their burgers cooked to medium; some like them medium-well. But, if you're eating pork burgers, *always* cook them well-done.

● Coals flare up? Use any of these fire fighters: cover the grill, space the hot coals farther apart, or take out coals. As a last resort, mist the fire with water.

Our best barbecue-burger secret? Put them in a grill basket and flip them all at once.

LAMB-BURGER PITAS

- ⅓ cup soft bread crumbs
- 2 tablespoons plain yogurt
- 1 teaspoon dried oregano, crushed
- ¼ teaspoon ground nutmeg
- 1 *or* 2 cloves garlic, minced
- 1 pound ground lamb
- ¼ cup crumbled feta cheese
- 2 large pita bread rounds, halved crosswise

Spinach leaves (optional)
Sliced ripe olives (optional)

Combine crumbs, yogurt, oregano, nutmeg, and garlic. Mix in lamb. Shape into eight ¼-inch-thick patties. Place *1 tablespoon* feta atop *each* of 4 patties. Top with remaining patties. Seal edges.

Grill, uncovered, directly over *medium-hot* coals for 7 minutes. Turn and grill to desired doneness, allowing 6 to 8 minutes more for medium. Serve in pita halves lined with spinach. Top with olives and additional cheese and yogurt. Makes 4 servings.

Nutrition information per serving: 286 cal., 22 g pro., 27 g carbo., 9 g fat, 67 mg chol., 175 mg sodium.

CAJUN-STYLE PORK BURGERS

- 1 4½-ounce can tiny shrimp, drained
- 1 beaten egg
- ⅓ cup soft bread crumbs

Cajun Seasoning (see recipe at right)
- ¾ pound ground pork
- 4 slices French bread, toasted

Peppy Relish (see recipe at right)

Finely chop *half* of the shrimp. In a small mixing bowl stir together egg, crumbs, and Cajun Seasoning. Mix in chopped shrimp and pork. Shape into four ¾-inch-thick patties.

Grill, on an uncovered grill, directly over *medium-hot* coals for 7 minutes. Turn and grill 6 to 10 minutes more or till well-done. Serve on bread; top with Peppy Relish. Makes 4 servings.

Cajun Seasoning: Combine ½ teaspoon *garlic salt,* ½ teaspoon ground *white pepper,* ½ teaspoon ground *red pepper,* ½ teaspoon ground *black pepper,* and ¼ teaspoon *dry mustard.*

Peppy Relish: Combine remaining shrimp; 1 small *tomato,* peeled, seeded, and chopped; 1 *green onion,* thinly sliced; 1 teaspoon finely chopped *jalapeño chili pepper;* and 1 small clove *garlic,* minced. Makes about ¾ cup.

Nutrition information per serving: 354 cal., 34 g pro., 25 g carbo., 12 g fat, 183 mg chol., 579 mg sodium.

BURRITO BURGERS

- 1 pound ground beef
- ¼ cup chopped canned green chili peppers, drained
- ¼ cup refried beans
- 2 slices process American cheese, halved diagonally
- 4 7-inch flour tortillas

Divide beef into fourths; pat each fourth into a 5-inch circle. Season with salt and pepper. Place *1 tablespoon* of the peppers and *1 tablespoon* of the beans on *one* side of *each* patty. Fold patties in half, forming semicircles; seal edges.

Grill, on an uncovered grill, directly over *medium-hot* coals for 7 minutes. Turn; grill to desired doneness, allowing 6 to 8 minutes more for medium. Top each patty with a halved cheese slice during last 2 minutes. Place tortillas on grill for a few seconds to heat. Serve patties in folded warm tortillas. If desired, top with shredded *lettuce,* halved *tomato slices,* sliced *green onion,* and *dairy sour cream.* Makes 4 servings.

Nutrition information per serving: 317 cal., 29 g pro., 16 g carbo., 15 g fat, 93 mg chol., and 323 mg sodium.

GARDEN-FRESH CUISINE

SWEET & SASSY ▪ CRISP & CRUNCHY
HOT & SPICY ▪ GOOD & NUTTY

By Lynn Hoppe

GINGERSNAP-BERRY PIE

Enjoy strawberry pie as never before! Heads will turn when you serve this glistening version with a blueberry bonus.

STORING TIP: Delicate berries deserve gentle treatment. Store strawberries loosely covered in the refrigerator up to a few days; store blueberries up to one week in the refrigerator. Rinse just before using.

RAZZLE-DAZZLE LEMONADE

Raspberries, lemon sherbet, and sparkling water blend into a surprisingly sprightly delight.

PLUM DUMPLINGS AND CREAM

Classic dishes provide a treasury of creative new recipe possibilities. In this plum spin-off of traditional apple dumplings, home-style and hearty go haute.

Sweet and sassy fruit temptations make captivating finales to your warm-weather meals.

CANTALOUPE MOUSSE

A velvety chocolate sauce, the epitome of indulgence, kisses every spoonful of this feathery-light fruit dessert. Divine!

PHOTOGRAPHS: MIKE JENSEN. FOOD STYLIST: JANET PITTMAN

GARDEN-FRESH CUISINE

BEAN AND BRIE SALAD

Whether you call them string beans, snap beans, or green beans, showcase them in this easy meatless main dish.

BUYING TIP: The hallmark of the perfect green bean is a long, straight pod that is free from blemishes and that snaps crisply when bent. Ridges or bulges on the pod? The bean will be tough.

HONEYDEW MELON WITH SAUTÉED FRUIT

Sautéed apricots and bananas in a zesty lime sauce raise refreshing honeydew melon slices to new heights of sophistication.

Crisp and crunchy fruits and vegetables contribute color, texture, nutrients, and great taste in these smashing treats.

TOASTY CARROT CRACKERS

Flaunt your flair for making the ordinary extraordinary. Serve the crispy wafers with cheese and avocado slices.

JICAMA-CUCUMBER RELISH

Expand your produce repertoire. Jicama, a root vegetable grown in tropical America, provides the extra crunch in this sweet pickle relish for sandwiches.

123

GARDEN-FRESH CUISINE

PEPPERY GRILLED TURKEY MIREPOIX

Mirepoix (pronounced mir PWA), French for sautéed vegetables and herbs, dresses slices of prime turkey breast.

FREEZING TIP: Freeze some of your zucchini crop for year-round eating. When adding frozen zucchini to a recipe, remember that you're also adding extra liquid; precook it slightly and drain it first.

SIZZLING SUMMER CHILI

Satisfy your penchant for chili with this sensational version that boasts summer's best—corn and zucchini.

Hot and spicy seasonings such as ground red pepper, jalapeño peppers, cumin, hot pepper sauce, and mustard seed fuel the fire in these bold recipes.

BLAZE-OF-GLORY SALSA

In the spirit of jazzing up fruits and vegetables, here's a kicky salsa guaranteed to be a titillating experience.

Mexicans spoon on salsa in much the same way Americans sprinkle on salt. Salsas, typically a mixture of tomatoes, chili peppers, and onion, accompany most Mexican foods—egg dishes, grilled meats, cold seafood, chicken, and tacos and other tortilla specialties.

125

GARDEN-FRESH CUISINE

Make a culinary statement with this bread that you customize yourself. Choose from four options—zucchini, carrot, pear, or peach. It's simple, summery, and super!

CHOOSE-A-FRUIT-OR-VEGETABLE BREAD

- 1 cup all-purpose flour
- ½ cup whole wheat flour
- ⅓ cup quick-cooking rolled oats
- 1 teaspoon baking soda
- ½ cup butter *or* margarine
- ½ cup sugar
- 2 eggs
- 2 tablespoons milk
- 1 teaspoon vanilla
- ½ teaspoon finely shredded lemon peel
- 1 cup finely shredded zucchini *or* carrots, peeled pears, *or* finely chopped peeled peaches
- ½ cup chopped walnuts

Combine flours, oats, and soda; set aside. In a large mixer bowl beat butter or margarine with an electric mixer on medium speed for 30 seconds. Add sugar; beat till fluffy, scraping sides of bowl often. Add eggs, milk, vanilla, and lemon peel; beat well. Stir in vegetable or fruit. Add flour mixture, a *third* at a time, beating on low speed till combined. Stir in walnuts.

Spread batter in a greased 5½-cup ring mold or 8x4x2-inch loaf pan. Bake in a 350° oven 35 to 40 minutes for ring mold or 55 to 60 minutes for loaf pan, or till a wooden toothpick inserted in center comes out clean. Cover with foil the last 10 minutes of baking. Cool 10 minutes. Remove from pan; cool on wire rack. Wrap and store overnight for easier slicing. Makes 1 loaf, 12 servings.

Nutrition information per slice: 180 cal., 4 g pro., 14 g carbo., 12 g fat, 67 mg chol., 180 mg sodium.

CANTALOUPE MOUSSE

1¾ cups cubed cantaloupe (about 1
    small cantaloupe)
  2 tablespoons sugar
  1 envelope unflavored gelatin
  ¼ cup water
  ½ cup whipping cream
1½ cups semisweet chocolate
    pieces (9 ounces)
  2 tablespoons shortening
Toasted coconut (optional)
Cantaloupe slices (optional)

For mousse, in a blender container or food processor bowl place cubed cantaloupe. Cover and blend or process till smooth. Set aside.

In a 1-quart saucepan stir together sugar and gelatin; stir in water. Let stand for 5 minutes. Cook and stir over low heat till gelatin is dissolved. Stir in blended cantaloupe. Chill in the refrigerator to the consistency of corn syrup, stirring occasionally.

Remove gelatin mixture from the refrigerator. (Gelatin will continue to set.) Beat the whipping cream with an electric mixer on low speed till soft peaks form (tips curl). When the gelatin mixture is partially set (consistency of unbeaten egg whites), gently fold in the whipped cream. Carefully pour mixture into four 6-ounce custard cups. Chill for 4 hours or till firm.

For sauce, in a heavy saucepan combine the chocolate pieces and shortening. Cook and stir over low heat till the chocolate begins to melt. Immediately remove the saucepan from heat. Stir till smooth.

To serve, spoon about *3 tablespoons* of the warm sauce into individual shallow bowls. Unmold *each* cantaloupe mousse and place atop chocolate sauce in bowls. Drizzle *1 to 2 teaspoons* of sauce over *each* mousse. Garnish with toasted coconut and cantaloupe slices, if desired. Makes 4 servings.

Nutrition information per serving:
305 cal., 4 g pro., 28 g carbo., 23 g fat, 41 mg chol., 16 mg sodium. U.S. RDA: 28% vit. A, 21% vit. C.

GINGERSNAP-BERRY PIE

Crushed gingersnaps, crushed vanilla wafers, and chopped walnuts make the delicious no-fuss crust for this pie—

  1 cup finely crushed gingersnaps
    (15 cookies)
  ¾ cup finely crushed vanilla wafers
    (18 cookies)
  ¼ cup finely chopped walnuts
  ⅓ cup butter *or* margarine, melted
  1 envelope unflavored gelatin
1¾ cups unsweetened white grape
    juice
  1 8-ounce package cream cheese,
    softened
  ¼ cup sugar
  1 teaspoon vanilla
2½ cups blueberries
1½ cups sliced strawberries
Citrus leaves

For crust, in a medium mixing bowl combine crushed gingersnaps, crushed vanilla wafers, and walnuts. Add melted butter or margarine. Toss to mix well. Press crumb mixture onto the bottom and 1½ inches up the sides of a 9-inch springform pan to form a firm, even crust. Bake in a 375° oven for 5 minutes. Cool completely on a wire rack before filling.

Meanwhile, in a medium saucepan soften gelatin in the grape juice for 5 minutes. Cook and stir over low heat till gelatin dissolves. Chill for 40 to 50 minutes or till mixture is partially set (consistency of unbeaten egg whites), stirring occasionally.

Meanwhile, in a small mixer bowl beat the cream cheese, sugar, and vanilla with an electric mixer on medium speed till smooth. Spread mixture over bottom of prepared crust. Spoon *half* of the gelatin mixture over cream cheese layer. Top with *1½ cups* of the blueberries, all of the sliced strawberries, and then the remaining blueberries. Spoon the remaining gelatin mixture over berries. Chill for 4 to 6 hours or till set.

To serve, loosen crust with a narrow spatula; remove the sides of the springform pan. Garnish with citrus leaves. Makes 12 to 16 servings.

Nutrition information per serving:
186 cal., 3 g pro., 22 g carbo., 10 g fat, 26 mg chol., 114 mg sodium. U.S. RDA: 27% vit. C.

PLUM DUMPLINGS AND CREAM

  ¼ cup sugar
  ¼ teaspoon ground nutmeg
  ½ of a 3-ounce package cream
    cheese, softened
1½ cups all-purpose flour
  ¼ teaspoon salt
  ½ cup butter *or* margarine
  4 to 5 tablespoons cold water
  6 plums, halved and pitted
Light cream *or* milk

In a small mixing bowl, stir together sugar and nutmeg. Set aside. In a small mixer bowl beat cream cheese with an electric mixer on medium speed till fluffy. Add *3 tablespoons* of the sugar-nutmeg mixture. Beat till well combined. Set aside.

For dough, in a medium mixing bowl stir together flour and salt. Cut in butter or margarine till pieces are the size of small peas. Sprinkle *1 tablespoon* of the cold water over part of the mixture; gently toss with fork. Push to one side of the bowl. Repeat till all is moistened. Form dough into a ball.

On a lightly floured surface roll dough into an 18x12-inch rectangle. Cut into six 6-inch squares.

For *each* dumpling, spread *2 teaspoons* of the cream cheese mixture on the cut side of a plum half. Top with another plum half. Place in the center of a dough square. Moisten dough edges with water. Fold corners to center and pinch to seal edges.

Place the dumplings in a shallow baking pan. Brush with some of the light cream or milk and sprinkle with the remaining sugar-nutmeg mixture. Bake dumplings in a 375° oven about 30 minutes or till pastry is lightly browned and plums are tender. Serve warm dumplings with cream. Serves 6.

Nutrition information per serving:
344 cal., 5 g pro., 41 g carbo., 19 g fat, 49 mg chol., 268 mg sodium. U.S. RDA: 18% vit. A, 15% thiamine, 12% riboflavin, 10% niacin.

RAZZLE-DAZZLE LEMONADE

1¼ cups water
¾ cup sugar
6 to 8 lemons
1 cup fresh raspberries *or* blueberries
1 pint lemon sherbet
3 cups carbonated water, chilled
Fresh raspberries *or* blueberries (optional)

For syrup, stir together water and sugar. Cook, stirring constantly, over medium heat for 1 to 2 minutes or till sugar is dissolved. Cool.

Finely shred *2 teaspoons* lemon peel. Squeeze the juice from lemons (about 1½ cups total). In a 4-cup pitcher stir together the cooled syrup, lemon peel, lemon juice, and the 1 cup fresh raspberries or blueberries. Cover. Chill well.

For *each* serving, place *1 scoop* of the lemon sherbet in a tall glass. Pour ½ *cup* of the syrup mixture and ½ *cup* of the carbonated water over sherbet in the glass. Garnish with additional fresh raspberries or blueberries, if desired. Makes 6 (10-ounce) servings.

Nutrition information per serving: 215 cal., 1 g pro., 53 g carbo., 1 g fat, 5 mg chol., 32 mg sodium. U.S. RDA: 54% vit. C.

BEAN AND BRIE SALAD

When Brie cheese is fully ripened, it has a soft, creamy texture that's not runny—

1 recipe Yogurt and Chive Dressing
1½ cups water
½ cup wheat berries
½ pound green beans, bias-sliced into 1-inch pieces (2 cups)
Savoy cabbage leaves
4 medium tomatoes, cut into wedges
2 4½-ounce wheels Brie cheese, cut into bite-size wedges (2 cups)
1 cup broken walnuts

Prepare Yogurt and Chive Dressing. In a small saucepan bring water to boiling. Add wheat berries. Reduce the heat. Simmer, covered, about 50 minutes or till the wheat berries are tender. Drain. Rinse with cold water. Drain well. Cover and chill thoroughly.

In a medium saucepan cook green beans, covered, in a small amount of boiling water for 15 to 20 minutes or just till tender. Drain. Rinse with cold water. Drain well. Cover and chill.

On 4 cabbage-lined plates arrange the green beans and tomato wedges. In a small mixing bowl stir together the chilled Yogurt and Chive Dressing and wheat berries. Spoon some of the wheat berry mixture into the center of each plate. Top each plate with some of the cheese wedges and walnuts. Makes 4 servings.

Yogurt and Chive Dressing: In a small mixing bowl stir together ½ cup *plain yogurt* or *dairy sour cream*, 2 tablespoons grated *Parmesan cheese*, 2 teaspoons snipped *chives* or *green onion tops*, and ⅛ teaspoon *paprika*. Cover and chill till serving time. Makes about ½ cup dressing.

Nutrition information per serving: 530 cal., 25 g pro., 26 g carbo., 39 g fat, 68 mg chol., 489 mg sodium. U.S. RDA: 34% vit. A, 55% vit. C, 22% thiamine, 33% riboflavin, 11% niacin, 30% calcium, 15% iron, 41% phosphorus.

TOASTY CARROT CRACKERS

If the dough is difficult to slice at room temperature, chill it before slicing—

¾ cup shredded carrot
⅓ cup water
1½ cups rolled oats
⅔ cup all-purpose flour
⅓ cup toasted wheat germ
1 tablespoon sesame seed
½ teaspoon garlic salt
¼ cup butter *or* margarine
Wheat germ
Swiss cheese slices (optional)
Avocado slices (optional)

In a small saucepan combine carrot and water. Bring to boiling. Reduce the heat. Simmer, covered, for 5 to 10 minutes or till carrot is tender. Drain.

Meanwhile, in a blender container or food processor bowl place oats. Cover and blend or process about 1 minute or till oats are evenly ground. Set aside.

Place carrot in blender container or food processor bowl. Cover and blend or process till smooth (about ½ cup puree). Set aside.

In a medium mixing bowl stir together ground oats, flour, the ⅓ cup wheat germ, sesame seed, and garlic salt. Cut in butter or margarine till mixture resembles coarse crumbs. Add carrot puree, kneading till moistened.

Shape dough into a 9-inch roll. Use a serrated knife to cut into ⅛-inch slices. Place on an ungreased baking sheet. Sprinkle with wheat germ. Flatten with the bottom of a glass. Bake in a 375° oven about 9 minutes or till edges are lightly browned. Transfer to a wire rack. Serve crackers with cheese and avocado slices, if desired. Makes about 60 crackers.

Nutrition information per cracker: 23 cal., 1 g pro., 3 g carbo., 1 g fat, 2 mg chol., 24 mg sodium.

JICAMA-CUCUMBER RELISH

Serve this crunchy vegetable relish on ham and rye sandwiches, hamburgers, or hot dogs, or as a zippy accompaniment to most any meal—

- 2 cups shredded, peeled jicama (½ pound)
- 2 cups shredded, seeded, unpeeled cucumber (about 1½ medium)
- ½ cup sliced pitted ripe olives
- ¼ cup chopped pimiento
- 1 tablespoon salt
- 1 cup sugar
- 1 cup vinegar
- 1 teaspoon mustard seed
- 1 teaspoon celery seed

In a large mixing bowl stir together the jicama, cucumber, olives, pimiento, and salt. Let mixture stand for 3 hours. Drain well.

In a large kettle or Dutch oven stir together the sugar, vinegar, mustard seed, and celery seed. Bring the mixture to boiling, stirring constantly, to completely dissolve the sugar. Stir in the drained vegetable mixture. Return entire mixture to boiling. Boil, uncovered, for 5 minutes.

Ladle the hot vegetable mixture into 3 hot, clean half-pint jars, leaving a ½-inch headspace in each. Wipe the jar rims and adjust the lids. Process the jars in a boiling water bath for 15 minutes (start timing when the water boils). Makes 3 half-pints of the relish.

Nutrition information per 2 tablespoons relish: 24 cal., 0 g pro., 6 g carbo., 0 g fat, 0 mg chol., and 146 mg sodium.

HONEYDEW MELON WITH SAUTÉED FRUIT

- 3 tablespoons butter *or* margarine
- 4 lime peel curls (optional)
- 1 tablespoon lime juice
- 1 tablespoon honey
- 2 medium bananas, bias-sliced into ¼-inch pieces
- 2 peaches *or* 4 apricots, peeled, pitted, and coarsely chopped
- ½ of a honeydew melon *or* cantaloupe, peeled, seeded, and cut into thin slices
- ¼ cup pine nuts, toasted

In a 10-inch skillet melt butter or margarine. Stir in lime juice and honey. Add bananas and peaches or apricots. Heat and stir about 2 minutes or till heated through.

On *each* of 4 small plates arrange some of the melon or cantaloupe slices in a fan shape. Top with some of the fruit mixture and pine nuts. Garnish with lime peel, if desired. Serves 4.

Microwave directions: In a 1½-quart microwave-safe casserole microcook butter or margarine, uncovered, on 100% power (high) for 45 to 60 seconds or till melted. Stir in lime juice and honey. Add bananas and peaches or apricots. Stir to coat. Cook, uncovered, on high for 1½ to 2 minutes or till heated through, stirring once. Continue as directed above.

Nutrition information per serving: 266 cal., 3 g pro., 38 g carbo., 14 g fat, 23 mg chol., and 108 mg sodium. U.S. RDA: 14% vit. A, 90% vit. C, and 18% thiamine.

PEPPERY GRILLED TURKEY MIREPOIX

- 4 turkey breast tenderloin steaks (about 1 pound total)
- 2 tablespoons butter *or* margarine, melted
- 1 large onion, finely chopped (about 1 cup)
- 1 medium carrot, finely chopped (about ½ cup)
- ½ cup sliced fresh mushrooms (about 1¼ ounces)
- 1½ teaspoons snipped fresh thyme *or* ½ teaspoon dried thyme, crushed
- ¼ teaspoon salt
- ⅛ to ¼ teaspoon ground red pepper
- 1 tablespoon snipped parsley
- Coarsely shredded zucchini
- Thyme sprigs (optional)

Grill turkey steaks, on an uncovered grill, directly over *medium* coals for 20 to 25 minutes or till steak is lightly browned and no longer pink, turning once and brushing occasionally with *1 tablespoon* of the melted butter.

Meanwhile, in a medium saucepan combine the onion, carrot, mushrooms, fresh or dried thyme, salt, red pepper, and the remaining 1 tablespoon melted butter or margarine. Cook, covered, over low heat for 10 to 12 minutes or just till the vegetables are tender. Stir in the parsley.

On *each* of 4 plates arrange some of the shredded zucchini. Place a grilled steak on each bed of shredded zucchini. Spoon some of the vegetable mixture over each steak. Garnish with thyme sprigs, if desired. Makes 4 servings.

Nutrition information per serving: 203 cal., 29 g pro., 6 g carbo., 7 g fat, 86 mg chol., 261 mg sodium. U.S. RDA: 37% vit. A, 11% riboflavin, 38% niacin, 13% iron, 27% phosphorus.

SIZZLING SUMMER CHILI

Anaheims are long green peppers that are mildly hot. Look for them in the produce section of your supermarket—

- 1 **pound boneless pork, cut into ½-inch cubes**
- 1 **small onion, chopped (¼ cup)**
- 1 **clove garlic, minced**
- 2 **tablespoons cooking oil**
- 2 **fresh ears of corn**
- 1 **15-ounce can tomato sauce**
- ½ **cup water**
- ¼ **cup raisins**
- 2 **fresh Anaheim chili peppers, seeded and finely chopped**
- ¼ **teaspoon salt**
- ¼ **teaspoon ground cumin**
- ¼ **teaspoon ground coriander**
- 1 **small zucchini, halved lengthwise and sliced**
- 1 **recipe Cheese and Onion Corn Bread**

In a 10-inch skillet cook pork, onion, and garlic in oil till pork is lightly browned and onion is tender.

Use a sharp knife to cut corn from cob. Add corn, tomato sauce, water, raisins, peppers, salt, cumin, and coriander to pork mixture. Bring to boiling. Reduce heat. Simmer, covered, for 30 minutes. Add zucchini. Cook, covered, about 10 minutes more or till pork is no longer pink. Serve chili over Cheese and Onion Corn Bread. Serves 4.

Cheese and Onion Corn Bread: In a medium mixing bowl combine 1 *egg,* one 7-ounce package *corn muffin mix,* ½ cup shredded *Monterey Jack cheese,* ⅓ cup *milk,* and 3 sliced *green onions,* stirring just till dry ingredients are moistened. Transfer the mixture to a greased 8x8x2-inch baking pan or a 9x5x3-inch loaf pan. Bake in a 400° oven about 20 minutes or till lightly browned and a wooden toothpick inserted near center comes out clean. Cut into squares or slice to serve.

Microwave directions: To prepare the Cheese and Onion Corn Bread in the microwave oven, prepare batter as above. Transfer the batter to an 8x8x2-inch square or an 8x1½-inch round microwave-safe baking dish. Be sure to spread the batter evenly in the baking dish. Micro-cook, uncovered, on 100% power (high) for 4 to 5 minutes or till a wooden toothpick inserted near the center of the corn bread comes out clean, giving the dish a half-turn once. Let the corn bread stand for 3 minutes. To serve, cut into squares or wedges.

Nutrition information per serving: 606 cal., 34 g pro., 68 g carbo., 23 g fat, 183 mg chol., 1,423 mg sodium. U.S. RDA: 36% vit. A, 40% vit. C, 51% thiamine, 35% riboflavin, 42% niacin, 19% calcium, 23% iron, 61% phosphorus.

BLAZE-OF-GLORY SALSA

Plan to use your salsa within two or three days. If it becomes watery, stir in some tomato paste or sauce—

- 2 **large tomatoes, peeled, seeded, and finely chopped**
- 3 **tablespoons finely chopped jalapeño chili pepper**
- 3 **tablespoons finely chopped onion**
- 3 **tablespoons finely chopped green pepper**
- 1 **tablespoon red wine vinegar**
- 1 **tablespoon snipped fresh coriander *or* 1 teaspoon dried coriander, crushed**
- ¼ **teaspoon salt**
- 2 **cloves garlic, minced**
- **Several dashes bottled hot pepper sauce**
- **Dash pepper**

In a medium mixing bowl stir together the tomatoes, jalapeño pepper, onion, green pepper, vinegar, coriander, salt, garlic, hot pepper sauce, and pepper. Cover and chill several hours or overnight, stirring occasionally. Makes about 1½ cups salsa.

Nutrition information per tablespoon salsa: 3 cal., 0 g pro., 1 g carbo., 0 g fat, 0 mg chol., 23 mg sodium. U.S. RDA: 10% vit. C.

PIÑA COLADA BREAD PUDDING

This delightful pudding features the flavors of the popular cocktail—

- 3 **slightly beaten eggs**
- 1 **3-ounce package cream cheese, softened and cut up**
- ½ **cup packed brown sugar**
- 3 **cups dry whole wheat bread cubes (about 4 slices)**
- 1 **8¼-ounce can crushed pineapple (juice pack)**
- 1 **cup coconut**
- ½ **cup milk**
- 1 **recipe Rum Whipped Cream (optional)**

In a large mixing bowl stir together the eggs, cream cheese, and brown sugar. Stir in whole wheat bread cubes, *undrained* pineapple, coconut, and milk.

Transfer pineapple mixture to a greased 10x6x2-inch baking dish. Bake in a 325° oven about 30 minutes or till a knife inserted near the center comes out clean. Transfer the bread pudding to a wire rack and cool slightly.

To serve, top the warm bread pudding with some of the Rum Whipped Cream, if desired. Makes 8 servings.

Rum Whipped Cream: In a small mixer bowl beat ½ cup *whipping cream* and 2 teaspoons *rum* with an electric mixer on low speed till soft peaks form (tips curl).

Nutrition information per serving: 212 cal., 5 g pro., 28 g carbo., 10 g fat, 117 mg chol., 121 mg sodium.

SEPTEMBER

The Idea Magazine For American Families

Better Homes and Gardens

September 1989 • $1.50

IN THIS ISSUE
- HEALTH
- TRAVEL
- LANDSCAPING
- PARENTING

MAKE-AHEAD GIFTS
That Family And Friends Will Cherish

GOOD EATING FOR GOOD HEALTH
35 Terrific Recipes For A Healthier You

REMARKABLE KITCHEN REMAKES
Great Ideas You Can Use

CREATIVE WINDOW DRESSINGS
With Ready-Made Curtains And Drapes

35 RECIPES FOR A HEALTHIER YOU

Feel better, look better, and live better with recipes and ideas from the newest BH&G® cookbook.

By Terri Pauser Wolf and Joy Taylor

EATING HEALTHY COOK BOOK

For more nutrition information and more than 200 recipes, get the just-released, 288-page *Eating Healthy Cook Book* for $24.95 at bookstores.

THE 7 SIMPLE GUIDELINES

1. Eat a variety of foods

2. Maintain an ideal weight

3. Avoid too much fat, saturated fat, and cholesterol

4. Eat foods with adequate starch and fiber

5. Avoid too much sugar

6. Avoid too much sodium

7. If you drink alcohol, do so in moderation

To encourage sensible eating, the U.S. Department of Agriculture and the U.S. Department of Health and Human Services promote these dietary guidelines for Americans.

THE WAY WE EAT TODAY

Give your meals a make-over. For example: *Honey-Orange Beef* (*above left*) uses 50 percent less fat than most stir-fried main dishes. *Italian Wheat Bread,* brown rice and bulgur pilaf, and fresh vegetables round out your vitamin, mineral, and fiber needs. Capitalize on fruit's natural sweetness by serving a baked apple for dessert.

Nutrition information per dinner: 631 cal., 33 g pro., 103 g carbo., 11 g fat, 58 mg chol., 414 mg sodium.

NUTRITION BASICS

Daily figures that help your figure—

USE THE NUMBERS

The dietary rules of thumb below are what most women, 23 to 50 years old, should strive to consume daily. In general, teenagers, pregnant women, and men need more calories.

CALORIES—2,000
PROTEIN—45 to 65 grams
FAT—85 grams
CHOLESTEROL—300 milligrams
SODIUM—1,100 to 3,300 milligrams
FIBER—25 to 35 grams

Healthful eating is easy when you practice a few new habits every day. To help you, we include nutrition information with every recipe.

SALAD-BAR SAVVY

Know-how makes a meal of a salad—

● **Be Selective.**
Go easy on the protein; choose two of the following popular salad-bar offerings: ¼ cup cottage cheese; 1 hard-cooked egg; 1 ounce of tuna, ham, turkey, or chicken; 3 to 4 tablespoons shredded Swiss or cheddar cheese; ⅓ cup garbanzo beans or peanuts; ¼ cup sunflower nuts. At any meal you need only 15 to 20 grams of protein.

● **Be Stingy.**
Spoon dressing on the side instead of on top. Be stingy; salad dressings tend to be high in sodium and fat. For even more calorie savings, dip your fork tines into the dressing, then spear the salad.

● **Be Creative.**
To make your own dressing, try vinegar and a little oil. You can even use cottage cheese as a salad dressing.

A DAY'S WORTH OF
M·E·N·U·S
For Busy Families

BREAKFAST In 10 minutes you'll be eating satisfying *Pineapple-Rice Compote*. Just quick-cook the ingredients and let them stand for a few minutes.

LUNCH Eat out, but eat smart. Be choosy. The average salad-bar lunch has 300 to 500 calories. See the tips at left for selective salad-bar dining.

DINNER Broiling *Pronto Mini Pizzas* on pita bread delivers fast cooking and jiffy cleanup. Add a side salad and then blend *Banana Shakers*.

TRIMMING FAT AND CHOLESTEROL

Beware of hidden fat. One slice of fruit pie can add up to 14 percent of your daily recommended fat intake of 85 g—10 potato chips, 9 percent; 1 cup chocolate milk, 10 percent; 1 cake doughnut, 12 percent; 1 avocado, 44 percent.

● ● ●

CITRUS WAFFLES WITH BLUEBERRY SAUCE
Say good-bye to cholesterol—replace whole eggs with extra egg whites in these waffles. One serving has only 1 mg compared to 200 mg in most other waffles.

FRUITED FLOATING ISLANDS AND MOCHA MERINGUES Removing the yolk eliminates 100 percent of the cholesterol in a whole egg. Make the most of cholesterol-free egg whites for low-fat desserts.

SAUCED SIRLOIN STEAK Enjoy a rich-tasting sauce over meat, but skip the high calories and guilt. Use low-fat yogurt and skim milk. Choose a lean cut of meat, trim fat, and broil to reduce your fat intake.

MORE WAYS TO CUT FAT AND CHOLESTEROL

- **Use nonstick spray coating.**
  Spray cool cooking utensils with this product (6 calories per spray) instead of greasing with butter, margarine, or shortening (30 calories per teaspoon).
- **Rely on low-fat dairy foods.**
  Good choices include skim milk, evaporated skim milk, low-fat yogurt, Neufchâtel cheese, low-fat mozzarella, and hard cheeses such as Parmesan or romano.
- **Select lean meats.**
  Beef—flank steak, sirloin, rib eye, extra-lean hamburger. Pork—extra-lean ham, loin chops. Lamb—leg of lamb. Veal—loin.
- **Limit whole eggs.**
  Eat no more than four eggs per week. Opt for poached or hard- or soft-cooked eggs. For scrambled or fried eggs, use nonstick spray coating.

SKIP THE SALT

Sodium shows up in many foods, often undetected. Even fresh foods such as celery, artichokes, and spinach contain notable amounts of sodium.

• • •

HONEY-GINGER CHICKEN Rely on sodium-reduced soy sauce and seasonings to minimize the sodium content while maximizing flavor.

MORE WAYS TO CUT SODIUM

- **Stash the shakers.**
Seasoning with salt at the table is unnecessary. A balanced diet provides plenty of sodium, which is in food naturally. A dash of salt here, or a pinch there, adds up; 1 teaspoon has 2,000 mg. The maximum amount recommended daily is 3,300 mg.
- **Try low-salt foods.**
Tomato sauce, soy sauce, bread, cheeses, bouillon cubes, and cereals are available in a sodium-reduced form. Look for labels with these words: sodium-free, low-sodium, sodium-reduced, unsalted, or no salt added.
- **Limit soft drinks.**
Cut back on the number of carbonated beverages you drink. Sodium is added in processing. A 12-ounce low-calorie cola has about 70 milligrams of sodium.
- **Read labels.**
Processed foods often contain sodium as a preservative and flavor enhancer. Foods with a nutrition label must list sodium content in milligrams. No nutrition label? The position of the word salt or sodium in an ingredient list is a clue to the amount inside.
- **Cut salt in breads.**
Some salt is necessary in yeast breads for good texture and palatable flavor, but in most recipes you can cut the amount of salt in half without losing quality.

A DAY'S WORTH OF M·E·N·U·S

To Make Ahead

BREAKFAST Make *Breakfast Apple Bars* ahead and freeze. Thaw them overnight in the refrigerator for a jiffy morning meal.

LUNCH Make and chill *Triple-Cheese Spread with Crudités*. The next noon just grab it plus *Fruit Juice Mousse* from the refrigerator.

DINNER Use your crockery cooker to slow-cook *All-Day Chicken Cassoulet*. Pair it with *Orange-Parsley Vinaigrette* and *Fruit Compote*.

CALORIE-CUTTING TACTICS

Small changes in the way you cook add up to big calorie savings every day—

USE REDUCED-CALORIE PRODUCTS
Retain the sweet flavor while you decrease the calories by using low-calorie fruit preserves. *Ladder Coffee Cake*—145 calories per serving.

SEASON WITH SPIRITS
Use wines and liquors in cooking to boost flavor while calories from the alcohol evaporate. *Brandied Beef*—228 calories per serving.

GO VEGETARIAN
Go meatless a few times a week. Fill up on vegetables and add moderate amounts of cheese, nuts, grains, and seeds for protein. *Harvest Potpie*—276 calories per serving.

THICKEN ON THE SLY
One tablespoon of tapioca, cornstarch, or arrowroot has the same thickening power as 2 tablespoons of flour for half the calories. *Curried Pork Stew*—289 calories per serving.

NONSTICK FRYING
Enjoy lightly breaded foods without a pang of guilt using nonstick spray coating instead of calorie-laden oil. *Parmesan Fish Fillets*—179 calories per serving.

SWEETEN NATURALLY
Get the sweetest taste for the fewest calories by using juice-pack fruits and naturally sweet fruit juices. *Pineapple Sherbet* and *Orange Sherbet*—81 and 91 calories per serving.

FIBER BOOSTING

Fiber isn't as easy to come by as sodium and fat. No one source gives you the recommended 25 grams per day.

• • •

BULGUR-STUFFED SALMON STEAKS Get 5 times more fiber than you would from a bread-crumb stuffing. Also try nuts, seeds, and grains.

ADD SOME FIBER

RICE Cooked long grain white rice has about 2 grams of fiber per ½ cup; double the fiber by using brown rice.

NUTS Get a small boost of fiber (about 1 gram in 1 tablespoon). Don't overdo it; nuts are high in fat.

BARLEY Bump up fiber in soups, salads, and ground-meat dishes—½ cup cooked has 2 grams of fiber.

OATS A steaming bowl in the morning gives you about 8 grams of fiber.

WHEAT In any form, wheat is full of fiber—1 cup of cooked bulgur has 9 grams of fiber.

A DAY'S WORTH OF
M·E·N·U·S
Perfect for One

BREAKFAST Use your blender for breakfast in seconds. Whip up *Peach Smoothie* and pair it with a peanut-butter-topped bagel for breakfast.

LUNCH For lunch in 15 minutes, prepare *Dilled Potato Salad* and the ingredients for *Cider-Turkey Soup* the night before.

DINNER Lean on light foods for supper for one. Try *Barbecued Beef on Lettuce,* steamed broccoli spears, and *Melon Salad Dessert.*

ITALIAN WHEAT BREAD

Wheat germ adds protein, iron, and B vitamins to the bread. Sprinkle extra wheat germ on the baking sheet for a crisp bottom crust—

2 to 2½ cups all-purpose flour
1 package active dry yeast
1 cup warm water (115° to 120°)
1 tablespoon cooking oil
1 teaspoon sugar
½ teaspoon salt
¾ cup toasted wheat germ
Nonstick spray coating
Toasted wheat germ

In a large mixer bowl combine *1 cup* of the flour and the yeast. In a small mixing bowl combine water, cooking oil, sugar, and salt; add to flour mixture. Beat with an electric mixer on low speed for ½ minute, scraping sides of bowl constantly. Beat on high speed for 3 minutes.

With a spoon, stir in the ¾ cup wheat germ and as much of the remaining flour as you can. On a lightly floured surface knead in enough of the remaining flour to make a moderately stiff dough that is smooth and elastic (6 to 8 minutes total). Place in a lightly greased bowl and turn once to grease surface. Cover and let rise in a warm place till double (1 to 1¼ hours).

Punch dough down. Shape into a large loaf about 15 inches long, tapering the ends. Spray a baking sheet with nonstick coating and sprinkle with additional wheat germ. Place loaf on baking sheet. Cover and let rise till nearly double (about 45 minutes).

With a sharp knife, make 3 or 4 diagonal slashes about ¼ inch deep across the top of the loaf. Bake in a 375° oven for 35 to 40 minutes or till done. Cool on a wire rack. Makes 1 loaf (15 servings).

Nutrition information per serving:
88 cal., 3 g pro., 15 g carbo., 2 g fat, 0 mg chol., 73 mg sodium. U.S. RDA: 14% thiamine.

HONEY-ORANGE BEEF

A meat and vegetable stir-fry that is delicately seasoned with ginger and curry, not salt—

1 pound beef top round steak
2¼ cups water
½ cup brown rice
½ cup bulgur
¾ cup orange juice
1 tablespoon honey
1 tablespoon sodium-reduced soy sauce
2 teaspoons cornstarch
¼ teaspoon ground ginger
¼ teaspoon curry powder
1 medium onion, thinly sliced and separated into rings
2 cups broccoli flowerets
Nonstick spray coating
1 tablespoon cooking oil
½ cup quartered cherry tomatoes

Partially freeze beef; bias-slice into thin bite-size strips. Set aside. In a large saucepan combine the water and uncooked brown rice. Bring to boiling; reduce heat. Simmer, covered, for 25 minutes. Stir in bulgur. Simmer, covered, for 15 to 20 minutes more or till rice is tender. Drain, if necessary.

Meanwhile, for sauce, in a small mixing bowl stir together orange juice, honey, soy sauce, cornstarch, ginger, and curry powder. Set aside.

In a medium saucepan cook onion in a small amount of boiling *water* for 5 minutes. Add broccoli; cook for 3 to 5 minutes more or till vegetables are crisp-tender. Drain. Set aside.

Pat meat dry with paper towels. Spray a wok or 10-inch skillet with nonstick coating. Preheat over high heat till a drop of water sizzles. Stir-fry *half* of the beef for 2 to 3 minutes or till done. Remove beef. Add cooking oil, if necessary. Stir-fry remaining beef for 2 to 3 minutes or till done. Return all beef to the skillet.

Stir sauce; add to the center of the wok or skillet. Cook and stir till thickened and bubbly. Cook and stir for 2 minutes more. Add onion and broccoli; heat through. Stir in tomatoes. Serve with rice mixture. Makes 5 servings.

Nutrition information per serving:
304 cal., 22 g pro., 40 g carbo., 7 g fat, 49 mg chol., 183 mg sodium. U.S. RDA: 32% vit. A, 96% vit. C, 15% thiamine, 14% riboflavin, 26% niacin, 20% iron.

PINEAPPLE-RICE COMPOTE

This fruity breakfast cereal is a super-simple way to start any day—

1 15¼-ounce can crushed pineapple (juice pack)
1⅓ cups orange juice
4 teaspoons brown sugar
Dash ground allspice
1⅓ cups quick-cooking rice
Ground allspice (optional)

In a saucepan stir together *undrained* pineapple, orange juice, brown sugar, and the dash allspice. Bring to boiling. Remove from heat; stir in rice. Cover and let stand for 5 minutes. Transfer to serving bowls. Sprinkle with additional allspice, if desired. Makes 4 servings.

Nutrition information per serving:
236 cal., 3 g pro., 56 g carbo., 0 g fat, 0 mg chol., 4 mg sodium. U.S. RDA: 70% vit. C, 20% thiamine.

BANANA SHAKERS

Freezing the sliced banana makes the drink colder and more refreshing—

1 cup vanilla ice milk
1 cup skim milk
1 cup unsweetened pineapple juice
2 ripe large bananas, peeled, sliced, and frozen
2 teaspoons vanilla

In a blender container combine ice milk, milk, pineapple juice, bananas, and vanilla. Cover and blend till mixture is smooth. Makes 4 servings.

Nutrition information per serving:
124 cal., 3 g pro., 20 g carbo., 4 g fat, 16 mg chol., 61 mg sodium. U.S. RDA: 12% vit. C, 11% riboflavin, and 13% calcium.

PRONTO MINI PIZZAS

Toasted pita bread rounds make easy crusts for these individual pizzas—

- 1 **pound fresh *or* frozen ground raw turkey**
- 4 **large whole wheat pita bread rounds**
- 1 **cup sliced fresh mushrooms**
- 1 **medium green pepper, chopped**
- ½ **cup chopped onion**
- 2 **cloves garlic, minced**
- 1 **cup sodium-reduced tomato sauce**
- ½ **teaspoon fennel seed, crushed**
- ¼ **teaspoon dried oregano, crushed**
- ½ **cup shredded mozzarella cheese (2 ounces)**

Thaw turkey, if frozen. Place pita bread rounds on a baking sheet. Broil about 3 inches from the heat about 1 minute on each side or till toasted. Set aside.

In a medium skillet combine turkey, mushrooms, green pepper, onion, and garlic. Cook over medium heat till turkey is light brown and vegetables are tender. Stir in tomato sauce, fennel seed, and oregano. Cook and stir for 1 minute more.

Divide turkey mixture evenly between the toasted pita rounds. Sprinkle with shredded cheese. Return to the broiler; broil about 3 inches from heat for 1 to 2 minutes or till cheese is melted. Makes 4 servings.

Nutrition information per serving: 430 cal., 40 g pro., 48 g carbo., 6 g fat, 81 mg chol., 172 mg sodium. U.S. RDA: 15% vit. A, 20% vit. C, 22% thiamine, 30% riboflavin, 51% niacin, 16% calcium, 32% iron.

CITRUS WAFFLES WITH BLUEBERRY SAUCE

To make Cinnamon Waffles, omit the orange peel and stir ½ teaspoon ground cinnamon into the flour mixture—

- 1 **recipe Blueberry Sauce**
- ¾ **cup all-purpose flour**
- ½ **teaspoon finely shredded orange peel**

Dash salt

- ¾ **cup skim milk**
- 3 **tablespoons cooking oil**
- 2 **egg whites**
- 2 **small bananas, sliced**

Prepare Blueberry Sauce and set aside. In a medium mixing bowl stir together flour, orange peel, and salt. In a glass measure stir together milk and oil. Add to flour mixture all at once. Stir till combined but still slightly lumpy.

In a small mixer bowl beat the egg whites till stiff peaks form (tips stand straight); gently fold into the flour-milk mixture, leaving a few fluffs of egg white. *Do not overmix.*

Pour *one-third* of the batter onto the grids of a preheated, lightly greased waffle baker. Close lid quickly; *do not open* during baking. Bake till steam stops escaping from sides of the baker. Use a fork to help lift the baked waffle off the grids.

To keep waffle warm for serving, arrange in a single layer on a wire rack placed on a baking sheet; place in a warm oven. Repeat with remaining batter to make 2 more waffles. Serve waffles topped with bananas and Blueberry Sauce. Makes 3 servings.

Blueberry Sauce: In a small saucepan combine 2 tablespoons *sugar* and 1 teaspoon *cornstarch.* Stir in 2 tablespoons *orange juice* till well mixed. Add ⅔ cup *fresh* or *frozen blueberries.* Cook and stir till thickened and bubbly. Cook and stir for 2 minutes more. Remove from heat. Slightly crush blueberries.

Nutrition information per serving: 386 cal., 9 g pro., 57 g carbo., 15 g fat, 1 mg chol., 112 mg sodium. U.S. RDA: 26% vit. C, 18% thiamine, 20% riboflavin, 11% niacin.

SAUCED SIRLOIN STEAK

Steamed brussels sprouts and new potatoes make an attractive side dish—

- 1 **2-pound beef top sirloin steak, cut 1½ inches thick**
- 1 **cup sliced fresh mushrooms**
- ¼ **cup shredded carrot**
- ¼ **cup chopped onion**
- 1 **tablespoon margarine *or* butter**
- 4 **teaspoons all-purpose flour**
- ½ **teaspoon dried basil, crushed**

Dash pepper

- ½ **cup plain low-fat yogurt**
- ½ **cup skim milk**

Trim fat from steak. Place meat on the unheated rack of a broiler pan. Broil meat 3 inches from the heat, turning halfway through cooking. (Allow 14 to 16 minutes total time for rare, 18 to 20 minutes total time for medium, and 25 to 30 minutes total time for well-done.)

Meanwhile, for sauce, in a medium saucepan cook mushrooms, carrot, and onion in hot margarine or butter till tender. Stir flour, basil, and pepper into yogurt; stir into mushroom mixture in saucepan. Add milk. Cook and stir till thickened and bubbly. Cook and stir for 1 minute more.

Sprinkle broiled steak with additional pepper. To serve, slice the meat diagonally across the grain into ¼-inch-thick slices. Arrange on a serving platter. Spoon some sauce over. Pass remaining sauce. Makes 6 servings.

Nutrition information per serving with 1 tablespoon sauce: 201 cal., 26 g pro., 5 g carbo., 8 g fat, 68 mg chol., 107 mg sodium. U.S. RDA: 19% riboflavin, 26% niacin, 17% iron.

FRUITED FLOATING ISLANDS

Surrounded by a sea of cherries, oranges, and apricot nectar, poached meringue puffs are tasty, no-cholesterol islands—

- 2 egg whites
- 3 tablespoons sugar
- 3 cups water
- 1½ cups fresh *or* frozen unsweetened pitted dark sweet cherries
- 1½ cups apricot nectar
- ¼ cup sugar
- 4 teaspoons cornstarch
- 1½ teaspoons finely shredded orange peel
- 2 oranges, peeled and sectioned

For meringue puffs, in a small mixer bowl beat egg whites with an electric mixer on medium speed till soft peaks form (tips curl). Gradually add the 3 tablespoons sugar, beating on high speed till stiff peaks form (tips stand straight).

In a 10-inch skillet heat water to simmering. Drop egg white mixture in 6 portions into water. Simmer, uncovered, about 5 minutes or till firm. Lift meringue puffs from water; drain on paper towels and place on waxed paper. Chill, uncovered, in the refrigerator till serving time.

Meanwhile, thaw cherries, if frozen. Cut cherries in half. In a medium saucepan stir together apricot nectar, the ¼ cup sugar, and cornstarch. Cook and stir till thickened and bubbly. Cook and stir for 2 minutes more. Gently stir in cherries, *1 teaspoon* of the orange peel, and orange sections. Cover and chill till serving time.

At serving time, spoon fruit mixture into 6 individual dessert dishes. Top each with a meringue puff. Sprinkle with remaining orange peel. Makes 6 servings.

Nutrition information per serving: 156 cal., 2 g pro., 38 g carbo., 1 g fat, 0 mg chol., 19 mg sodium. U.S. RDA: 20% vit. A, 46% vit. C.

MOCHA MERINGUES

For a meringue that fluffs rather than flops, be sure to start with a clean bowl and beaters. This no-fat, no-cholesterol dessert is bound to be a hit—

- 2 egg whites
- ½ teaspoon vanilla
- ¼ teaspoon cream of tartar
- ½ cup sugar
- 1¼ cups skim milk
- ½ cup water
- ¼ cup sugar
- 2 tablespoons cornstarch
- 2 tablespoons unsweetened cocoa powder
- 2 tablespoons coffee liqueur
Sliced fresh fruit (optional)

For meringue shells, cover a baking sheet with brown paper. Draw 6 circles, 3½ inches in diameter, on the paper.

In a small mixer bowl beat the egg whites, vanilla, and cream of tartar with an electric mixer on medium speed till soft peaks form (tips curl). Gradually add the ½ cup sugar, beating on high speed till stiff peaks form (tips stand straight) and the sugar is almost dissolved.

Immediately pipe or spoon beaten egg-white mixture into a shell shape in each circle on the paper-lined baking sheet. Bake in a 300° oven for 30 minutes. Turn off the heat; let shells dry in the oven with the door closed for at least 1 hour more. Peel off paper.

Meanwhile, for filling, in a heavy medium saucepan combine milk, water, the ¼ cup sugar, cornstarch, and cocoa powder. Cook and stir over medium heat till thickened and bubbly. Cook and stir for 2 minutes more. Remove from heat. Stir in coffee liqueur. Pour filling into a bowl. Cover surface with clear plastic wrap. Chill, without stirring, till serving time.

To serve, spoon filling into individual meringue shells. Serve with fruit, if desired. Makes 6 servings.

Nutrition information per serving: 149 cal., 3 g pro., 35 g carbo., 0 g fat, 0 mg chol., 56 mg sodium.

HONEY-GINGER CHICKEN

Look for sodium-reduced soy sauce in the Oriental-food or special-diet section of the grocery store—

- 3 tablespoons honey
- 1 teaspoon finely shredded orange peel
- 1 tablespoon orange juice
- 2 teaspoons sodium-reduced soy sauce
- ¼ teaspoon coarsely ground pepper
- ⅛ teaspoon ground ginger
- 2 whole medium chicken breasts (about 1½ pounds total), skinned, boned, and halved lengthwise
Steamed green beans (optional)
Whole wheat rolls (optional)
Fruit salad (optional)

In a small mixing bowl stir together honey, orange peel, orange juice, soy sauce, pepper, and ginger. Place chicken, bone side up, on the unheated rack of a broiler pan. Broil 5 to 6 inches from the heat for 20 minutes. Turn chicken over. Broil for 10 to 20 minutes more or till chicken is tender, brushing with the honey mixture the last minute of broiling. Brush again before serving. Serve with green beans, rolls, and fruit salad, if desired. Makes 4 servings.

Nutrition information per serving: 192 cal., 27 g pro., 14 g carbo., 3 g fat, 72 mg chol., 169 mg sodium. U.S. RDA: 58% niacin.

BREAKFAST APPLE BARS

Honey sweetens these moist and fruity oat bars—

Nonstick spray coating
- ½ cup whole wheat flour
- ½ cup quick-cooking rolled oats
- ½ teaspoon baking soda
- ¼ teaspoon ground cinnamon
- ¼ cup cooking oil
- ¼ cup applesauce
- 3 tablespoons honey
- ½ teaspoon vanilla
- ½ of a 6-ounce package (¾ cup) mixed dried fruit bits
- ¼ cup chopped walnuts

Spray a 10x6x2-inch baking dish with nonstick coating. In a medium mixing bowl stir together flour, oats, baking soda, and cinnamon; set aside.

In a small mixing bowl stir together cooking oil, applesauce, honey, and vanilla. Add the applesauce mixture to flour mixture; stir till combined. Stir in fruit bits and nuts.

Spread the batter evenly in the prepared baking dish. Bake in a 350° oven for 15 to 20 minutes or till a wooden toothpick inserted near the center comes out clean. Cool in the dish on a wire rack. Cut into 16 bars.

Store in a tightly covered container at room temperature or in the freezer. Makes 8 servings.

Nutrition information per serving (2 bars): 182 cal., 3 g pro., 23 g carbo., 10 g fat, 0 mg chol., and 75 mg sodium.

TRIPLE-CHEESE SPREAD WITH CRUDITÉS

A trio of cottage, Swiss, and Parmesan cheeses in the spread provides complete protein for a meatless lunch—

- 1 cup low-fat cottage cheese
- ½ cup shredded Swiss cheese (2 ounces)
- ¼ cup grated Parmesan cheese
- 2 tablespoons skim milk
- ⅛ teaspoon dried dillweed
- ⅛ teaspoon pepper
- ¼ cup unsalted sunflower nuts
- ¼ cup finely shredded carrot
- 1½ cups assorted fresh vegetables (cauliflower flowerets, cucumber spears, bias-sliced carrots, *or* green pepper wedges)

In a blender container or food processor bowl combine cheeses, milk, dillweed, and pepper. Cover and blend or process till smooth. Transfer to a storage container. Stir in sunflower nuts and carrot. Cover and chill. Serve with fresh vegetables. Makes 1⅓ cups (4 servings).

Nutrition information per serving: 253 cal., 20 g pro., 10 g carbo., 16 g fat, 23 mg chol., 405 mg sodium. U.S. RDA: 51% vit. A, 45% vit. C, 27% thiamine, 15% riboflavin, 31% calcium, and 11% iron.

ORANGE-PARSLEY VINAIGRETTE

This citrus dressing gives the simplest tossed salad extraordinary flavor—

- 3 tablespoons olive *or* salad oil
- 1 teaspoon finely shredded orange peel
- 3 tablespoons orange juice
- 2 tablespoons finely snipped parsley
- 1 tablespoon vinegar
- ¼ teaspoon dried marjoram, crushed
Dash pepper

In a small screw-top jar combine oil, peel, juice, parsley, vinegar, marjoram, and pepper. Cover and shake well to mix. Chill. Shake again just before using. Makes about ½ cup (4 servings).

Nutrition information per 2 tablespoons: 97 cal., 0 g pro., 2 g carbo., 10 g fat, 0 mg chol., 1 mg sodium. U.S. RDA: 14% vit. C.

FRUIT JUICE MOUSSE

- 1 teaspoon unflavored gelatin
- ⅔ cup cold water
- ½ of a 6-ounce can (⅓ cup) frozen apple juice concentrate
- ¼ teaspoon finely shredded lemon peel
- 2 teaspoons lemon juice
- ¼ teaspoon ground cinnamon
- 1 small apple, cored, peeled, and shredded
- ½ of a 4-ounce container frozen whipped dessert topping, thawed
Apple slices

In a medium saucepan soften gelatin in water for 5 minutes. Over low heat, stir till gelatin is dissolved. Remove from heat. Stir in apple juice concentrate, lemon peel, lemon juice, and cinnamon. Chill till partially set (consistency of unbeaten egg whites).

Fold in shredded apple and dessert topping. Transfer to 4 individual dessert glasses or a 2-cup bowl or soufflé dish. Chill for 3 to 24 hours. Before serving, top with apple slices. Serves 4.

Nutrition information per serving: 105 cal., 1 g pro., 17 g carbo., 4 g fat, 0 mg chol., 6 mg sodium.

CIDER-TURKEY SOUP

- ¾ cup apple cider *or* apple juice
- 3 tablespoons sliced green onion
- ½ teaspoon grated gingerroot
- ⅛ teaspoon salt
- ⅛ teaspoon dried basil, crushed
- ⅔ cup cubed cooked turkey
- ¼ cup shredded zucchini
- ¼ cup shredded carrot
- ⅛ teaspoon finely shredded orange peel

In a small saucepan combine cider or juice, ¼ cup *water*, green onion, gingerroot, salt, basil, and dash *pepper*. Bring to boiling; reduce heat. Cover and simmer for 5 minutes. Add turkey, zucchini, carrot, and orange peel. Return to boiling; reduce heat. Cover and simmer for 3 to 5 minutes more or till heated through. Makes 1 serving.

Nutrition information per serving: 275 cal., 29 g pro., 28 g carbo., 5 g fat, 72 mg chol., 354 mg sodium. U.S. RDA: 64% vit. A, 149% vit. C, 14% riboflavin, 29% niacin, 16% iron.

ALL-DAY CHICKEN CASSOULET

Cook the navy beans the night before. Then in the morning, put all the ingredients in the crockery cooker to simmer till dinnertime—

- ½ cup dry navy beans
- 4 cups water
- 1½ to 2 pounds chicken pieces, skin removed
- ¾ cup sodium-reduced tomato juice
- ½ cup chopped celery
- ½ cup sliced carrot
- ½ cup chopped onion
- 1 clove garlic, minced
- 1 bay leaf
- 1 teaspoon instant beef bouillon granules
- ½ teaspoon dried basil, crushed
- ½ teaspoon dried oregano, crushed
- ½ teaspoon dried sage, crushed
- ¼ teaspoon paprika

Rinse beans. In a medium saucepan combine *half* of the water and all of the beans. Bring to boiling. Cook, uncovered, for 10 minutes. Drain. Add the remaining water. Return to boiling; reduce heat. Cover and simmer about 1½ hours or till beans are tender. Drain; cover and chill.

In an electric crockery cooker combine drained beans, chicken pieces, tomato juice, celery, carrot, onion, garlic, bay leaf, bouillon granules, basil, oregano, sage, and paprika. Cover and cook on low-heat setting for 8 to 10 hours. Remove and discard bay leaf. Serves 4.

Nutrition information per serving: 249 cal., 28 g pro., 20 g carbo., 6 g fat, 67 mg chol., 190 mg sodium. U.S. RDA: 44% vit. A, 16% vit. C, 15% thiamine, 12% riboflavin, 40% niacin, 19% iron.

FRUIT COMPOTE

- 1 cup sliced fresh *or* frozen strawberries
- ½ cup fresh *or* frozen blueberries
- ½ cup fresh *or* frozen peach slices, halved
- ¼ teaspoon finely shredded orange peel
- 1 cup orange-pineapple juice *or* orange juice
- Toasted coconut (optional)

Combine fruits, orange peel, and juice. Divide fruit mixture evenly among four 1-cup freezer containers. Seal, label, and freeze. Before serving, let stand at room temperature about 3 hours or till thawed. Or, thaw in the refrigerator for 6 to 8 hours. Sprinkle with toasted coconut, if desired. Makes 4 servings.

Nutrition information per serving: 59 cal., 1 g pro., 14 g carbo., 0 g fat, 0 mg cholesterol, 2 mg sodium. U.S. RDA: 82% vit. C.

PARMESAN FISH FILLETS

- 4 fresh *or* frozen fish fillets (1 pound total)
- 1 beaten egg white
- 2 tablespoons water
- ½ cup finely crushed sodium-reduced wheat wafers
- 3 tablespoons grated Parmesan cheese
- 2 tablespoons finely snipped parsley
- Nonstick spray coating

Thaw fish, if frozen. Pat dry with paper towels. In a small mixing bowl stir together egg white and water.

In another mixing bowl stir together crushed wafers, Parmesan cheese, and snipped parsley. Dip fish into egg-white mixture, then into Parmesan mixture to coat.

Spray a large skillet with nonstick coating. Preheat the skillet on medium-high heat. Cook crumb-coated fish in the hot skillet for 6 to 8 minutes or till fish flakes easily with a fork, turning once. Makes 4 servings.

Nutrition information per serving: 179 cal., 25 g pro., 9 g carbo., 4 g fat, 63 mg chol., 249 mg sodium. U.S. RDA: 10% thiamine, 10% riboflavin, 16% niacin, 13% calcium.

LADDER COFFEE CAKE

This recipe makes two coffee cakes. Wrap and freeze one coffee cake for a later treat—

- 2 to 2½ cups all-purpose flour
- 2 tablespoons unsalted sunflower nuts, chopped
- 1 package active dry yeast
- ½ cup skim milk
- 3 tablespoons sugar
- 3 tablespoons margarine *or* butter
- ¼ teaspoon salt
- 2 egg whites
- ½ teaspoon finely shredded orange peel
- Nonstick spray coating
- ½ cup low-calorie orange marmalade

In a large mixer bowl combine *1 cup* of the flour, sunflower nuts, and yeast. In a small saucepan heat milk, sugar, margarine or butter, and salt just till warm (115° to 120°), stirring constantly. Add to flour mixture; add egg whites and peel. Beat with an electric mixer on low speed for ½ minute. Beat on high speed for 3 minutes.

Using a spoon, stir in as much of the remaining flour as you can. On a floured surface knead in enough of the remaining flour to make a moderately soft dough that is smooth and elastic (3 to 5 minutes total). Shape into a ball. Place in a lightly greased bowl and turn once to grease surface. Cover and let rise in a warm place till double (about 45 minutes).

Punch dough down. Cover and let rest for 10 minutes. Divide dough in half. Spray a baking sheet with nonstick coating. On the baking sheet roll *half* of the dough into a 10-inch square. Spread *half* of the marmalade down the center third of the dough. With kitchen shears, snip sides toward center into strips about 1 inch wide and 3 inches long. Fold strips over marmalade, alternating sides in a V-shaped pattern. Repeat with the remaining dough and marmalade.

Cover and let rise till nearly double (30 to 40 minutes). Bake in a 350° oven for 20 to 25 minutes or till golden. Cool thoroughly on a wire rack. Makes 2 coffee cakes (12 servings).

Nutrition information per serving: 145 cal., 4 g pro., 24 g carbo., 4 g fat, 0 mg chol., 93 mg sodium. U.S. RDA: 12% thiamine.

HARVEST POTPIE

The bulk of the protein comes from the Monterey Jack and cottage cheeses—

- 1½ cups sliced and halved zucchini
- 1 cup sliced fresh mushrooms
- 1 small parsnip, peeled and cubed
- 1 cup frozen whole kernel corn
- ¾ cup chopped green pepper
- 1 clove garlic, minced
- 1 cup frozen peas
- 1 8-ounce can sodium-reduced tomato sauce
- 1 teaspoon sugar
- 1 teaspoon dried oregano, crushed
- 1 teaspoon chili powder
- ½ teaspoon dried basil, crushed
- 2 cups shredded Monterey Jack cheese (8 ounces)
- 1 tablespoon all-purpose flour
- 2 tablespoons shortening
- ½ cup all-purpose flour
- ⅓ cup cream-style cottage cheese, sieved

In a large saucepan bring a small amount of water to boiling. Add zucchini, mushrooms, parsnip, frozen corn, green pepper, and garlic. Cook, covered, about 4 minutes or till parsnip is crisp-tender; drain.

Stir in frozen peas, tomato sauce, sugar, oregano, chili powder, and basil. Bring to boiling; reduce heat. Simmer, uncovered, for 2 minutes. Toss shredded Monterey Jack cheese with 1 tablespoon flour; stir into vegetable mixture. Spoon into an 8x1½-inch round baking dish or a 1½-quart casserole.

For pastry, cut shortening into the ½ cup flour till pieces are the size of small peas. Add cottage cheese; stir with a fork till moistened. If necessary, stir in a little water. Form dough into a ball. On a lightly floured surface roll dough into an 8-inch circle. Cut into 6 wedges; prick with a fork.

Arrange pastry wedges on top of the hot vegetable mixture. Bake in a 375° oven for 25 to 30 minutes or till pastry is light brown. Makes 6 servings.

Nutrition information per serving:
276 cal., 17 g pro., 27 g carbo., 12 g fat, 22 mg chol., 301 mg sodium. U.S. RDA: 41% vit. A, 99% vit. C, 17% thiamine, 21% riboflavin, 15% niacin, 32% calcium, 16% iron.

BRANDIED BEEF

- 1 pound boneless beef round steak, cut ½ to ¾ inch thick
- ⅓ cup water
- ¼ cup brandy *or* apple juice
- 2 tablespoons vinegar
- 1 clove garlic, minced
- ¼ teaspoon dried dillweed
- ⅛ teaspoon ground allspice
- ⅛ teaspoon pepper
- 2 large carrots, bias sliced
- 1 9-ounce package frozen French-style green beans
- 1 medium onion, cut into wedges
- 2 teaspoons cornstarch
- ¼ teaspoon instant beef bouillon granules
- Nonstick spray coating
- 2 teaspoons cooking oil

Partially freeze beef; bias-slice into thin bite-size strips. Place meat in a plastic bag set in a bowl. For marinade, in a small bowl stir together water, brandy or apple juice, vinegar, garlic, dillweed, allspice, and pepper; pour over meat in bag. Close bag. Marinate in the refrigerator for several hours or overnight, turning the bag occasionally. Drain meat, reserving marinade.

In a medium saucepan combine carrots, beans, and onion. Add ½ cup *water*. Bring to boiling; reduce heat. Simmer, covered, about 8 minutes or till vegetables are crisp-tender; stir to separate beans. Drain and keep warm.

For sauce, in a small mixing bowl stir together cornstarch and ¼ cup cold *water*. Stir in reserved marinade and bouillon granules. Set aside.

Pat meat dry with paper towels. Spray a wok or 10-inch skillet with nonstick coating. Preheat over high heat till a drop of water sizzles. Stir-fry *half* of the beef for 2 to 3 minutes or till done. Remove beef. Add cooking oil, if necessary. Stir-fry remaining beef for 2 to 3 minutes or till done. Return all beef to the skillet.

Stir sauce; add to the center of the wok or skillet. Cook and stir till thickened and bubbly. Cook and stir for 2 minutes more.

To serve, arrange vegetables on a serving platter; spoon meat mixture atop. Sprinkle with pepper. Serves 4.

Nutrition information per serving:
228 cal., 23 g pro., 11 g carbo., 7 g fat, 61 mg chol., 101 mg sodium. U.S. RDA: 86% vit. A, 13% vit. C, 14% riboflavin, 23% niacin, 19% iron.

CURRIED PORK STEW

- ½ pound lean boneless pork, cut into ¾-inch cubes
- ½ cup chopped onion
- 1 clove garlic, minced
- 2 teaspoons curry powder
- 1 16-ounce can tomatoes, cut up
- 2 medium carrots, sliced
- 2 medium potatoes, cut into bite-size pieces (2⅓ cups)
- 2 tablespoons raisins
- 1 tablespoon quick-cooking tapioca
- 1 large apple, cored and cut into thin wedges
- 2 tablespoons snipped parsley
- ¼ cup unsalted peanuts

Cook meat, onion, garlic, and curry powder till onion is tender and meat is brown. In a 2-quart casserole combine *undrained* tomatoes, carrots, potatoes, raisins, tapioca, and ¼ cup *water*. Add meat mixture; mix well. Cover and bake in a 350° oven for 50 to 60 minutes or till meat and vegetables are nearly tender. Stir in apple and parsley. Bake, covered, about 15 minutes more or till meat and vegetables are tender. Sprinkle with peanuts. Makes 4 servings.

Nutrition information per serving:
289 cal., 17 g pro., 37 g carbo., 10 g fat, 33 mg chol., 195 mg sodium. U.S. RDA: 104% vit. A, 71% vit. C, 27% thiamine, 13% riboflavin, 30% niacin, 15% iron.

DILLED POTATO SALAD

- 2 whole tiny new potatoes, cubed
- ¼ cup chopped cucumber
- 2 radishes, sliced
- 2 tablespoons chopped green *or* red sweet pepper
- 2 tablespoons plain low-fat yogurt
- 1 teaspoon vinegar
- ⅛ teaspoon dried dillweed
- Cucumber slices (optional)

Cook potatoes in boiling water for 8 to 10 minutes. Drain. Combine potatoes, cucumber, radishes, and green pepper. Combine yogurt, vinegar, dillweed, dash *salt*, and dash *pepper*. Add to potato mixture; toss to coat. Cover and chill. Serve with cucumber slices. Serves 1.

Nutrition information per serving:
106 cal., 4 g pro., 22 g carbo., 1 g fat, 2 mg chol., 162 mg sodium. U.S. RDA: 77% vit. C.

PINEAPPLE SHERBET

      3 **cups skim milk**
      1 **15¼-ounce can crushed**
         pineapple (juice pack)
     ¾ **cup evaporated skim milk**
      1 **6-ounce can pineapple juice**
         concentrate, thawed
     ⅓ **cup sugar**
     ½ **teaspoon vanilla**
Mint sprigs (optional)

In a mixing bowl stir together skim milk, *undrained* pineapple, evaporated milk, pineapple juice concentrate, sugar, and vanilla. Stir till sugar dissolves.

Freeze in a 4- or 5-quart ice-cream freezer according to manufacturer's directions. Serve scoops in dessert dishes. Garnish with mint sprigs, if desired. Makes 7½ cups (15 servings).

Nutrition information per ½-cup serving: 81 cal., 3 g pro., 18 g carbo., 0 g fat, 1 mg chol., 40 mg sodium. U.S. RDA: 14% vit. C, 11% calcium.

ORANGE SHERBET

      1 **envelope unflavored gelatin**
     ¼ **cup cold water**
     ½ **of a 6-ounce can (⅓ cup) frozen**
         orange juice concentrate,
         thawed
     ½ **cup orange marmalade**
      2 **8-ounce cartons vanilla low-fat**
         yogurt
Orange slices, quartered (optional)

In a small saucepan soften gelatin in cold water for 5 minutes. Over low heat, stir till gelatin is dissolved. Remove from heat. Stir in orange juice concentrate and marmalade. Stir in yogurt. Turn the yogurt mixture into a 9x9x2-inch pan; cover and freeze about 3 hours or till firm.

With a fork, break the frozen mixture into chunks; place in a large chilled mixer bowl. Beat with an electric mixer on medium speed till fluffy. Return to the pan. Cover and freeze for at least 2 hours or till firm.

Serve scoops in dessert dishes. Garnish with orange slice quarters, if desired. Makes 4 cups.

Nutrition information per ½-cup serving: 91 cal., 4 g pro., 18 g carbo., 1 g fat, 3 mg chol., 38 mg sodium. U.S. RDA: 25% vit. C, 10% calcium.

BULGUR-STUFFED SALMON STEAKS

      4 **fresh** *or* **frozen salmon** *or* **halibut**
         steaks, cut 1 inch thick
      1 **cup bulgur**
     ¼ **cup snipped parsley**
      2 **tablespoons sliced green onion**
      1 **teaspoon ground coriander**
      2 **tablespoons margarine** *or* **butter,**
         melted
      1 **tablespoon lemon juice**
Wilted romaine (optional)
Strips of lemon peel (optional)

Thaw fish, if frozen. Pat dry with paper towels. Combine bulgur and 2 cups hot *water.* Let stand for 30 minutes; drain well. Combine bulgur, parsley, green onion, coriander, ⅛ teaspoon *salt,* and ⅛ teaspoon *pepper;* set aside.

Stir together the melted margarine and lemon juice; reserve *1 tablespoon.* Add remaining lemon mixture to bulgur mixture; toss to coat.

Spoon *half* the bulgur filling into a 3-quart casserole. Place fish on top. Spoon remaining filling into the center cavity of each fish steak. Cover loosely with foil. Bake in a 375° oven for 15 minutes; brush fish with reserved lemon mixture. Bake, covered, for 5 to 10 minutes more or till fish flakes easily with a fork. Serve with romaine and lemon peel, if desired. Serves 4.

Nutrition information per serving: 496 cal., 31 g pro., 29 g carbo., 28 g fat, 85 mg chol., 201 mg sodium. U.S. RDA: 20% vit. A, 16% vit. C, 16% thiamine, 22% riboflavin, 24% calcium, and 18% iron.

PEACH SMOOTHIE

      1 **8½-ounce can peach slices (juice**
         pack), chilled
     ¼ **cup nonfat dry milk powder**
      1 **teaspoon vanilla**
Dash ground nutmeg
      2 **ice cubes**

In a blender container combine all ingredients except ice cubes. Cover and blend till smooth. Add ice cubes. Cover and blend till combined. Serves 1.

Nutrition information per serving: 200 cal., 11 g pro., 41 g carbo., 0 g fat, 5 mg chol., 152 mg sodium. U.S. RDA: 31% vit. A, 17% vit. C, 29% riboflavin, 33% calcium.

BARBECUED BEEF ON LETTUCE

      4 **ounces lean ground beef**
      2 **tablespoons chopped onion**
     ⅓ **cup water**
      1 **tablespoon tomato paste**
      1 **teaspoon red wine vinegar** *or*
         vinegar
     ¼ **teaspoon sugar**
     ¼ **teaspoon chili powder**
     ⅛ **teaspoon celery seed**
Dash Worcestershire sauce
      1 **cup shredded lettuce**

In a small skillet cook beef and onion till beef is brown and onion is tender. Drain off fat. Stir in water, tomato paste, vinegar, sugar, chili powder, celery seed, and Worcestershire sauce. Bring to boiling; reduce heat. Simmer, uncovered, for 8 to 10 minutes or to desired consistency. Place shredded lettuce on a serving plate. Top with the meat mixture. Makes 1 serving.

Nutrition information per serving: 224 cal., 25 g pro., 8 g carbo., 10 g fat, 80 mg chol., 205 mg sodium. U.S. RDA: 20% vit. A, 23% vit. C, 10% thiamine, 14% riboflavin, 29% niacin, 23% iron.

MELON SALAD DESSERT

Enjoy it as a salad or dessert—

     ½ **of a small cantaloupe**
      1 **tablespoon plain low-fat yogurt**
      1 **tablespoon frozen whipped**
         dessert topping, thawed
Pinch dried mint
      1 **tablespoon sliced celery**
      1 **tablespoon chopped walnuts**
Leaf lettuce

Remove seeds from the cantaloupe. With a melon ball cutter, scoop cantaloupe into balls. With a spoon, carefully scoop any remaining cantaloupe from the shell and cut into bite-size pieces; reserve the pieces for another use. Reserve the shell.

In a small mixing bowl combine yogurt, dessert topping, and mint. Add cantaloupe balls, celery, and walnuts. Toss to coat. Line the cantaloupe shell with lettuce. Spoon cantaloupe mixture into shell. Makes 1 serving.

Nutrition information per serving: 137 cal., 4 g pro., 18 g carbo., 7 g fat, 1 mg chol., 36 mg sodium. U.S. RDA: 108% vit. A, 117% vit. C.

OCTOBER

The Idea Magazine for American Families

Better Homes and Gardens

October 1986 • $1.50

IN THIS ISSUE
- CRAFTS
- HEALTH
- REMODELING

DECORATING CONTEST WINNERS!
15 Idea-Filled Pages For You

MICROWAVE COOKING
New Recipes,
New Techniques!

TODAY'S PARENTS:
HOW WELL ARE THEY DOING?
80,000 Readers Tell Us
What They Think!

EDUCATION'S DIRTY LITTLE SECRET
What Every Parent Should Know

INDOOR BLOOMS ALL WINTER!
Pot Up Some Flowering Bulbs

A MASTER SUITE RETREAT

Rooms You Love
To Come Home To

MICROWAVE
— COOKING —
NEW RECIPES, NEW TECHNIQUES
FROM 3 COOKING PROS

By Lynn Hoppe

WEEKNIGHT DINNERS AND WEEKEND FEASTS
Microwave recipes to fit every occasion.

Christy and daughter Brittin cook together.

"The first step— think microwave! Before cooking a favorite dish, consider adapting it to the microwave."
—**Christy Heaps**

When Christy Heaps got her first micro- wave, she went to work con- verting family-style and gourmet specialties to the new appliance. Today, Chris- ty uses her recipes to show her Atlanta microwave cooking students what the Heapses know firsthand— that speedy micro-cooking measures up in every way.

Photographs: Rick Taylor
Field editor: Ruth L. Rieter

Fast-cooking chicken and a make-ahead salad are weekday winners.

ON-CALL MEAL

When family schedules don't mesh, the Heapses help themselves to a meal they can fix fast. Christy makes *Julienne Vegetable Salad* ahead. Family mem- bers cook their own *Fancy Baked Chicken.* Bulgur rounds out the meal.

Coat chicken for color.

Cut up for even cooking.

CHICKEN TETRAZZINI

SCALLOPS NEWBURG

SOLE FLORENTINE WITH MORNAY SAUCE

NO-FUSS GOURMET RECIPES

Christy particularly enjoys teaching gourmet microwave cooking classes. Three of her favorites—*Scallops Newburg, Chicken Tetrazzini,* and *Sole Florentine with Mornay Sauce*—earn rave reviews from students and family, husband Thom and children, Brook and Brittin.

FOLD FISH FILLETS
To prevent the thin ends of fish fillets from overcooking, fold them over spinach filling. Secure with a toothpick.

MAKE A SAUCE
A plus for microwave sauce making—measure, mix, and cook the pasta sauce in the same measuring cup.

CHOOSE THE RIGHT DISH
To allow for boiling and stirring of recipes, such as the scallops, choose a dish with *twice* the volume of the mixture.

MICROWAVE COOKING

MAKE-AHEAD MEALS FOR ONE OR A FEW

Cook, freeze, reheat—keys to meals in minutes.

Dick touts using the micro-wave to its full potential.

"Whether you're cooking for one or a crowd, the micro-wave oven and the freezer make a terrific team."
—**Dick Difino**

Nine years ago, Dick Difino hung up his three-piece suit and donned an apron. Dick, now a Chicago microwave cooking teacher, says, "When I bought my first microwave, I read all I could find and did a lot of experimenting."

Dick promotes the convenience of make-ahead microwave meals. "When cooking for myself, I micro-cook a recipe for three or four servings. I eat one portion and individually freeze the rest for other nights. Even for dinner parties, I micro-cook and freeze part of the meal."

Photographs: Jim Hedrich

Dick freezes stuffed peppers in individual portions.

DINING ALONE

Dick suggests that you undercook *Italian Stuffed Peppers* before freezing them. If you cook the peppers too long at first, they'll get mushy when you reheat them. If needed, you can add time later, but you can't take cooking time away.

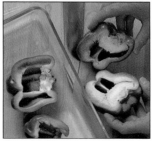

Precook the peppers.

Wrap individually; freeze.

GARLIC-BUTTER
VEGETABLES

Dick chats with guests
before dinner.

CRANBERRY-DIJON
CHICKEN

GINGER-MOLASSES CAKE
WITH ORANGE SAUCE

SNAPPY SNACK
CRACKERS

FREEING THE COOK AT MEALTIME

So he can spend more time with his guests, Dick prepares the *Ginger-Molasses Cake with Orange Sauce, Snappy Snack Crackers,* and the *Cranberry-Dijon Chicken* in advance. The day of the dinner party, he arranges and micro-cooks the platterful of *Garlic-Butter Vegetables.*

COOK IN SEQUENCE
Because different vegetables require different cooking times, start with the longest-cooking vegetables.

ARRANGE CHICKEN
For even microwave cooking, arrange chicken pieces with the meatiest portions to the outside of the dish.

TEST FOR DONENESS
The cake is done when you can scrape the wet surface with a toothpick and find a crumb texture underneath.

MICROWAVE
COOKING

NUTRITIOUS FOODS TEENS LIKE TO FIX

High school students learn healthful eating in microwave cooking class.

Carol's students get hands-on cooking experience.

"In my classes, I stress that healthful eating and microwave cooking are complementary."
—Carol Trench

H ome economist Carol Trench saw her first microwave in 1955. "The oven, then as big as a built-in oven, so intrigued me that I had to learn more."

In her course at a suburban Minneapolis high school, Carol combines nutrition and microwave cooking. She says the subjects go together well. When you micro-cook, you can get by with little or no added fat or water. The result—fewer calories, greater appeal, and better nutrient retention.

Photographs: Mike Jensen
Field editor: Pat Carpenter

Students duplicate Carol's popular pizzas at home.

PIZZA, PLEASE!

"I try to give my students healthful microwave versions of the foods they love," says Carol. Carol's 15 microwave pizza recipes are a hit with her teenage students. She tops **French Pizza** with a cream cheese mixture and fresh vegetables.

Arrange on browning griddle.

Spread toppers on crust.

LEMONY CHILI

CHEESE AND CORN CASSEROLES

SPAGHETTI SQUASH WITH PARMESAN SAUCE

GOOD AND HEALTHFUL EATING

Carol's students rate these recipes a 10. *Cheese and Corn Casseroles* include a favorite vegetable. The pastalike strands in *Spaghetti Squash with Parmesan Sauce* surprise many of her students. *Lemony Chili* with a pleasant blend of herbs and spices transcends the generation gap.

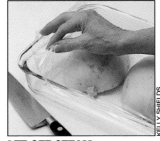

LET OFF STEAM
Vent clear plastic wrap by folding back a small corner of wrap at the edge of the microwave-safe baking dish.

COOK INDIVIDUALLY
So that the egg mixture gets done in the center, rearrange and rotate the corn casseroles twice during cooking.

USE A NIFTY GADGET
A steamer-cooker utensil provides an easy and safe way to cook ground beef for the chili and to drain fat.

151

Christy Heaps

JULIENNE VEGETABLE SALAD

- 6 cloves garlic
- 1 medium zucchini, cut into julienne strips
- 2 stalks celery, cut into julienne strips
- 2 medium carrots, cut into julienne strips
- ¼ of a green or red sweet pepper, cut into julienne strips
- 2 green onions, sliced
- ¼ cup sliced fully cooked ham cut into strips (1¼ ounces)
- 1 egg
- ¼ cup white wine vinegar
- 1 tablespoon Dijon-style mustard
- 1 cup olive oil or cooking oil
- ½ cup grated Parmesan cheese

In a 2-cup microwave-safe measure combine garlic and ¾ cup *water*. Cover with microwave-safe plastic wrap. Vent by leaving a small area unsealed at edge. Micro-cook on 100% power (high) 2 minutes. Uncover; cook on 50% (medium) 5 minutes more. Drain. Set aside.

In a 1½-quart microwave-safe casserole combine zucchini, celery, carrots, pepper, green onions, and 2 tablespoons *water*. Cook, covered, on high for 5 to 7 minutes or till vegetables are crisp-tender. Drain. Stir in ham.

For dressing, in a blender container or food processor bowl combine garlic, egg, vinegar, and mustard. Cover; blend or process for 5 seconds. With blender or food processor running, add oil through opening in lid in a slow, steady stream. Stir in Parmesan, ¼ teaspoon *salt*, and ¼ teaspoon *pepper*.

Toss ⅔ *cup* dressing with warm vegetables. Store remaining dressing, covered, in the refrigerator for up to 1 week. Makes 6 servings.

Conventional directions: In a small saucepan combine garlic and ¾ cup *water*. Bring to boiling. Reduce heat. Cover and simmer for 3 minutes or till tender. Drain. Set aside.

In a saucepan combine vegetables and ½ cup *water*. Bring to boiling. Reduce heat. Cover and simmer for 7 to 9 minutes. Drain. Stir in ham. Prepare dressing and serve as above.

Nutrition information per serving: 190 cal., 4 g pro., 5 g carbo., 18 g fat, 26 mg chol., 224 mg sodium. U.S. RDA: 146% vit. A, 22% vit. C.

FANCY BAKED CHICKEN

To allow for busy family members who need to eat at different times, prepare the bulgur and crumb mixtures ahead and store in the refrigerator. Later, coat a breast half and cook it for 3 to 4 minutes on high. Heat ¾ cup of the bulgur mixture for 1 to 1½ minutes on high—

- 2 cups boiling water
- 1 cup bulgur
- 1 teaspoon instant chicken bouillon granules
- ⅛ teaspoon pepper
- 2 tablespoons butter or margarine
- ¼ cup fine dry seasoned bread crumbs
- 2 tablespoons grated Parmesan cheese
- ¼ teaspoon garlic powder
- ⅛ teaspoon paprika
- 2 medium whole chicken breasts (about 1½ pounds total), skinned, boned, and halved lengthwise

To cook bulgur, in a 1-quart microwave-safe casserole micro-cook water, bulgur, bouillon granules, and pepper, covered, on 100% power (high) for 4 to 5 minutes or till done, stirring once.

In a 1-cup microwave-safe measure cook butter, uncovered, on high for 45 to 60 seconds or till melted. In a shallow dish combine crumbs, cheese, garlic powder, and paprika. Brush one side of *each* chicken piece with some of the melted butter. Coat the same side with some of the crumb mixture.

Place chicken, crumb side up, on a microwave-safe rack in a 12x7½x2-inch microwave-safe baking dish. Sprinkle with remaining crumbs and drizzle with remaining butter. Cover with waxed paper. Cook on high for 6 to 7 minutes or till chicken is tender, giving the dish a half-turn once. Serve with bulgur mixture. Makes 4 servings.

Conventional directions: To cook bulgur, in a medium saucepan combine water, bulgur, bouillon granules, and pepper. Bring to boiling. Reduce heat. Simmer, covered, for 12 to 15 minutes or till done. Coat chicken as above.

Place, crumb side up, in a shallow baking pan. Add remaining crumbs and butter. Bake in a 375° oven 25 minutes or till done. Serve with bulgur.

Nutrition information per serving: 231 cal., 29 g pro., 5 g carbo., 10 g fat, 91 mg chol., 226 mg sodium. U.S. RDA: 60% niacin, 23% phosphorus.

CHICKEN TETRAZZINI

- 2 whole large chicken breasts (about 2 pounds total), skinned, boned, and cut into bite-size pieces
- ½ cup chopped green or red sweet pepper
- ¼ cup butter or margarine
- ¼ cup all-purpose flour
- 2 teaspoons instant chicken bouillon granules
- ¼ teaspoon pepper
- 1 cup water
- 1 cup milk
- ½ cup shredded Swiss cheese (2 ounces)
- 8 ounces spaghetti, cooked and drained
- 1 4-ounce can sliced mushrooms, drained
- 12 rich round crackers, crushed

In a 2-quart microwave-safe casserole combine chicken and green or red pepper. Micro-cook, covered, on 100% power (high) for 6 to 8 minutes or till chicken is no longer pink, stirring once. Drain. Cover and set aside.

For sauce, in a 4-cup microwave-safe measure cook butter or margarine, uncovered, on high about 45 seconds or till melted. Stir in flour, bouillon granules, and pepper. Stir in water and milk. Cook on high for 5 to 7 minutes or till thickened and bubbly, stirring every minute. Stir in cheese.

In the 2-quart casserole combine chicken mixture, sauce, cooked spaghetti, and mushrooms. Sprinkle cracker crumbs on top. Cook, uncovered, on high for 1 to 3 minutes or till heated through. Makes 6 servings.

Conventional directions: In a large skillet cook chicken and green or red pepper in butter or margarine about 5 minutes or till chicken is brown and pepper is tender. Combine flour, bouillon granules, and pepper; stir in water and milk. Add to skillet. Cook and stir till thickened and bubbly. Stir in cheese, spaghetti, and mushrooms.

Transfer the mixture to a 2-quart casserole. Sprinkle with crumbs. Bake, uncovered, in a 350° oven for 20 to 25 minutes or till heated through.

Nutrition information per serving: 439 cal., 29 g pro., 43 g carbo., 16 g fat, 81 mg chol., 600 mg sodium. U.S. RDA: 23% vit. A, 28% vit. C, 33% thiamine, 21% riboflavin, 56% niacin, 20% calcium, 15% iron, 34% phosphorus.

SCALLOPS NEWBURG

Use sea scallops that measure about 1 inch. Cut up any larger scallops—

- **1 pound fresh *or* frozen sea scallops**
- **3 cups sliced fresh mushrooms**
- **4 green onions, sliced**
- **¼ cup dry white wine**
- **¼ cup butter *or* margarine**
- **3 tablespoons all-purpose flour**
- **½ teaspoon dried thyme, crushed**
- **⅛ teaspoon pepper**
- **½ cup milk**
- **½ teaspoon Worcestershire sauce**
- **Several dashes bottled hot pepper sauce**
- **2 tablespoons butter *or* margarine**
- **½ cup fine dry bread crumbs**
- **2 tablespoons snipped parsley**
- **Green onions (optional)**

To thaw frozen scallops, in a 1-quart microwave-safe casserole micro-cook the frozen scallops, uncovered, on 50% power (medium) about 7 minutes or till nearly thawed, removing thawed portions twice. Drain and remove scallops from the casserole. Set aside.

In the same 1-quart casserole combine mushrooms and green onions. Cook, covered, on 100% power (high) for 3 to 4 minutes or till onion is tender. Drain. Stir in scallops and wine. Cook, covered, on high for 2 to 2½ minutes or till scallops are opaque, stirring once. Drain, reserving ½ cup liquid. (Add water, if necessary, to equal ½ cup.)

For sauce, in a medium microwave-safe mixing bowl cook the ¼ cup butter or margarine, uncovered, on high about 45 seconds or till melted. Stir in flour, thyme, and pepper. Stir the reserved liquid, milk, Worcestershire sauce, and hot pepper sauce into the flour mixture. Cook, uncovered, on high for 2 to 3 minutes or till thickened and bubbly, stirring every minute. Stir the sauce into scallop mixture. Spoon into 4 ungreased individual 10-ounce casseroles.

For topping, in a 1-cup microwave-safe measure cook the 2 tablespoons butter or margarine, uncovered, on high for 30 to 45 seconds or till melted. Stir in the bread crumbs and parsley. Sprinkle topping over scallop mixture in casseroles. Cook, uncovered, on high about 30 seconds or till casseroles are heated through. Garnish with green onion, if desired. Makes 4 servings.

Conventional directions: Thaw scallops, if frozen. In a covered 10-inch skillet cook mushrooms and onion in 2 tablespoons *water* for 2 to 3 minutes or till onion is tender. Drain. Stir in the scallops and wine. Cook, covered, for 4 to 5 minutes or till scallops are opaque. Drain, reserving ½ cup liquid. (Add water, if necessary, to equal ½ cup.)

For sauce, in a 1½-quart saucepan heat the ¼ cup butter or margarine till melted. Stir in flour, thyme, and pepper. Stir in the reserved liquid, milk, Worcestershire sauce, and hot pepper sauce. Cook and stir till thickened and bubbly. Cook and stir for 1 minute more. Stir in the scallop mixture. Spoon into 4 individual ungreased 10-ounce casseroles.

For topping, in a saucepan heat the remaining butter till melted. Stir in the bread crumbs and parsley. Sprinkle over scallop mixture. Place casseroles in a 15x10x1-inch baking pan. Bake, uncovered, in a 350° oven for 10 to 15 minutes or till heated through.

Nutrition information per serving: 346 cal., 24 g pro., 26 g carbo., 15 g fat, 81 mg chol., 625 mg sodium. U.S. RDA: 15% vit. A, 18% thiamine, 28% riboflavin, 24% niacin, 15% calcium, 22% iron, 39% phosphorus.

SOLE FLORENTINE WITH MORNAY SAUCE

- **6 fresh *or* frozen sole, walleye, *or* flounder fillets (1 to 1¼ pounds)**
- **2 cups chopped fresh spinach**
- **1 cup frozen cut broccoli, chopped**
- **2 tablespoons water**
- **1 stalk celery, sliced (½ cup)**
- **1 small onion, chopped (¼ cup)**
- **2 fresh mushrooms, sliced**
- **3 tablespoons butter *or* margarine**
- **½ cup herb-seasoned stuffing mix**
- **2 tablespoons all-purpose flour**
- **½ teaspoon instant chicken bouillon granules**
- **⅛ teaspoon ground nutmeg**
- **Dash pepper**
- **1 cup milk**
- **Lemon slices (optional)**

To thaw frozen fish, in an 8x8x2-inch microwave-safe baking dish micro-cook fish, uncovered, on 50% power (medium) for 3 to 5 minutes or till nearly defrosted, separating and rearranging the fillets once. Let stand for 5 minutes.

In a medium microwave-safe mixing bowl combine spinach, broccoli, and water. Cook, covered, on 100% power (high) for 4 minutes. Drain well. Cut large chunks of broccoli in half. Add celery, onion, mushrooms, and *1 tablespoon* butter. Cook, covered, on high for 3 minutes. Stir in stuffing mix. Cover and let stand for 2 to 3 minutes for stuffing to absorb moisture.

Place about ⅓ cup of the stuffing mixture in center of *each* fish fillet. Roll ends over stuffing. Secure with a wooden toothpick. Transfer fish, seam side down, to the 8x8x2-inch dish. Cover with microwave-safe plastic wrap. Vent by leaving a small area unsealed at the edge. Cook on high for 6 to 8 minutes or till fish flakes easily when tested with a fork, rotating the dish a quarter-turn twice. Let stand while preparing sauce.

For sauce, in a 4-cup microwave-safe measure cook remaining butter or margarine, uncovered, on high for 1 minute. Stir in flour, bouillon granules, nutmeg, and pepper. Add milk. Cook, uncovered, on high for 2 to 3 minutes or till thickened and bubbly, stirring twice. Cook and stir for 30 seconds more. Transfer fish to a serving platter. Top with sauce. Garnish with lemon slices, if desired. Makes 6 servings.

Conventional directions: Thaw fish, if frozen. For stuffing, in a medium saucepan combine broccoli, celery, onion, and ¼ cup *water*. Cover and cook for 3 minutes. Add spinach and mushrooms. Cover and cook about 3 minutes more or till the vegetables are crisp-tender. Drain well. Return the vegetables to saucepan. Stir in *1 tablespoon* butter or margarine and the stuffing mix. Cover and let stand for 2 to 3 minutes for stuffing to absorb moisture.

Stuff fillets as above. Place in a 10x6x2-inch baking pan. Cover with foil. Bake in a 350° oven for 20 to 25 minutes or till fish flakes with a fork.

For sauce, in a saucepan heat the remaining butter till melted. Stir in flour, bouillon granules, nutmeg, and pepper. Add milk. Cook and stir till thickened and bubbly. Cook and stir for 1 to 2 minutes more. Serve as above.

Nutrition information per serving: 247 cal., 23 g pro., 15 g carbo., 10 g fat, 66 mg chol., 416 mg sodium. U.S. RDA: 40% vit. A, 18% vit. C, 10% thiamine, 15% riboflavin, 14% niacin, 18% calcium, 29% phosphorus.

153

Dick Difino

ITALIAN STUFFED PEPPERS

- 3 large green peppers
- 1 pound ground beef
- 1 medium onion, chopped (½ cup)
- 1 clove garlic, minced
- 1 7½-ounce can tomatoes, cut up
- ½ cup halved, sliced, pitted ripe olives
- ½ of a 6-ounce can (⅓ cup) tomato paste
- 2 teaspoons chili powder
- 1 teaspoon sugar
- ¼ teaspoon salt
- 2½ cups crisp rice cereal
- 1 cup shredded cheddar cheese (4 ounces)

Halve the peppers lengthwise. Discard seeds and membranes. Arrange peppers, cut side up, in a 12x7½x2-inch microwave-safe baking dish. Cover with microwave-safe plastic wrap. Vent by leaving a small area unsealed at the edge of the dish. Micro-cook on 100% power (high) for 4 to 5 minutes or till crisp-tender. Drain. Sprinkle the insides of the peppers with salt.

In a 2-quart microwave-safe casserole combine beef, onion, and garlic. Cook, uncovered, on high for 4 to 5 minutes or till done, stirring twice. Drain. Stir in *undrained* tomatoes, olives, tomato paste, chili powder, sugar, and salt. Stir in cereal. Spoon about ¾ cup meat mixture into *each* pepper half.

For immediate serving: For each serving, transfer a pepper half to a microwave-safe individual casserole. Cover with microwave-safe plastic wrap. Vent by leaving a small area unsealed at the edge of the dish. Cook on 50% power (medium) for 3 to 4 minutes or till heated through and green pepper is tender, giving the dish a half-turn once. Uncover and top with cheese. Cook on medium for 30 seconds. Let stand, covered, for 3 minutes. Makes 6 servings.

For later serving: Wrap the pepper halves individually in moisture- and vaporproof wrap. Freeze for up to 2 months. For each serving, unwrap one pepper half. Transfer to a microwave-safe individual casserole. Cover with microwave-safe plastic wrap. Vent by leaving a small area unsealed.

Cook on 70% power (medium-high) for 4 minutes. Uncover. Cook on 50% power (medium) for 5 to 7 minutes or

till heated through and the pepper is nearly tender, giving the dish a half-turn once. Top pepper with cheese. Cook on medium for 30 seconds. Let stand, covered, for 3 minutes.

Conventional directions: Prepare peppers as above. Cook peppers in boiling water for 5 minutes. Drain well. Sprinkle insides with salt.

In a large skillet cook beef, onion, and garlic till meat is brown. Drain. Stir in *undrained* tomatoes, olives, tomato paste, chili powder, sugar, and salt. Stir in cereal. Spoon mixture into pepper halves.

Transfer peppers to a 13x9x2-inch baking pan. Cover with foil. Bake in a 350° oven for 25 minutes. Uncover and sprinkle with cheese. Bake for 5 minutes more or till cheese is melted.

Nutrition information per serving: 342 cal., 21 g pro., 22 g carbo., 20 g fat, 71 mg chol., 650 mg sodium. U.S. RDA: 41% vit. A, 145% vit. C, 21% thiamine, 26% riboflavin, 31% niacin, 18% calcium, 26% iron, 26% phosphorus.

CRANBERRY-DIJON CHICKEN

- 1 2½- to 3-pound broiler-fryer chicken, cut up
- 1 8-ounce can whole cranberry sauce
- 1 medium onion, finely chopped
- ½ cup catsup
- 2 tablespoons Dijon-style mustard
- 1 tablespoon brown sugar
- 1 tablespoon Worcestershire sauce
- ½ teaspoon salt
- 2 tablespoons water
- 2 tablespoons vinegar
- 4 teaspoons cornstarch
- 2 tablespoons snipped parsley
- 3 cups hot cooked rice

In a 12x7½x2-inch microwave-safe baking dish arrange the chicken with meatiest parts toward outside of dish. Cover with waxed paper. Micro-cook on 100% power (high) for 8 minutes, rearranging pieces twice. Drain off fat.

Combine cranberry sauce, onion, catsup, mustard, brown sugar, Worcestershire sauce, and salt. Spoon over chicken. Cover with waxed paper. Cook on high for 10 to 12 minutes or till chicken is tender, basting chicken and giving dish a half-turn once. Remove

chicken, reserving cranberry mixture. Skim fat from cranberry mixture.

Stir together water, vinegar, and cornstarch. Stir into cranberry mixture. Cook, uncovered, on high for 2 minutes or till thickened and bubbly, stirring every minute. Cook, uncovered, on high for 30 seconds more. (If chilling, return chicken to dish.) Stir parsley into rice. Serve chicken and sauce over parslied rice. Serves 6.

To make ahead: Let chicken with sauce cool. Chill up to 24 hours.

At serving time, cook chicken, covered, on 70% power (medium-high) for 8 to 10 minutes or till heated through, giving the dish a half-turn and rearranging chicken twice.

Conventional directions: In a large skillet brown chicken in 2 tablespoons hot *cooking oil* for 10 to 15 minutes. Drain off fat. Combine ingredients for cranberry mixture as above. Spoon over chicken. Cover and simmer for 30 to 40 minutes or till chicken is tender.

Transfer the chicken to a platter. Skim fat from cranberry mixture. Stir together water, vinegar, and cornstarch. Stir into cranberry mixture. Cook and stir till thickened and bubbly. Cook and stir 2 minutes more. Serve.

Nutrition information per serving: 312 cal., 30 g pro., 29 g carbo., 8 g fat, 89 mg chol., 694 mg sodium. U.S. RDA: 12% riboflavin, 48% niacin, 14% iron, 25% phosphorus.

SNAPPY SNACK CRACKERS

- 1 cup butter *or* margarine
- ½ cup grated Parmesan cheese
- 1 teaspoon celery salt
- 1 teaspoon paprika
- ½ teaspoon garlic powder
- ½ teaspoon onion powder
- 1 16-ounce package oyster crackers (10 cups)

In a 4-quart microwave-safe bowl micro-cook butter, uncovered, on 100% power (high) for 1 to 2 minutes or till melted. Stir in cheese, celery salt, paprika, garlic powder, and onion powder. Add crackers. Toss to coat.

Cook, uncovered, on high for 2 to 3 minutes or till hot, stirring every minute. Cool. Store in an airtight container for up to 1 week. Makes 10 cups.

Nutrition information per ½-cup serving: 192 cal., 3 g pro., 16 g carbo., 13 g fat, 27 mg chol., 477 mg sodium.

GINGER-MOLASSES CAKE WITH ORANGE SAUCE

- ⅔ cup molasses
- ½ cup butter *or* margarine
- 1 cup all-purpose flour
- ⅔ cup regular rolled oats
- 1 tablespoon sugar
- 1 tablespoon finely shredded orange *or* lemon peel
- ½ teaspoon baking soda
- ½ teaspoon salt
- ½ teaspoon ground ginger
- ¼ teaspoon ground cloves
- ½ cup milk
- 1 recipe Orange Sauce *or* Lemon Sauce

In a 2-cup microwave-safe measure combine molasses and butter or margarine. Micro-cook, uncovered, on 100% power (high) for 1 to 2 minutes or till butter is melted.

Combine flour, oats, sugar, peel, baking soda, salt, ginger, and cloves. Stir in molasses mixture and milk. Pour into a greased 8x8x2-inch microwave-safe baking dish.

Cook, uncovered, on 50% power (medium) for 10 minutes, giving the dish a quarter-turn every 2 minutes. Cook, uncovered, on high for 1 to 2 minutes more, giving the dish a quarter-turn twice. (To check for doneness, scrape the moist surface of the cake with a wooden toothpick to look for a crumb texture underneath.)

Let stand, uncovered, for 20 minutes before serving. Cut into squares. Serve with Orange Sauce or Lemon Sauce. Makes 9 servings.

Orange Sauce: In a 4-cup microwave-safe measure combine ¼ cup *sugar* and 2 tablespoons *cornstarch*. Stir in ¾ cup *water*, 1 tablespoon *butter* or *margarine*, 1 teaspoon finely shredded *orange peel*, and 1 cup *orange juice*. Cook, uncovered, on high for 5 to 6 minutes or till thickened and bubbly, stirring every minute.

Lemon Sauce: In a 4-cup microwave-safe measure combine 1 cup *water*, 1 cup *milk*, one 3⅛-ounce package regular *lemon pudding mix*, 1 tablespoon finely shredded *lemon peel*, and 1 tablespoon *lemon juice*. Cook, uncovered, on high for 5 to 7 minutes or till boiling, stirring every minute.

Conventional directions: In a saucepan heat molasses and butter till butter is melted. Prepare batter as above. Pour into a greased 8x8x2-inch baking pan. Bake in a 375° oven for 25 to 30 minutes or till done. Cool 10 minutes on a wire rack. Remove from pan.

Meanwhile, for Orange Sauce, in a small saucepan combine sugar, cornstarch, and orange peel. Stir in the water and orange juice. Cook and stir till thickened and bubbly. Cook and stir 2 minutes more. Remove from heat and stir in butter or margarine till melted.

For Lemon Sauce, in a small saucepan combine water, milk, pudding mix, lemon peel, and lemon juice. Cook and stir till boiling. Serve as above.

Nutrition information per serving with Orange Sauce: 286 cal., 3 g pro., 41 g carbo., 13 g fat, 33 mg chol., 317 mg sodium. U.S. RDA: 10% vit. A, 14% vit. C, 20% thiamine, 16% riboflavin, 16% niacin, 14% calcium, 36% iron.

GARLIC-BUTTER VEGETABLES

To keep the cooked vegetables neatly arranged on the platter, before removing the plastic wrap, tilt the platter in the direction of the vent to drain—

- 2 cups broccoli flowerets
- 1 cup cauliflower flowerets
- 2 tablespoons water
- 1 medium zucchini, sliced ¼ inch thick
- 1 cup fresh mushrooms
- 1 green *or* red sweet pepper, cut into thin strips
- 1 recipe Garlic Butter

On a large microwave-safe platter arrange broccoli and cauliflower around outer edges. Sprinkle with water. Cover with microwave-safe plastic wrap. Vent by leaving a small area unsealed at the edge. Micro-cook on 100% power (high) for 2 minutes. Place zucchini, mushrooms, and pepper in center. Cook, covered, on high for 3 to 5 minutes more or till vegetables are crisp-tender. Carefully drain liquid. Drizzle with Garlic Butter. Makes 6 servings.

Garlic Butter: In a 1-cup microwave-safe measure stir together ¼ cup *butter* or *margarine*; ⅛ teaspoon *pepper*; 1 clove *garlic*, quartered; and dash *salt*. Cook on high about 1 minute or till melted. Discard garlic pieces.

Nutrition information per serving: 93 cal., 2 g pro., 5 g carbo., 8 g fat, 21 mg chol., and 112 mg sodium. U.S. RDA: 47% vit. A, 108% vit. C.

Carol Trench

FRENCH PIZZA

For a crisp crust with golden color, use a microwave browning crisper/griddle—

- 1 package (8) refrigerated crescent rolls
- 2 3-ounce packages cream cheese
- ¼ cup mayonnaise *or* salad dressing
- 1½ teaspoons dried dillweed
- Dash garlic powder
- 2 cups desired pizza toppers (chopped cauliflower, broccoli flowerets, shredded carrot, chopped green pepper, sliced pitted ripe olives, *or* sliced mushrooms)

If using a 10-inch-round microwave browning crisper/griddle, preheat the griddle on 100% power (high) for 4 minutes. For crust, unroll crescent rolls. Carefully arrange triangles in a circle on the hot griddle or on a lightly greased 12-inch microwave-safe pizza dish, pressing edges together.

Micro-cook on 50% power (medium) for 6 minutes (12 minutes if using a pizza dish), giving the griddle or dish a half-turn twice. If using a browning griddle, loosen edges and invert onto a serving platter.

In a 4-cup microwave-safe measure cook cream cheese on high for 30 to 45 seconds or till softened. Stir in mayonnaise or salad dressing, dillweed, and garlic powder. Spread over crust. Arrange pizza toppers over all. Serve immediately or chill for several hours or overnight. Makes 6 servings.

Conventional directions: For the crust, unroll crescent rolls. Arrange triangles in a circle on a greased 12-inch pizza pan. Bake in a 375° oven for 8 to 10 minutes or till light brown.

Stir together the *softened* cream cheese, mayonnaise or salad dressing, dillweed, and garlic powder. Spread over crust. Arrange pizza toppers over all. Serve as above.

Nutrition information per serving: 314 cal., 6 g pro., 19 g carbo., 25 g fat, 37 mg chol., 455 mg sodium. U.S. RDA: 84% vit. A, 44% vit. C, 10% thiamine, 10% riboflavin, 10% iron, and 20% phosphorus.

CHEESE AND CORN CASSEROLES

These individual main-dish casseroles are done when you shake the dishes and the custards appear almost set—

- 1 10-ounce package frozen whole kernel corn
- ¼ cup chopped onion
- ¼ cup chopped green pepper
- 1 tablespoon butter *or* margarine
- 3 beaten eggs
- 1 cup shredded American cheese (4 ounces)
- ½ cup milk
- Several dashes bottled hot pepper sauce
- 1 tablespoon sunflower nuts *or* toasted wheat germ

In a 1½-quart microwave-safe casserole combine corn, onion, green pepper, and butter or margarine. Micro-cook, uncovered, on 100% power (high) for 4 to 6 minutes or till vegetables are tender, stirring once.

Stir in eggs, cheese, milk, and hot pepper sauce. Spoon mixture into 4 ungreased 8-ounce microwave-safe soufflé dishes or casseroles. Cook, uncovered, on high for 4½ to 5½ minutes or till almost set, rearranging and rotating the dishes twice.

Let stand for 5 minutes. Sprinkle with sunflower nuts or toasted wheat germ. Serve immediately. Makes 4 main-dish servings.

Conventional directions: In a medium saucepan bring ½ cup *water* to boiling. Add corn, onion, and green pepper. Return to boiling. Reduce heat. Cover and simmer for 5 minutes or till vegetables are tender. Drain.

Stir in butter or margarine, eggs, cheese, milk, and hot pepper sauce. Spoon into 4 ungreased 8-ounce soufflé dishes or casseroles. Bake in a 325° oven for 30 to 35 minutes or till set. Sprinkle with sunflower nuts or toasted wheat germ. Serve as above.

Nutrition information per serving:
265 cal., 14 g pro., 20 g carbo., 15 g fat, 236 mg chol., 437 mg sodium. U.S. RDA: 17% vit. A, 19% vit. C, 20% riboflavin, 23% calcium, 28% phosphorus.

SPAGHETTI SQUASH WITH PARMESAN SAUCE

- 1 2- to 2½-pound spaghetti squash
- 1 cup sliced celery
- ½ cup chopped onion (1 medium)
- ½ cup chopped green *or* red sweet pepper
- 2 tablespoons butter *or* margarine
- 1 tablespoon all-purpose flour
- ½ teaspoon dry mustard
- Dash pepper
- ¾ cup milk
- 2 slices process Swiss cheese, cut up (2 ounces)
- ¼ cup grated Parmesan cheese

Halve squash lengthwise. Use a large spoon to scoop seeds from the squash halves. Place halves, cut side down, in a 12x7½x2-inch microwave-safe baking dish. Cover with microwave-safe plastic wrap. Vent by leaving a small area unsealed at edge of dish. Micro-cook on 100% power (high) for 10 to 14 minutes or till pulp can just be pierced with a fork, giving dish a half-turn twice. Let stand, covered, while making sauce.

For sauce, in a 4-cup microwave-safe measure combine celery, onion, green pepper, and butter or margarine. Cover with waxed paper. Cook on high for 3 to 4 minutes or till onion is tender. Stir in flour, mustard, and pepper. Stir in milk. Cook, uncovered, on high for 1 to 3 minutes or till thickened and bubbly, stirring every minute. Cook on high 30 seconds more. Stir in cheeses.

Using a kitchen fork, shred and separate the squash pulp into strands. Pile the squash onto a warm serving platter. Top with sauce. Makes 4 to 6 main-dish servings.

Conventional directions: Place halved and seeded squash in a Dutch oven. Add 2 inches *water*. Bring to boiling. Reduce heat. Cover and simmer for 25 to 35 minutes or till tender. Drain.

Meanwhile, for sauce, in a medium saucepan cook celery, onion, and green or red pepper in butter till vegetables are tender. Stir in flour, mustard, and pepper. Add milk all at once. Cook and stir till thickened and bubbly. Cook and stir for 1 to 2 minutes more. Stir in cheeses till melted. Serve as above.

Nutrition information per serving:
217 cal., 10 g pro., 15 g carbo., 13 g fat, 39 mg chol., 446 mg sodium. U.S. RDA: 26% vit. A, 43% vit. C, 116% thiamine, 110% riboflavin, 26% calcium, 19% phosphorus.

LEMONY CHILI

- 1 pound ground pork *or* beef
- ½ cup chopped onion (1 medium)
- ¼ cup chopped green pepper
- 1 clove garlic, minced
- 2 15½-ounce cans chili beans
- 1 4-ounce can mushroom stems and pieces
- ½ cup chili sauce
- 1 tomato, chopped
- 2 tablespoons lemon juice
- 1 tablespoon chili powder
- 1 teaspoon dry mustard
- ¼ teaspoon ground cumin
- ⅛ teaspoon dried oregano, crushed (optional)
- **Dash ground coriander (optional)**
- **Dash pepper (optional)**
- **Dash bottled hot pepper sauce**
- **Shredded cheddar cheese (optional)**
- **Dairy sour cream (optional)**

Crumble ground meat into a 2-quart microwave-safe steamer-cooker utensil or casserole. Add onion, green pepper, and garlic. Micro-cook, covered, on 100% power (high) for 4 to 6 minutes or till no pink remains in meat, stirring twice to break up meat. Drain.

In the bottom of the steamer or in the casserole combine meat mixture, *undrained* beans, *undrained* mushrooms, chili sauce, tomato, lemon juice, chili powder, dry mustard, cumin, oregano (if desired), coriander (if desired), pepper (if desired), and hot pepper sauce. Cook, covered, on high for 12 to 14 minutes or till heated through, stirring twice. If desired, serve with cheddar cheese and sour cream. Makes 5 or 6 servings.

Conventional directions: In a 12-inch skillet cook meat, onion, green pepper, and garlic till meat is brown and vegetables are tender. Drain fat. Stir in remaining ingredients *except* cheese and sour cream as above. Bring to boiling. Reduce heat. Cover and simmer for 10 minutes. Serve with cheese and sour cream, if desired.

Nutrition information per serving:
360 cal., 30 g pro., 41 g carbo., 9 g fat, 64 mg chol., 518 mg sodium. U.S. RDA: 22% vit. A, 26% vit. C, 15% thiamine, 16% riboflavin, 31% niacin, 36% iron, 39% phosphorus.

NOVEMBER

The Idea Magazine For American Families

PART 2
1986 DECORATING
CONTEST WINNERS!
Rooms You Love To Come Home To

Better Homes
and Gardens

IN THIS ISSUE
- TRAVEL
- MONEY
- HEALTH
- EDUCATION

HOLIDAY MAKE-AHEADS
Dazzling Desserts, Hors d'Oeuvres,
Cookies, Breads

November 1986
● $1.50

TODAY'S NEW SOLAR HOUSES
With Yesteryear Charm

PERSONALITY KITCHENS
How To Make
Your Kitchen
Suit Your Style

Coping With
Meddling
Grandparents

Flowering
Houseplants
That Just Won't
Stop Blooming!

The Hot
New Cars
For Under
$6,500

DAZZLING HORS D'OEUVRES

READY WHEN YOU ARE FOR ENTERTAINING

Create these stunning, savory tidbits before the holiday rush begins; later whisk them out of storage to wow your guests. What better way to celebrate the spirit of the season—minus any last-minute frazzle or hassle.

CRAB-FILLED PHYLLO BITES
Pop the frozen bundles in the oven; bake till golden.

STRIPED SALMON 'N' PARSLEY ROUNDS
Thaw, glaze, and garnish the night before.

SPECKLED VEGETABLE TERRINE
Just 30 minutes from freezer to party buffet.

VEAL-SPINACH PÂTÉ EN CROÛTE
Flaky, sumptuous—no clue that it's made ahead.

SUGAR- AND NUT-GLAZED BRIE
Warm the whiskey-kissed topper and creamy cheese.

PEPPER-COATED CHEESE WHEEL
Let the colorful coating tickle your taste buds.

SPECTACULAR DESSERTS

INDULGE YOUR GUESTS IN A SWEET BUFFET

Stash these marvelous do-ahead treats in your freezer or refrigerator. Like magic, serve one or all at a holiday open house or to end a festive dinner. Either way, they're perfect choices for sweetening the season.

CREAM-FILLED HAZELNUT CAKE
Brimming with nuts; ideal to freeze.

HOLIDAY CRANBERRY TORTE
Ready for drop-in guests in just 20 minutes.

GLAZED FINGER TARTS
Thaw as many delightful tarts as you need: 2 to 15.

LIQUEUR-LACED FRUITCAKES
A holiday must. Give the minicakes as gifts.

PUFFED COCONUT PASTRY DIAMONDS
Bake these frozen gems for an airy, warm dessert.

CHOCOLATE-PRALINE PUMPKIN PIE
Lift pumpkin pie to delectable new heights.

FANCY BREADS
ONE YEAST DOUGH MAKES ALL *THREE*

Take a big bite out of holiday baking by making just one recipe of Rich Yeast Dough. Ease the time crunch even further: mix and freeze the dough up to three months ahead.

STAR-BURST BREAD WITH HERB BUTTER
Flavor with anise, caraway, and fennel seed.

SHAPING THE STAR

Coil the end of each dough rope. Then, curve the center of each dough rope slightly to create the star shape.

FESTIVE
PINWHEEL ROLLS
Bake all 20 rolls; freeze.
Take them out as needed.

ALMOND
BREAD CROWN
The crowning touch to
any holiday brunch.

CREATING PINWHEELS

To form the pinwheel shape, fold every other dough tip over the jam in the center. Then, pinch the points together securely. Brush with milk; sprinkle with nuts.

FORMING A CROWN

Using a ruler to measure and sharp scissors to snip, cut the thin rope of dough at 1-inch intervals. This creates the crown's points.

FESTIVE COOKIES
ONE BUTTERY DOUGH MAKES THEM ALL

Fill your holiday cookie tray with Crackled Crescents, Little Snow People, and Zigzag Cookie Shapes.

Take this rich dough and make more than seven dozen cookies in all—

CRACKLED CRESCENTS: Add chocolate pieces, shape crescents, bake, and dip in chocolate, then nuts or coconut.

LITTLE SNOW PEOPLE: Shape the dough into balls, assemble, decorate with candy, and bake. Decorate with chocolate hats, colored frosting, and powdered sugar.

ZIGZAG COOKIE SHAPES: Roll, cut out, bake, and zigzag icing over.

FESTIVE COOKIE DOUGH

- 3½ cups all-purpose flour
- 1 teaspoon baking powder
- 1 cup butter *or* margarine, softened
- 1 8-ounce package cream cheese, softened
- 2 cups sugar
- 1 egg
- 1 teaspoon vanilla
- ¼ teaspoon almond extract
- ¼ teaspoon coconut flavoring (optional)

In a medium mixing bowl stir together flour and baking powder. Set aside.

In a large mixer bowl beat butter or margarine and cream cheese with an electric mixer on medium speed for 30 seconds. Add sugar; beat till fluffy. Add egg, vanilla, almond extract, and coconut flavoring; beat well. Gradually add flour mixture to creamed mixture, beating well after each addition. Divide dough into thirds (about 2 cups each). Cover and chill overnight. *Or,* place in moisture- and vaporproof plastic bags. Seal, label, and freeze up to 3 months.

SPECKLED VEGETABLE TERRINE

    1 cup chopped broccoli stems
    2 large carrots
    1 cup finely chopped onion
    1 clove garlic, minced
    2 tablespoons butter or margarine
    2 teaspoons instant chicken
       bouillon granules
    1 15-ounce can garbanzo beans,
       drained
 1½ cups soft bread crumbs (2 slices)
    ½ cup whipping cream
    ½ teaspoon dried savory, crushed
    ¼ teaspoon pepper
    4 beaten eggs
    2 tablespoons diced pimiento
Carrot-rope garnish (optional)
Cooked broccoli spear (optional)

Cook broccoli stems in a small amount of boiling water for 10 to 15 minutes or till tender. Drain; set aside.

Meanwhile, cut carrots lengthwise into quarters. In a skillet cook carrots, covered, in a small amount of boiling water for 10 to 15 minutes or till tender. Drain; set aside.

Cook onion and garlic in hot butter till tender but not brown. Remove from heat; set aside.

Combine 1 tablespoon hot *water* and bouillon granules. Stir to dissolve; set aside.

With a potato masher, mash garbanzo beans. Stir in onion mixture, bouillon mixture, bread crumbs, whipping cream, savory, and pepper. Stir in cooked broccoli, eggs, and pimiento.

Pour ¼ of the mixture into a well-greased 8x4x2-inch loaf dish. Lay 3 carrot strips lengthwise over the mixture. Pour another ¼ of the mixture over. Lay 2 carrot strips lengthwise over mixture. Pour another ¼ of the mixture atop. Lay remaining 3 carrot strips lengthwise over mixture. Pour remaining mixture over, spreading evenly.

Cover tightly with foil. Set in a 13x9x2-inch baking pan in a 350° oven. Pour hot water around dish to a depth of 1 inch. Bake about 1½ hours or till set. Cool in dish. Cover; chill up to 2 days. (Or, if you own a microwave oven, seal, label, and freeze up to 1 month.)

To serve: If loaf is frozen, place in a microwave oven. Cover with waxed paper. Micro-cook on 30% power (medium-low) about 20 minutes or till a sharp knife can be inserted in the center, giving dish a quarter-turn every 5 minutes. Let stand for 10 to 15 minutes.

Unmold the thawed or chilled loaf onto a serving platter lined with curly carrot ropes, if desired. Top with a broccoli spear and a carrot rope, if desired. Cut into ½-inch-wide slices. Serves 16.

Note: Our Test Kitchen does not recommend refrigerator thawing as the dense loaf takes too long to thaw.

Nutrition information per slice: 106 cal., 4 g pro., 9 g carbo., 6 g fat, 83 mg chol., 213 mg sodium. U.S. RDA: 58% vit. A, 11% vit. C.

CRAB-FILLED PHYLLO BITES

    1 6-ounce can crabmeat, drained,
       flaked, and cartilage removed
    ½ cup shredded Swiss cheese
    1 2-ounce can mushroom stems
       and pieces, drained and chopped
    ¼ cup crushed shredded wheat
       wafers (6 crackers)
    2 tablespoons snipped parsley
    ½ teaspoon onion powder
    ½ cup butter or margarine, melted
    6 sheets frozen phyllo dough
       (16x13-inch rectangles), thawed

For filling, combine crabmeat, Swiss cheese, mushrooms, crushed wafers, parsley, onion powder, and dash *pepper.* Drizzle with *1 tablespoon* of the butter. Toss to mix well. Set aside.

Unfold phyllo; spread 1 sheet flat. (Cover remaining sheets with damp towel while working.) Brush sheet with some of the remaining butter. Top with another sheet; brush with butter. Top with another sheet; brush.

Cut buttered phyllo stack lengthwise into fourths, then crosswise into fifths (makes twenty 3¼-inch squares). Place about *1 rounded teaspoon* filling in the center of *each* square. Bring edges of square up to top of filling. Press together; twist slightly to form bundle. Place bundles upright in 2 greased 9x9x2- or 8x8x2-inch baking pans. Repeat with remaining phyllo sheets and filling.

Brush all bundles with some of the remaining butter. Wrap baking pans in moisture- and vaporproof wrap. Seal, label, and freeze up to 6 months.

To serve: Uncover pans. Bake bundles in a 375° oven for 15 to 20 minutes or till golden. Makes 40 appetizers.

Nutrition information for each appetizer: 36 cal., 1 g pro., 1 g carbo., 3 g fat, 12 mg chol., 86 mg sodium.

SUGAR- AND NUT-GLAZED BRIE

    ¼ cup packed brown sugar
    ¼ cup broken walnuts, pecans,
       macadamia nuts, almonds, or
       hazelnuts (filberts)
    1 tablespoon whiskey or brandy
    1 14-ounce round Brie cheese
       (about 5 inches in diameter)
Apple wedges, seedless grapes, and
    crackers
Lemon juice

Stir together sugar, nuts, and whiskey. Cover. Chill up to 1 week. (Or, seal, label, and freeze up to 6 months in a moisture- and vaporproof freezer container.)

To serve: If frozen, let sugar mixture stand 1 hour at room temperature.

Place Brie in a 9-inch pie plate. Bake in a 500° oven 4 to 5 minutes or till slightly softened. Sprinkle sugar mixture atop; bake 2 to 3 minutes more or till the sugar is melted and cheese is heated through but not melted. Brush apple with lemon juice. Serve fruit and crackers with cheese. Serves 16 to 20.

Nutrition information per cheese slice: 110 cal., 5 g pro., 4 g carbo., 8 g fat, 25 mg chol., 157 mg sodium.

PEPPER-COATED CHEESE WHEEL

    1 8-ounce container soft-style
       cream cheese with chives
 1¼ cups shredded Muenster cheese
    1 3½-ounce package sliced
       pepperoni, finely chopped
    2 teaspoons paprika
    ½ teaspoon ground red pepper
Assorted crackers

Combine the cream cheese, Muenster cheese, and pepperoni. Shape into a 4x½-inch wheel shape. On waxed paper combine paprika and red pepper. Pat wheel in pepper mixture till coated. Cover. Chill several hours or till firm. Refrigerate up to 1 week. (Or, wrap in moisture- and vaporproof wrap. Seal, label, and freeze up to 3 months.)

To serve: If wheel is frozen, thaw overnight in refrigerator. Score top of wheel into diamond shapes. Cut into wedges. Serve with crackers. Makes 14 to 16 servings.

Nutrition information per cheese wedge: 131 cal., 5 g pro., 1 g carbo., 12 g fat, 32 mg chol., 271 mg sodium. U.S. RDA: 10% vit. A.

VEAL-SPINACH PÂTÉ EN CROÛTE

- ¾ **pound ground veal**
- 1 **medium onion, chopped (½ cup)**
- 2 **cloves garlic, minced**
- 4 **ounces chicken livers**
- ½ **cup dry white wine**
- 3 **eggs**
- ¼ **cup fine dry seasoned bread crumbs**
- 1 **tablespoon cornstarch**
- 1 **10-ounce package frozen chopped spinach, thawed and well drained**
- ½ **of a 17½-ounce package (1 sheet) frozen puff pastry**
- 1 **slightly beaten egg yolk**

Cook veal, onion, and garlic till veal is browned. Add livers. Cook and stir over high heat about 7 minutes or till liver is no longer pink. Drain. Cool slightly.

In a food processor bowl combine veal mixture and wine. Cover. Process till smooth. Add *two* of the eggs, *2 tablespoons* of the bread crumbs, cornstarch, and ¼ teaspoon *each salt* and *pepper.* Cover. Process till smooth. Transfer to a bowl. (Or, grind veal mixture through the fine blade of a food grinder. Repeat if necessary. Transfer to a bowl. Stir in wine, eggs, bread crumbs, cornstarch, salt, and pepper till smooth.) Cover. Chill about 1½ hours or till thickened.

Meanwhile, in clean food processor bowl combine remaining egg, spinach, and the remaining *2 tablespoons* bread crumbs. Cover. Process till smooth. (Or, finely chop spinach. Stir in egg and bread crumbs till smooth.)

Grease four 4½x2½x1½-inch loaf pans. For *each* loaf, spread *3 tablespoons* veal mixture in the bottom of the pan. Top with *one-fourth* of the spinach mixture. Top with *3 tablespoons* veal mixture. Cover with foil. Place in a shallow baking pan. Pour hot water around loaf pans to a depth of ½ inch. Bake in a 325° oven for 30 minutes or till a knife inserted near centers comes out clean. Cool 15 minutes. Remove loaves from pans.

Meanwhile, let pastry stand at room temperature 20 minutes. On a floured surface unfold pastry sheet. Roll into a 17x15-inch rectangle. With a fluted pastry wheel, cut eight ½-inch-wide strips off 1 short side of the rectangle. Cut the strips in half crosswise, forming sixteen 7½x½-inch strips. Set aside. Cut remaining pastry in half

lengthwise, then in half crosswise, forming four 7½x6½-inch rectangles.

Place *one* of the baked loaves in a shallow baking pan. Top with *one* pastry rectangle, tucking edges of pastry under loaf about ½ inch. Combine egg yolk and 1 tablespoon *water;* brush some over pastry.

Arrange *two* of the reserved pastry strips diagonally across top of loaf. Arrange *two* more strips in opposite direction, forming a diamond pattern. Tuck strips under bottom. Repeat with the remaining loaves, pastry rectangles, egg mixture, and pastry strips. Brush loaves with remaining egg mixture. Seal, label, and freeze up to 3 months.

To serve: Thaw loaves overnight in the refrigerator. Bake in a 425° oven for 20 to 25 minutes or till golden. Serve warm. Cut each loaf into 4 slices. Makes 4 loaves, 16 servings total.

Nutrition information per serving: 110 cal., 7 g pro., 6 g carbo., 6 g fat, 112 mg chol., 119 mg sodium. U.S. RDA: 53% vit. A, 14% riboflavin, 10% iron.

STRIPED SALMON 'N' PARSLEY ROUNDS

- 1 **8-ounce package cream cheese, softened**
- 1 **8-ounce container sour cream dip with chives**
- 1 **7¾-ounce can red salmon, drained and skin and bones removed**
- 1 **tablespoon diced pimiento**
- 1 **cup snipped parsley**
- ½ **cup sliced green onion**
- 1 **teaspoon dried dillweed**
- 1 **1-pound loaf unsliced whole wheat bread**
- ½ **teaspoon unflavored gelatin**
- ¾ **cup mayonnaise**
- ½ **cup whipping cream**
- **Whole pimientos**
- **Fresh chives *or* green onion tops**
- **Ripe olives, slivered**

Beat cream cheese and dip till smooth; divide in half. Stir salmon and diced pimiento into *half* of the mixture. Cover and chill for 30 minutes or till spreadable. Stir parsley, green onion, and dillweed into remaining mixture.

Trim crusts from bread loaf. Slice loaf lengthwise into ½-inch-wide slices. Using a rolling pin, gently flatten each slice; cover and set aside.

Spread salmon mixture over *half* of the bread slices. Spread parsley mixture over remaining bread slices. Cut slices lengthwise into 3 strips.

On 1 end of a large baking sheet, with salmon mixture toward the inside, wrap *half* of the salmon strips, end to end, into 1 pinwheel. Starting at outer end of salmon strips, with parsley mixture toward the inside, wrap *half* of the parsley strips, end to end, around the salmon strips (see photo, below). Repeat

for second round on the same baking sheet with the remaining strips, *except* begin with parsley strips and end with salmon strips. Cover. Freeze till firm. Remove from baking sheet. Wrap in moisture- and vaporproof wrap. Seal, label, and freeze up to 1 month.

To serve: The day before serving, remove rounds from freezer. In a small saucepan add gelatin to 2 tablespoons *cold water.* Let stand 5 minutes. Cook and stir over low heat till gelatin is dissolved. Remove from heat; cool slightly. Combine mayonnaise and cream. Stir in gelatin mixture.

Place rounds on a wire rack over waxed paper. Spoon *half* of the mayonnaise mixture over *each* round, allowing mixture to drip down over sides and spreading to coat evenly.

For garnish, use hors d'oeuvre or small cookie cutters to cut leaves from whole pimientos. Use chives for stems. Place olive slivers in centers of leaves. Chill 1 hour or till gelatin is set. Cover with plastic wrap. Chill overnight. Cut into thin wedges to serve. Makes 2 rounds, 16 to 20 servings each.

Nutrition information per serving: 136 cal., 4 g pro., 8 g carbo., 10 g fat, 21 mg chol., 160 mg sodium.

CREAM-FILLED HAZELNUT CAKE

- ¼ cup all-purpose flour
- ½ teaspoon baking powder
- ¼ teaspoon ground cinnamon
- ½ cup butter *or* margarine
- ⅔ cup sugar
- 3 egg yolks
- 1 cup finely ground toasted hazelnuts (filberts), walnuts, *or* pecans
- 3 egg whites
- 1½ cups whipping cream
- ¼ cup sugar
- 2 tablespoons finely ground toasted hazelnuts (filberts), walnuts, *or* pecans

Grease bottom of an 8x1½-inch round baking pan. Line bottom with waxed paper; grease paper. Set aside.

Combine the flour, baking powder, and cinnamon. Beat butter for 30 seconds. Add the ⅔ cup sugar; beat till fluffy. Beat in egg yolks. Beat in flour mixture. Stir in ½ *cup* of the nuts.

Wash beaters and bowl well. Beat egg whites till stiff peaks form (tips stand straight). Fold into nut mixture. Transfer to the prepared pan.

Bake in a 350° oven 30 to 35 minutes or till a wooden toothpick inserted near center comes out clean. Cool on rack 10 minutes. Remove from pan; remove waxed paper. Cool completely.

For easier slicing, chill cake. Use a long serrated knife to split cake horizontally into 2 layers. Transfer 1 layer to a freezer-proof plate.

Beat cream and ¼ cup sugar till stiff peaks form. Reserve *half* of the cream mixture (about 1½ cups). Fold ½ cup nuts into remaining mixture; spread atop cake layer on plate. Top with remaining cake layer. Spread reserved cream over top and sides of cake.

Out of paper, cut patterns such as six 2x1-inch diamonds; place on top of cake. Sprinkle the 2 tablespoons nuts over cake to form a design. Carefully remove paper patterns.

Place uncovered cake on plate in freezer for 30 to 45 minutes or till cream frosting is frozen. Wrap cake in moisture- and vaporproof wrap. Seal well, label, and freeze up to 2 weeks.

To serve: Place in refrigerator several hours or till thawed. Serves 16.

Nutrition information per serving: 302 cal., 3 g pro., 19 g carbo., 24 g fat, 129 mg chol., 117 mg sodium. U.S. RDA: 16% vit. A.

LIQUEUR-LACED FRUITCAKES

- 2 cups all-purpose flour
- 1 cup whole wheat flour
- 1 teaspoon baking powder
- 1 cup orange juice
- ¼ cup light corn syrup
- 1 teaspoon lemon extract
- 24 ounces whole candied red *or* green cherries (4 cups)
- 1 pound diced mixed candied fruits and peels (2½ cups)
- 2 cups raisins
- 1 cup chopped pecans
- 1 cup butter *or* margarine
- 1 cup packed brown sugar
- 4 eggs
- Amaretto, orange liqueur, crème de cacao, crème de cassis, *or* other desired liqueur *or* brandy
- Liqueur Glaze
- Pecan halves *or* candied red *or* green cherry halves

Grease and flour a 10-inch fluted tube pan and twelve 2¾-inch fluted muffin cups. Set aside.

Combine all-purpose flour, whole wheat flour, and baking powder. Combine orange juice, corn syrup, and lemon extract. Combine candied cherries, fruits and peels, raisins, and chopped pecans. Set aside.

Beat butter or margarine for 30 seconds. Add brown sugar; beat till fluffy. Add eggs, one at a time, beating well after each addition. Add flour mixture and orange juice mixture alternately to beaten mixture, beating after each addition just till combined. Fold fruit mixture into batter.

Place about ¼ cup batter in *each* prepared muffin cup. Place remaining batter in prepared tube pan. Bake in a 300° oven 30 to 40 minutes for muffin pan and 70 minutes for tube pan or till toothpick inserted near centers comes out clean. Cool in muffin pan for 10 minutes and in tube pan for 15 minutes; remove from pans. Cool.

Cut cheesecloth into pieces large enough to wrap around cakes. Moisten cheesecloth pieces with desired liqueur or brandy. Wrap cakes in moistened cheesecloth. Wrap in foil or clear plastic wrap, or place in airtight containers.

Store at least 1 week in refrigerator. (Store 3 to 4 weeks for a more blended flavor, remoistening cheese-cloth weekly with ⅓ *cup* liqueur or brandy for the large cake and ½ *cup* total liqueur for minicakes.)

To serve: Unwrap cakes. Drizzle with Liqueur Glaze. Top with pecan halves or candied cherry halves. Makes 1 large cake and 12 minicakes, about 36 servings total.

Liqueur Glaze: Combine 1 cup sifted *powdered sugar* and 2 to 4 tablespoons *amaretto, orange liqueur, crème de cacao, crème de cassis,* or desired *liqueur* or *brandy*. Makes about ⅓ cup.

Nutrition information per serving: 280 cal., 3 g pro., 51 g carbo., 8 g fat, 44 mg chol., 94 mg sodium.

GLAZED FINGER TARTS

- 1 package 1-layer-size white cake mix
- ½ cup cherry-vanilla yogurt
- 1 egg
- ½ cup currant jelly *or* peach preserves
- Candied red and green cherries, halved and cut into thin petals, *or* green gumdrops and red cinnamon candies (optional)

Grease and lightly flour 15 sandbakelser molds. Place on a baking sheet.

For batter, combine cake mix, yogurt, and egg. Fill molds about ⅔ full with batter (about 2 tablespoons batter in each mold).

Bake in a 350° oven for 15 to 18 minutes or till a wooden toothpick inserted near the centers comes out clean. Cool on wire rack for 10 minutes. Remove tarts from molds; cool completely on the rack.

In a small saucepan combine jelly or preserves and 1 tablespoon *water*. Heat and stir till melted. Strain the preserves through a small sieve. Brush over tart tops and sides.

If desired, place about 8 cherry petals on top of each tart, forming a flower. (Or, roll out gumdrops on a sugared surface; cut out holly leaves with an hors d'oeuvre or small cookie cutter. Arrange on top of tarts with cinnamon candies.) Let stand till jelly or preserves set. Transfer to a freezer container. Seal, label, and freeze up to 3 months.

To serve: Thaw at room temperature for 2 hours. Makes 15 tarts.

Nutrition information per tart: 114 cal., 2 g pro., 22 g carbo., 2 g fat, 19 mg chol., 124 mg sodium.

CHOCOLATE-PRALINE PUMPKIN PIE

Pastry for Single-Crust Pie
1 16-ounce can pumpkin
¾ cup sugar
1 teaspoon pumpkin pie spice
3 eggs
1 5-ounce can evaporated milk
½ cup milk
½ cup semisweet chocolate pieces
Whipped cream
Praline Topper

Prepare and roll out pastry. Line a 9-inch pie plate. Trim to ½ inch beyond edge. Flute edge high; *do not prick.*

Combine the pumpkin, sugar, and pumpkin pie spice. Add eggs; beat till combined. Stir in evaporated milk and milk. Transfer *½ cup* of the pumpkin mixture to a small heavy saucepan. Pour the remaining pumpkin mixture into prepared pastry.

Add chocolate pieces to pumpkin mixture in the saucepan. Cook and stir over low heat till melted. Spoon chocolate-pumpkin mixture over pumpkin filling in pastry. Gently swirl with a thin spatula to marble.

Cover the edge of the pie with foil. Bake in a 375° oven for 25 minutes. Remove foil; bake for 25 to 30 minutes more or till a knife inserted near center comes out clean. Cool on a wire rack. Cover with an inverted 10-inch paper plate. Wrap in moisture- and vaporproof wrap. Seal, label, and freeze for up to 3 months.

To serve: Thaw pie, loosely covered, for 24 hours in the refrigerator. Dollop with whipped cream and sprinkle with Praline Topper. Serves 8.

Pastry for Single-Crust Pie: Combine 1¼ cups *all-purpose flour* and ¼ teaspoon *salt.* Cut in ⅓ cup *shortening* till pieces resemble small peas. Sprinkle 1 tablespoon *cold water* over part of mixture; gently toss with a fork. Push to side of bowl. Repeat till all is moistened (use 3 to 4 tablespoons cold water). On a floured surface flatten dough with hands. Roll into a 12-inch circle.

Praline Topper: In a heavy small skillet stir together ½ cup coarsely chopped *pecans*, ¼ cup *sugar*, and 1 tablespoon *butter* or *margarine.* Cook and stir over medium heat 6 to 8 minutes or till sugar melts and turns a rich brown

color. Spread mixture on a buttered baking sheet or foil; separate into clusters. Cool. Break clusters into small chunks. Store in an airtight container at room temperature up to 1 month.

Nutrition information per serving: 442 cal., 8 g pro., 55 g carbo., 23 g fat, 115 mg chol., 139 mg sodium. U.S. RDA: 255% vit. A, 15% thiamine, 16% riboflavin, 10% calcium, 14% iron, and 16% phosphorus.

PUFFED COCONUT PASTRY DIAMONDS

½ of a 17½-ounce package
(1 sheet) frozen puff pastry
1 egg yolk
¼ cup flaked coconut
2 teaspoons brown sugar
1 egg white

Let frozen pastry stand at room temperature for 20 minutes. Meanwhile, stir together egg yolk, coconut, and sugar. Set aside.

On a lightly floured surface unfold pastry. Use a fluted pastry wheel to trim five ¼-inch-wide strips off 1 side of the pastry square; set strips aside. Using a cookie cutter or cardboard cutout as a guide, cut remaining dough into twelve 3½x2½-inch diamonds.

Place *six* of the diamonds in a shallow ungreased baking pan; spoon about *1 teaspoon* of the coconut mixture atop *each.* Combine the egg white and 1 tablespoon *water;* brush some around edges of pastry diamonds. Top with remaining pastry diamonds. Press together gently. Brush tops with more egg-white mixture.

Place the reserved pastry strips around top outside edges of diamonds; trim to fit. If desired, cut additional strips or decorative shapes from the remaining pastry scraps; brush with any remaining egg-white mixture and place on top crust. Wrap diamonds in moisture- and vaporproof wrap. Seal, label, and freeze up to 3 months.

To serve: Unwrap the diamonds. Bake, uncovered, in a 400° oven about 15 minutes or till golden. Serve warm. Makes 6 servings.

Nutrition information per serving: 122 cal., 2 g pro., 11 g carbo., 8 g fat, 45 mg chol., 118 mg sodium.

HOLIDAY CRANBERRY TORTE

½ of a 10¾-ounce frozen loaf
pound cake, thawed
1 14-ounce can (1¼ cups)
***sweetened condensed* milk**
1 10-ounce package frozen
cranberry-orange relish, thawed
2 cups whipping cream
Whipped cream
Chocolate Decorations

Line bottom of a 9-inch springform pan with a circle of waxed paper. Set aside.

Thinly trim off ends of cake. Cut cake into fifteen ¼-inch-thick slices. Trim the top crust off *eight* slices; cut in half crosswise. Arrange, trimmed side down, around sides of prepared pan. Cut the remaining cake slices in half lengthwise and arrange, spoke fashion, around bottom of pan so they overlap slightly near center of pan. Set aside.

Stir together condensed milk and cranberry-orange relish. Beat 2 cups cream till stiff peaks form; fold into relish mixture. Turn into pan. Wrap in moisture- and vaporproof wrap. Seal, label, and freeze up to 2 months.

To serve: Let stand at room temperature 20 minutes. Trim cake on sides even with top. Remove sides of springform pan. Invert onto serving platter. Peel off waxed paper. Pipe on whipped cream; top with Chocolate Decorations. Makes 12 to 16 servings.

Chocolate Decorations: Cook and stir 3 ounces of coarsely chopped *chocolate-flavored confectioners' coating* over low heat till it begins to melt. Remove from heat; stir till smooth.

Line a baking sheet with waxed paper. Fit a decorating bag with a No. 5 writing tip. When the coating is cool enough to handle, spoon it into bag.

For each decoration, on lined baking sheet pipe a tall, narrow triangle about 2½ inches high. Then pipe a wider upside-down triangle, about 1½ inches high, over first triangle, having bottom points meet. Then pipe a short, wide triangle, about 1 inch high, on top of second triangle, having all bottom points meet. Chill till firm.

Carefully remove decorations from waxed paper. Transfer to a freezer container. Seal, label, and freeze.

Nutrition information per serving: 383 cal., 5 g pro., 42 g carbo., 22 g fat, 92 mg chol., 117 mg sodium. U.S. RDA: 17% vit. A, 14% riboflavin, 15% calcium, 15% phosphorus.

RICH YEAST DOUGH

6½ cups all-purpose flour
2 packages active dry yeast
1½ cups milk
¾ cup butter *or* margarine
½ cup packed brown sugar
½ teaspoon salt
5 eggs

Combine *3 cups* of the flour and yeast. Heat and stir milk, butter, sugar, and salt just till warm (115° to 120°) and butter is almost melted. Add to flour mixture; add eggs. Beat with an electric mixer on low speed for ½ minute. Beat on high speed 3 minutes. Stir in enough remaining flour to make a soft dough.

Place in a lightly greased bowl. Turn once to grease surface. Cover; let rise in warm place till double (1 to 1½ hours). Stir dough down (it will be sticky). Divide into thirds.

To chill, place each portion in a plastic bag; tie, leaving ample space for expansion. Chill for 2 to 24 hours. To freeze, wrap each portion in moisture- and vaporproof wrap. Seal, label, and freeze up to 3 months. To use, thaw dough overnight in the refrigerator.

STAR-BURST BREAD WITH HERB BUTTER

⅓ recipe Rich Yeast Dough
(see recipe, above)
1 egg yolk
1 tablespoon milk
1 teaspoon caraway seed
1 teaspoon fennel seed
1 teaspoon aniseed
½ cup butter *or* margarine,
softened

Punch down Rich Yeast Dough. Divide into 8 pieces. On a lightly floured surface roll pieces into 9-inch-long ropes.

Coil 1 rope; place in center of a lightly greased baking sheet. Moisten end of another rope; press into center of coil. Repeat with remaining ropes, arranging spoke fashion. Coil outer end of each rope (see photo, page 162). Curve ropes slightly. Cover; let rise in a warm place till double (30 to 45 minutes).

Combine egg yolk and milk; brush onto dough. Top with ½ *teaspoon* of *each* seed. Bake in a 375° oven about 20 minutes, covering with foil the last 5 minutes to prevent overbrowning. Remove; cool. Crush remaining seeds; add to butter. Serve with bread. Serves 12.

To freeze: Wrap in moisture- and vaporproof wrap. Seal, label, and freeze up to 3 months. Thaw at room temperature for 4 to 6 hours.

Nutrition information per serving: 222 cal., 4 g pro., 21 g carbo., 14 g fat, 94 mg chol., 165 mg sodium. U.S. RDA: 10% vit. A, 11% thiamine.

FESTIVE PINWHEEL ROLLS

⅓ recipe Rich Yeast Dough
(see recipe, left)
8 teaspoons butter *or* margarine,
softened
¼ cup red raspberry, apricot, *or*
cherry preserves, *or* blackberry
jam
Milk
Finely chopped walnuts *or* pecans

Punch down Rich Yeast Dough. Divide in half. Cover; chill *half* of the dough. On a lightly floured surface roll remaining dough into a 15x12½-inch rectangle. Cut rolled dough into three 12½x5-inch rectangles. Spread 1 rectangle with *2 teaspoons* of the butter. Top with another rectangle. Repeat with another *2 teaspoons* of the butter and last dough rectangle.

Cut rectangle in half lengthwise, then cut crosswise into fifths to make ten 2½-inch squares. Place squares 1 inch apart on a greased baking sheet.

For each square, cut 1-inch slits from the center to *each* corner. Spoon about ½ *teaspoon* preserves or jam into center. Fold *every other point* to center to form a pinwheel. Pinch points in center together (see photo, page 163).

Brush centers with milk. Sprinkle nuts atop; press in centers to seal. Cover; let rise in a warm place 20 minutes. Repeat with remaining dough portion.

Gently press closed the tips of any rolls that have opened during rising. Bake in a 375° oven about 12 minutes or till golden. Cool on a wire rack. If desired, spoon additional preserves or jam and nuts onto centers. Makes 20.

To freeze: Place baked rolls in a moisture- and vaporproof freezer container. Seal, label, and freeze up to 3 months. Thaw at room temperature.

Nutrition information per roll: 111 cal., 2 g pro., 15 g carbo., 5 g fat, 34 mg chol., 67 mg sodium.

ALMOND BREAD CROWN

⅓ recipe Rich Yeast Dough
(see recipe, left)
½ cup almond paste
¼ cup packed brown sugar
1 egg
¾ cup sifted powdered sugar
Milk
¼ cup sliced almonds, coarsely
chopped

Punch down Rich Yeast Dough. Reserve *one-fourth* of the dough. On a lightly floured surface roll remaining dough into an 18x10-inch rectangle.

Crumble almond paste into a small mixer bowl; add brown sugar and egg. Beat till combined. Spread the almond mixture over dough rectangle to within ½ inch of edges. Roll up from a long side. Moisten and pinch seam to seal.

Roll a 6x3-inch piece of cardboard into a tube 3 inches high and 1½ inches in diameter; wrap with foil. Grease the outside of the foil. Stand the tube in the center of a greased 9x1½-inch round baking pan. Coil dough roll, seam side down, around tube in pan, pinching ends of dough together to seal.

Roll reserved dough into a 24-inch rope. Lay around the top outside edge of dough in pan; moisten and pinch ends together to seal. With scissors, snip about halfway through dough rope at 1-inch intervals (see photo, page 163). Cover; let rise in a warm place till nearly double (about 40 minutes).

Bake in a 350° oven for 20 minutes; remove tube. Bake for 15 to 20 minutes more or till bread sounds hollow when tapped. Cover the bread with foil during the last 10 minutes of baking to prevent overbrowning. Remove bread from pan. Cool on a wire rack.

For glaze, combine powdered sugar and milk (about 3 teaspoons) to make a glaze of drizzling consistency. Spoon over bread. Sprinkle with almonds. Makes 12 servings.

To freeze: Omit glaze. Wrap the baked bread in moisture- and vaporproof wrap. Seal, label, and freeze up to 6 months. Thaw overnight in refrigerator. To serve, glaze as directed above.

Nutrition information per serving: 248 cal., 6 g pro., 36 g carbo., 9 g fat, 73 mg chol., 94 mg sodium. U.S. RDA: 13% thiamine, 15% riboflavin, 11% iron, 11% phosphorus.

CRACKLED CRESCENTS

⅓ **recipe Festive Cookie Dough (see recipe, page 164)**
1 **6-ounce package (1 cup) miniature semisweet chocolate pieces**
1 **tablespoon shortening**
Chopped coconut, pearl sugar, finely chopped pistachio nuts, *or* finely chopped semisweet chocolate

If frozen, thaw Festive Cookie Dough in the refrigerator overnight. Or, place the dough in a microwave-safe mixing bowl; cover with waxed paper. Microcook on 10% power (low) about 5 minutes or till thawed.

If necessary, let dough stand at room temperature for 20 minutes for easier handling. Stir in ½ *cup* of the chocolate pieces. Shape dough into 1-inch balls. Roll into logs about 2 inches long. Place on an ungreased cookie sheet. Bend and pinch ends to form crescents (see photo, below).

Bake in a 375° oven for 8 to 10

minutes or till edges are firm and bottoms light brown. Cool on a wire rack.

Line a baking sheet with waxed paper; set aside. Heat and stir remaining chocolate pieces and shortening over low heat till melted. Remove from heat. Dip 1 end of each cookie into the melted chocolate mixture. Roll end in coconut, pearl sugar, pistachio nuts, or chopped chocolate. Place dipped cookies on lined cookie sheet; chill till chocolate is set. Makes about 36 cookies.

Nutrition information per cookie: 85 cal., 1 g pro., 11 g carbo., 5 g fat, 9 mg chol., 27 mg sodium.

LITTLE SNOW PEOPLE

⅓ **recipe Festive Cookie Dough (see recipe, page 164)**
Miniature semisweet chocolate pieces
Red cinnamon candies
¾ **cup sifted powdered sugar**
Milk *or* light cream
Several drops green food coloring
Milk chocolate kisses *or* bite-size chocolate-covered peanut butter cups, halved
Sifted powdered sugar

If frozen, thaw Festive Cookie Dough in the refrigerator overnight. For each snow person, shape dough into 3 balls: one 1-inch ball, one ¾-inch ball, and one ½-inch ball. Place on an ungreased cookie sheet in decreasing sizes with sides touching. Press together slightly.

Press 2 chocolate pieces in the smallest ball for eyes. Press 1 red cinnamon candy in the middle ball and 2 cinnamon candies in the largest ball for buttons (see photo, below).

Bake in a 325° oven about 18 minutes or till edges are firm and bottoms are light golden brown. Cool 1 minute; carefully transfer to a wire rack; cool.

To make icing of piping consistency, combine the ¾ cup powdered sugar and 2 to 3 teaspoons milk. Stir in food coloring. To make hats, attach halved kisses or peanut butter cups to heads with icing. With decorating bag, writing or star tip, and remaining icing, pipe bow ties, belts, scarves, or stocking caps. Lightly sprinkle snow people with powdered sugar. Makes about 16.

Nutrition information per cookie: 169 cal., 2 g pro., 25 g carbo., 8 g fat, 22 mg chol., 66 mg sodium.

ZIGZAG COOKIE SHAPES

Reroll dough scraps on a surface dusted with equal parts flour and powdered sugar. It makes the cookies more tender than using flour alone—

⅓ **recipe Festive Cookie Dough (see recipe, page 164)**
1 **cup sifted powdered sugar**
¼ **teaspoon vanilla**
Milk
Several drops red food coloring
Several drops green food coloring

If frozen, thaw Festive Cookie Dough in the refrigerator overnight. Or, place the dough in a microwave-safe mixing bowl; cover with waxed paper. Microcook on 10% power (low) about 5 minutes or till thawed.

On a lightly floured surface or pastry cloth roll the chilled or thawed dough ⅛ inch thick. Cut with a 2½-inch fluted round or other shaped cookie cutter. Place on an ungreased cookie sheet (see photo, below).

Bake in a 375° oven for 6 to 8 minutes or till edges are firm and bottoms are light golden brown. Remove and cool on a wire rack.

To make a glaze of piping consistency, combine powdered sugar, vanilla, and 3 to 4 teaspoons milk. Divide glaze in half. To *one* of the halves, add red food coloring; mix well. To remaining half, add green food coloring; mix well. With a decorating bag and writing tip, pipe both pink and green icing over cookies in a random zigzag fashion. Makes about 36 cookies.

Nutrition information per cookie: 63 cal., 1 g pro., 10 g carbo., 3 g fat, 9 mg chol., 27 mg sodium.

DECEMBER

HOLIDAY FAVORITES UPDATED

MORE HEALTHFUL, EASIER TO FIX

By Lynn Hoppe and Terri Pauser Wolf

CHRISTMAS DINNER

Merry up the most joyful of feasts with this
simplified, more nutritious version.

CRANBERRY-ORANGE SALAD

Brown the *Garlic-Chive Rolls* while you carve the roasted *Mushroom-Capped Turkey Breast.* Skip the gravy and serve a mushroom sauce with half the fat.

For a fix-and-forget (but not forgotten!) side dish, try *Two-Grain Apple Pilaf.* It provides 4 grams of fiber. A bed of fresh spinach with crisp jicama supplies extra vitamins and fiber to *Cranberry-Orange Salad.* Keep the meal simple with a steamed vegetable.

Come dessert, you'll be ready to savor lightened *Pumpkin-Chiffon Pie.*

Photographs: Ron Crofoot
Food stylist: Judy Tills

172

GARLIC-CHIVE ROLLS

MUSHROOM-CAPPED TURKEY BREAST

PUMPKIN-CHIFFON PIE

TWO-GRAIN APPLE PILAF

HOLIDAY APPETIZERS

MORE HEALTHFUL, EASIER TO FIX

'Tis the season for good food, drink, and togetherness. Add to the spirit with trouble-free party fare that has a wellness bonus—lower in sodium, fat, and cholesterol plus more fiber and vitamins.

SPICY WASSAIL AND APPLE EGGNOG

Toast to the health of all with low-fat, low-cholesterol eggnog and 38-calorie wassail!

BOSTON BROWN BREAD CANAPÉS

These glistening appetizer treats start with an egg-yolk-free quick bread.

SALMON ZUCCHINI PÂTÉ   Celebrate with a full-flavored, low-cholesterol pâté.

QUICHE WITH POTATO CRUST
Surprise! The crust has no fat or sodium.

PEPPERED SMOKY CHEESE DIP

Classic cheese logs provide the inspiration for this dip made from reduced-calorie cream cheese enriched with pureed carrots.

HOLIDAY MAIN DISHES

MORE HEALTHFUL, EASIER TO FIX

You expect holiday entrées to look special, taste special. These do! You search for entrées that are good and healthful. These are!

SPIRITED APPLE CHICKEN BREASTS

Poach the chicken in wine—the flavor is great, but the alcohol (and calories!) cooks away.

OYSTER STEW WITH VEGETABLES

This traditional soup is brightened with mixed vegetables, and abundantly rich without cream.

CAJUN PORK PINWHEELS
You can have it all—juicy, moist meat that's lean, too.

LEMON-CURRANT GLAZED HAM
Dress up a low-sodium, boneless ham in holiday colors.

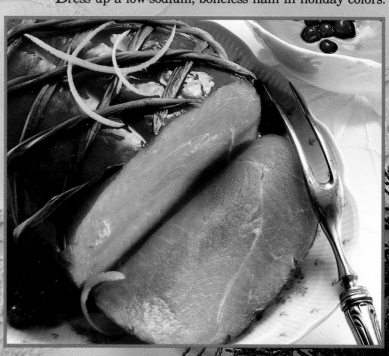

BEEF WITH LIGHT YORKSHIRE PUDDING
Popoverlike Yorkshire pudding fulfills your family's expectations. Shhh. Don't tell—this version is good for them!

HOLIDAY DESSERTS

MORE HEALTHFUL, EASIER TO FIX

Yes, you can have Christmas goodies without the guilt! These Christmas-present recipes from holidays past cut the surplus calories and fat and the extra work.

STAR-BURST FRUIT TRIFLE
This dessert offers the ease of convenience foods— frozen fruit and low-calorie pudding mix.

HONEY COOKIES AND MERINGUE STARS
Compared to sugar cookies, Honey Cookies shine in the calorie, sodium, and cholesterol departments. Meringue Stars are just slightly more fattening than air.

YULETIDE LOG Limit fat and sodium in your holiday indulging with this cake roll.

SWEET POTATO CHEESECAKE
Enjoy rich-tasting cheesecake with a third fewer calories.

FESTIVE FRUITCAKE

Laden with fruit, nuts, and spices, but with one difference: dried fruit bits replace sugary candied fruit.

Christmas Dinner

MUSHROOM-CAPPED TURKEY BREAST

- 1 cup chopped fresh mushrooms
- ¼ cup sliced green onion
- ¼ cup dry sherry
- ¼ teaspoon salt
- ¼ teaspoon dried basil, crushed
- ¾ cup soft bread crumbs (1 slice)
- 1 2½- to 3-pound turkey breast half with bone
- 2 teaspoons cooking oil
- ¼ teaspoon paprika
- ½ cup sliced fresh mushrooms
- 1 tablespoon sliced green onion
- 1 tablespoon margarine or butter
- 1 tablespoon cornstarch
- ½ cup chicken broth
- ½ cup skim milk

In a skillet cook 1 cup chopped mushrooms, ¼ cup green onion, sherry, salt, and basil over medium-high heat for 3 to 4 minutes or till liquid has evaporated. Stir in bread crumbs. Remove from heat. Set aside.

Use a sharp knife to cut along turkey bone; discard bone. Rinse turkey. Pat dry. Pull skin away, leaving it attached along one edge. Spread mushroom mixture over meat. Replace skin. Secure with wooden toothpicks. Combine oil and paprika. Brush over skin.

Place turkey, skin side up, on a rack in a 13x9x2-inch baking pan. Cover with foil. Insert a meat thermometer through foil into the center of turkey. Roast in a 325° oven for 1¾ to 2 hours or till thermometer registers 170°, uncovering after 1½ hours. Let stand for 10 minutes before slicing.

For sauce, cook ½ cup mushrooms and 1 tablespoon onion in hot margarine or butter till liquid has evaporated. Stir in cornstarch. Add chicken broth and milk. Cook and stir till thickened and bubbly. Cook 2 minutes more. Pass sauce with turkey. Makes 6 servings.

Microwave directions: In a 4-cup microwave-safe measure micro-cook 1 cup chopped mushrooms, ¼ cup green onion, sherry, salt, and basil, uncovered, on 100% power (high) for 8 minutes or till liquid has evaporated.

Prepare turkey as directed. Place turkey, skin side up, on rack in a 12x7½x2-inch microwave-safe baking dish. Cover with waxed paper. Cook on high for 25 to 35 minutes or till a thermometer registers 165°, giving the dish a half-turn 3 times. If necessary, shield with foil. Let stand, covered, 10 minutes or till thermometer registers 170°.

For sauce, in a 2-cup microwave-safe measure cook ½ cup mushrooms, 1 tablespoon onion, and margarine or butter, uncovered, on high for 1½ to 2 minutes. Stir in cornstarch. Add chicken broth and milk. Cook, uncovered, on high for 2 to 3 minutes or till bubbly. Pass sauce with turkey.

Nutrition information per serving: 250 cal., 39 g pro., 8 g carbo., 5 g fat, 103 mg chol., 266 mg sodium. U.S. RDA: 17% riboflavin, 52% niacin, 14% iron, 33% phosphorus.

TWO-GRAIN APPLE PILAF

Look for fiber-rich wheat berries (unpolished whole wheat kernels) at a health-food store—

- 2½ cups water
- 1 teaspoon instant chicken bouillon granules
- ½ cup wheat berries
- ½ cup regular brown rice
- 1 tablespoon dried minced onion
- ½ teaspoon dried sage, crushed
- 2 apples or pears, cored and coarsely chopped
- 2 tablespoons snipped parsley

In a medium saucepan combine water and bouillon granules; bring to boiling. Stir in wheat berries, rice, onion, and sage. Return to boiling. Reduce heat. Cover and simmer about 45 minutes or till wheat berries and rice are tender.

Stir in apples or pears. Cover and simmer for 5 to 10 minutes more or till fruit is tender. Drain liquid, if necessary. Stir in parsley. Makes 6 servings.

Nutrition information per serving: 123 cal., 3 g pro., 27 g carbo., 1 g fat, 0 mg chol., 65 mg sodium, 4 g fiber.

CRANBERRY-ORANGE SALAD

We dubbed this a nifty variation on classic cranberry-orange relish—

- 2 cups cranberries
- ½ cup water
- ¼ cup sugar
- ½ pound torn fresh spinach (6 cups)
- 3 oranges, peeled and thinly sliced
- 8 ounces jicama or celery root, peeled and cut into thin strips (1 cup)
- ½ cup broken walnuts, toasted
- ¼ cup white wine vinegar
- 2 tablespoons walnut or salad oil
- 2 tablespoons honey

In a medium saucepan combine cranberries, water, and sugar. Bring to boiling, stirring to dissolve sugar. Gently boil, covered, about 2 minutes or just till cranberry skins pop. Transfer to a medium mixing bowl. Cover and chill. Drain, reserving *1 tablespoon* liquid.

On 6 salad plates arrange spinach, orange slices, jicama or celery root, cranberries, and walnuts.

For dressing, in a small mixing bowl combine reserved cranberry liquid, vinegar, oil, and honey. Cover and shake well. Drizzle over salads. Makes 6 servings.

Microwave directions: In a 1-quart microwave-safe casserole combine the cranberries, water, and sugar. Micro-cook, covered, on 100% power (high) for 3 to 5 minutes or till mixture bubbles and berries pop, stirring after 2 minutes. Continue as directed above.

Nutrition information per serving: 184 cal., 4 g pro., 28 g carbo., 8 g fat, 0 mg chol., 46 mg sodium. U.S. RDA: 77% vit. A, 77% vit. C, 10% calcium, 12% iron.

GARLIC-CHIVE ROLLS

Lessen hectic holiday-dinner preparation by making your rolls ahead and freezing them—

3¾ to 4¼ cups all-purpose flour
1 package quick-rising active dry yeast
1 cup skim milk
¼ cup sugar
¼ cup shortening
2 tablespoons dried snipped chives
½ teaspoon salt
½ teaspoon garlic powder
3 egg whites
Nonstick spray coating
Skim milk

In a large mixer bowl combine *2 cups* of the flour and yeast. In a medium saucepan heat the 1 cup milk, sugar, shortening, chives, salt, and garlic powder just till mixture is warm (115° to 120°) and shortening is almost melted, stirring constantly. Add milk mixture to flour mixture. Add egg whites. Beat with an electric mixer on low speed for ½ minute, scraping sides of bowl constantly. Beat on high speed for 3 minutes.

Using a spoon, stir in as much of the remaining flour as you can. On a lightly floured surface knead in enough of the remaining flour to make a moderately stiff dough that is smooth and elastic (6 to 8 minutes total). Shape into a ball. Place in a bowl. Cover and let rest in a warm place for 20 minutes.

Punch dough down. Divide into 18 portions. Cover. Let rest for 10 minutes. Spray 18 muffin cups with nonstick spray coating. Shape dough into desired rolls and place in muffin cups.* Cover. Let rise till nearly double (20 to 25 minutes).

Brush tops lightly with additional skim milk. Bake in a 375° oven for 10 minutes. *Do not brown.* Remove from pan. Cool on a wire rack. Wrap in moisture- and vaporproof wrap. Seal, label, and freeze.

To serve, partially uncover rolls. Let stand at room temperature about 10 minutes. Uncover completely. Bake on an ungreased baking sheet in a 400° oven for 8 to 10 minutes or till golden.

*To shape rolls: Shape each dough portion into a ball. Place 1 ball in each muffin cup. With a sharp knife, cut 1 slit across the top.

Or, halve each dough portion. Shape each half into a ball. Place two balls in each muffin cup.

Or, on a lightly floured surface roll each portion into a 10-inch rope. Tie in a loose knot. Place one knot, smooth side up, in each muffin cup.

Nutrition information per roll: 126 cal., 4 g pro., 21 g carbo., 3 g fat, 0 mg chol., 75 mg sodium.

PUMPKIN-CHIFFON PIE

We substituted skim milk and whipped dessert topping mix for the usual whipping cream found in chiffon pies. The result? A savings of 10 grams fat and 20 milligrams cholesterol per serving—

½ of a 15-ounce package folded refrigerated unbaked piecrusts (1 crust)
1 envelope unflavored gelatin
¾ cup water
2 tablespoons sugar
1 cup canned pumpkin
1½ teaspoons pumpkin pie spice
¼ teaspoon salt
2 egg whites
2 tablespoons sugar
1 1.4-ounce envelope whipped dessert topping mix
½ cup skim milk
Ground cinnamon

For crust, follow package directions to fit crust into a 9-inch pie plate. For decorative edge, make ¼-inch cuts at ½-inch intervals around the edge of the crust. Fold every other piece toward the center of the pie. Generously prick the bottom and sides of the crust with a fork. Bake in a 450° oven for 9 to 11 minutes or till golden. Cool.

For filling, in a small saucepan add gelatin to water. Let stand for 5 minutes. Stir in 2 tablespoons sugar. Cook and stir over low heat till sugar and gelatin dissolve. Cool.

In a large mixing bowl stir together pumpkin, pumpkin pie spice, and salt. Stir cooled gelatin mixture into pumpkin mixture. Chill in the freezer about 15 minutes or till slightly thickened, stirring occasionally. Remove from the freezer (gelatin mixture will continue to set).

In a small mixer bowl immediately begin beating egg whites with an electric mixer on medium speed till soft peaks form (tips curl). Gradually add the 2 tablespoons sugar, beating on high speed till stiff peaks form (tips stand straight). When gelatin mixture is partially set, fold in the stiff-beaten egg whites. Wash bowl and beaters.

In the same small mixer bowl prepare dessert topping according to package directions *except* use the ½ cup skim milk. Reserve ½ cup of the whipped topping for topping each serving and chill.

Fold remaining whipped topping into gelatin mixture. If necessary, chill filling till it mounds when spooned. Pile filling into prepared crust. Chill in the refrigerator at least 3 hours or till set.

Sprinkle cinnamon through a decorative stencil placed over pie. If necessary, stir reserved topping. Top each serving with topping. Makes 8 servings.

Nutrition information per serving: 198 cal., 3 g pro., 24 g carbo., 10 g fat, 0 mg chol., 319 mg sodium. U.S. RDA: 133% vit. A.

APPLE EGGNOG

Fat-free evaporated skim milk whipped to heavenly heights replaces the heavy cream in this eggnog—

- 2 **13-ounce cans (1⅔ cups each) evaporated skim milk**
- 2 **slightly beaten egg whites**
- 1 **beaten egg**
- ¼ **cup sugar**
- ½ **teaspoon ground cinnamon**
- 2¼ **cups apple juice, chilled**
- 1 **teaspoon vanilla**

Ice cubes
- 1 **recipe Poached Apple Slices**

Ground nutmeg

About 1¼ hours before serving, place ¾ cup of the evaporated skim milk in a small mixer bowl. Chill in the freezer about 30 minutes or till ice crystals form around the edge.

Meanwhile, in a medium saucepan combine egg whites, egg, sugar, cinnamon, and remaining evaporated skim milk. Cook over medium heat till slightly thickened, stirring constantly. *Do not boil.* Remove from heat. Transfer mixture to a 3-quart mixing bowl. Cover and chill for 15 minutes.

Meanwhile, beat the chilled evaporated milk from the freezer with an electric mixer on high speed about 3 minutes or till soft peaks form (tips curl). Set aside.

Stir apple juice and vanilla into egg mixture. Fold in whipped milk. Pour into a punch bowl. Place in a larger bowl or sink partially filled with ice. Let stand in ice for 30 minutes.

Top *each* serving with Poached Apple Slices. Sprinkle with ground nutmeg. Makes 16 (4-ounce) servings.

Poached Apple Slices: Core and thinly slice 1 medium *apple.* Place apple slices in a small skillet. Add enough *water* to cover. Bring to boiling. Reduce heat. Cover and simmer for 3 minutes. Remove from skillet. Drain well.

Nutrition information per serving: 76 cal., 4 g pro., 14 g carbo., 1 g fat, 19 mg chol., 65 mg sodium. U.S. RDA: 10% riboflavin, 14% calcium, 10% phosphorus.

SPICY WASSAIL

- 2 **32-ounce jars low-calorie cranberry juice cocktail**
- 2 **cups water**
- 1 **6-ounce can frozen pineapple-orange *or* orange juice concentrate, thawed**
- 12 **inches stick cinnamon**
- 3 **whole cloves**
- ½ **cup whiskey (optional)**

Orange slices
Stick cinnamon

In a large kettle or Dutch oven combine cranberry juice, water, juice concentrate, the 12 inches stick cinnamon, and cloves. Bring to boiling. Reduce heat. Cover and simmer for 10 minutes.

Remove cinnamon and cloves. Stir in whiskey, if desired. Ladle juice mixture into cups and serve with orange slices and additional stick cinnamon. Makes 20 (4½-ounce) servings.

Microwave directions: In a 4- or 4½-quart microwave-safe casserole combine cranberry juice, water, juice concentrate, the 12 inches stick cinnamon, and cloves. Micro-cook, uncovered, on 100% power (high) for 12 to 15 minutes or till flavors are blended. Remove spices and stir in whiskey, if desired. Serve as directed.

Nutrition information per serving: 38 cal., 0 g pro., 10 g carbo., 0 g fat, 0 mg chol., and 0 mg sodium. U.S. RDA: 42% vit. C.

BOSTON BROWN BREAD CANAPÉS

To get the interesting shapes, we baked our bread in round decorative tins—

- 1½ **cups whole wheat flour**
- 1¼ **cups all-purpose flour**
- ½ **cup yellow cornmeal**
- ½ **teaspoon baking powder**
- ½ **teaspoon baking soda**
- ¼ **teaspoon salt**
- 4 **egg whites**
- ½ **cup molasses**
- ⅓ **cup sugar**
- 2 **tablespoons cooking oil**
- 1¼ **cups skim milk**
- 4 **teaspoons vinegar**

Nonstick spray coating
Assorted fresh *or* dried fruit pieces and nuts
- 1 **recipe Orange Aspic**

In a large mixing bowl stir together whole wheat flour, all-purpose flour, cornmeal, baking powder, baking soda, and salt. Set aside.

In a large mixer bowl combine egg whites, molasses, sugar, and cooking oil. Beat with an electric mixer on high speed. Stir skim milk into vinegar. Add flour mixture and milk mixture alternately to molasses mixture, beating after each addition just till combined.

Spray two 8½x3-inch round decorative tins or two 7½x3½x2-inch loaf pans generously with nonstick spray coating. (If using decorative tins, seal one end of tin with 2 thicknesses of foil sprayed with nonstick spray coating. Close with the cap, being careful not to tear the foil.)

Turn *2 cups* molasses mixture into *each* pan. (If using decorative tins, seal other end with 2 thicknesses of foil sprayed with nonstick spray coating. Close with cap. Place horizontally on a baking sheet.)

Bake in a 350° oven for 55 to 60 minutes for decorative tins or till a long wooden toothpick inserted in centers comes out clean (45 to 50 minutes for loaf pans). Cool in pans for 10 minutes. Remove from pans. Cool on a wire rack. Wrap and store overnight.

Thinly slice loaves. (If desired, use cookie cutters to cut decorative shapes from the rectangular slices. Reserve leftover pieces of bread for another purpose.) Transfer slices to a baking sheet. Arrange the fruit and/or nuts on each slice. Slowly spoon partially set Orange Aspic over fruit. Chill 2 hours or till aspic is firm. Makes about 50 canapés.

Orange Aspic: In a small saucepan add 2 envelopes *unflavored gelatin* to ⅔ cup cold *orange juice.* Let stand 5 minutes to soften gelatin. Cook and stir over low heat till dissolved. Stir in ½ teaspoon finely shredded *orange peel* and 2 cups additional *orange juice.* Chill till mixture is partially set (consistency of unbeaten egg whites).

Nutrition information per canapé: 60 cal., 2 g pro., 11 g carbo., 1 g fat, 0 mg chol., 34 mg sodium.

SALMON ZUCCHINI PÂTÉ

We found foot-long Chinese green beans in an Oriental market. Cook them as you would regular green beans—

Nonstick spray coating
  4 ounces fresh *or* frozen salmon *or*
    other fish fillets
Boiling water
1½ teaspoons unflavored gelatin
  ¼ cup cold water
  1 4½-ounce can shrimp, drained
    and rinsed
  1 medium zucchini, shredded
    (1⅓ cups)
  1 8-ounce package Neufchâtel
    cheese, softened and cut up
  3 green onions, thinly sliced
  ⅓ cup plain low-fat yogurt
  2 tablespoons creamy buttermilk
    salad dressing
Cooked Chinese green beans *or*
    shredded zucchini (optional)
Salmon caviar (optional)
Sliced sweet potatoes, melba rounds,
    cocktail rye bread, sliced
    zucchini, *or* sliced turnip

Spray an 8-inch skillet with nonstick spray coating. Add fish. Add boiling water to almost cover. Simmer, covered, for 5 to 7 minutes or till fish flakes easily when tested with a fork. Drain.

To soften gelatin, in a small saucepan add gelatin to cold water. Let stand for 5 minutes. Cook and stir over low heat till gelatin is dissolved.

In a blender container or food processor bowl blend or process shrimp, covered, till chopped. Add cooked fish, gelatin mixture, the 1⅓ cups zucchini, cheese, green onions, yogurt, and dressing. Cover and blend till nearly smooth.

Spray a 3-cup decorative mold with nonstick spray coating. Spread fish mixture evenly in mold. Cover and chill about 6 hours or till firm.

To serve, unmold onto a plate lined with Chinese green beans or shredded zucchini, if desired. Garnish with salmon caviar, if desired. Serve with sweet potatoes or other vegetables or breads. Makes 2⅔ cups (40 servings).

Microwave directions: If fish is frozen, unwrap and place in a 10x6x2-inch microwave-safe baking dish. Cover with vented microwave-safe plastic wrap. Micro-cook on 30% power (medium-low) for 2 to 3 minutes or till thawed, turning fish over and separating after 1 minute. Rinse and pat dry.

Arrange fish in the dish. Cover with vented microwave-safe plastic wrap. Cook on 100% power (high) 1½ to 2 minutes or till fish flakes easily, rearranging fish and giving dish a half-turn once. Set aside. In a microwave-safe custard cup add gelatin to water. Let stand for 5 minutes. Cook on high for 30 to 40 seconds or till dissolved, stirring once. Continue as directed.

Nutrition information per tablespoon with 3 sweet potato slices: 58 cal., 3 g pro., 5 g carbo., 3 g fat, 14 mg chol., 52 mg sodium. U.S. RDA: 72% vit. A.

PEPPERED SMOKY CHEESE DIP

  5 8-inch flour tortillas
  1 8-ounce container reduced-
    calorie cream cheese, softened
  1 4½-ounce jar strained carrot
    baby food
  3 tablespoons sliced green onion
  2 tablespoons grated Parmesan
    cheese
  1 tablespoon plain low-fat yogurt
  ¼ teaspoon dry mustard
  ¼ teaspoon ground red pepper
  ⅛ teaspoon garlic powder
Several drops hickory seasoning
Carrot slice (optional)
Crisp-cooked halved brussels
    sprouts *or* other vegetable
    dippers, chilled

For tortilla wedges, stack tortillas. Cut whole stack into 8 wedges to make 40 wedges total. Spread evenly in a single layer on 2 baking sheets. Bake in a 375° oven for 10 to 15 minutes or till wedges are dry and crisp.

For dip, beat cream cheese with an electric mixer on medium speed 30 seconds. Add carrot, green onion, Parmesan cheese, yogurt, mustard, red pepper, garlic powder, and hickory seasoning. Beat till smooth. Cover and chill for 2 hours.

To serve, spoon dip onto a serving platter. If desired, sprinkle with additional red pepper. Use a canapé cutter to make cutout in carrot slice and place atop dip. Serve with tortilla wedges, brussels sprouts, or other vegetables. Makes 1½ cups (24 servings).

Nutrition information per tablespoon with 3 brussels sprouts: 109 cal., 5 g pro., 12 g carbo., 5 g fat, 15 mg chol., 114 mg sodium. U.S. RDA: 39% vit. A, 57% vit. C, 10% phosphorus.

QUICHE WITH POTATO CRUST

Egg whites stand in for some of the whole eggs in this cholesterol-trimmed broccoli filling—

Nonstick spray coating
  2 medium potatoes, thinly sliced
  1 10-ounce package frozen
    chopped broccoli, thawed
  ⅔ cup thinly sliced green onion
  1 2-ounce jar sliced pimiento
  4 egg whites
  1 egg
  ⅓ cup plain low-fat yogurt
  ¼ cup skim milk
1½ teaspoons snipped fresh basil *or*
    ½ teaspoon dried basil, crushed
  ⅛ teaspoon garlic powder
  ⅛ teaspoon pepper
Dash salt
  ½ cup shredded mozzarella cheese
    (2 ounces)
  ¼ cup grated Parmesan cheese
Fresh basil (optional)

Spray a 10-inch skillet with nonstick spray coating. In the skillet cook potatoes, covered, over medium-low heat for 10 to 15 minutes or till tender, turning occasionally. Remove from heat.

Spray a 9-inch quiche dish or pie plate with nonstick spray coating. Arrange potato slices over bottom and around sides of dish, overlapping potatoes to form a decorative edge.

In a medium saucepan cook broccoli and green onion in a small amount of water, covered, about 4 minutes or till just tender. Drain well. Reserve 1 pimiento strip for garnish. Drain and chop remaining pimiento.

In a medium mixing bowl stir together egg whites, egg, yogurt, milk, basil, garlic powder, pepper, and salt. Stir in the broccoli mixture, chopped pimiento, mozzarella cheese, and *2 tablespoons* of the Parmesan cheese. Turn into the prepared dish. Sprinkle with remaining Parmesan cheese.

Cover the dish edges with foil. Bake in a 375° oven for 10 minutes. Remove foil. Bake about 15 minutes more or till a knife inserted just off-center comes out clean. Let stand for 10 minutes before serving. Garnish with reserved pimiento and fresh basil, if desired. Makes 12 servings.

Nutrition information per serving: 67 cal., 6 g pro., 7 g carbo., 2 g fat, 28 mg chol., 112 mg sodium. U.S. RDA: 17% vit. C, 11% calcium.

SPIRITED APPLE CHICKEN BREASTS

Simply remove the skin from the halved chicken breasts and you eliminate 4 grams of fat and 10 milligrams of cholesterol per serving—

- 1 **14-ounce jar spiced apple rings**
- • *or* **one 16-ounce jar spiced crab apples**
- ½ **cup dry white wine**
- 1 **teaspoon dried minced onion**
- 1 **teaspoon instant chicken bouillon granules**
- 3 **whole medium chicken breasts (about 2¼ pounds total), skinned, boned, and halved lengthwise**
- 1 **16-ounce package frozen loose-pack French-style green beans**
- 2 **teaspoons margarine *or* butter**
- 1 **teaspoon cornstarch**

Drain apple rings or crab apples, reserving ¼ cup of the syrup. Cut crab apples or apple rings into quarters or halves. Set aside.

In a 10-inch skillet combine wine, onion, and bouillon granules. Rinse chicken. Pat dry. Add chicken breasts. Bring to boiling. Reduce heat. Cover and simmer 12 to 15 minutes or till chicken is tender. Use a slotted spoon to remove chicken, reserving cooking liquid. Cover chicken and keep warm.

Meanwhile, cook green beans according to the package directions. Drain. Add margarine, tossing to coat.

For sauce, boil cooking liquid vigorously, uncovered, about 3 minutes or till reduced to ⅓ cup. Pour reduced cooking liquid through a cheesecloth-lined sieve. Return to skillet.

In a small mixing bowl stir reserved apple syrup into cornstarch. Stir into liquid in skillet. Cook and stir till slightly thickened and bubbly. Cook and stir for 2 minutes more.

Arrange beans on serving platter. Place chicken on top of beans. Garnish with apple rings or crab apples. Spoon sauce over chicken. Makes 6 servings.

Microwave directions: In a 12x7½x2-inch microwave-safe baking dish, arrange the chicken breasts with thickest portions toward the outside of the dish. Cover with vented microwave-safe plastic wrap. Micro-cook on 100% power (high) for 6 to 8 minutes or till chicken is tender, giving the dish a half-turn once. Cover and keep warm.

In a 1½-quart microwave-safe casserole cook beans and 2 tablespoons *water*, covered, on high for 7 to 9 minutes or till crisp-tender. Drain beans. Toss with margarine.

In a 2-cup microwave-safe measure combine reserved syrup, wine, onion, bouillon granules, and *1 tablespoon* cornstarch. Cook, uncovered, on high 1½ to 2½ minutes or till thickened and bubbly, stirring every minute. Cook 30 seconds more. Serve as directed.

Nutrition information per serving: 256 cal., 28 g pro., 23 g carbo., 5 g fat, 72 mg chol., 143 mg sodium. U.S. RDA: 17% vit. C, 10% thiamine, 10% riboflavin, 60% niacin, and 23% phosphorus.

LEMON-CURRANT GLAZED HAM

We think sodium-reduced ham, available in most supermarkets, is a great convenience food. It's already cooked, and comes boneless for easy slicing—

- 1 **2- to 2½-pound sodium-reduced fully cooked boneless ham**
- ½ **cup red currant jelly**
- ¼ **cup dry red wine**
- 1 **tablespoon lemon juice**
- ¼ **cup chicken broth**
- 2 **teaspoons cornstarch**
- **Steamed green onion tops**
- **Orange peel cut into thin strips**
- **Fresh lingonberries (optional)**

Use a sharp knife to make diagonal cuts about ½ inch deep and 1 inch apart in the top of ham. Place ham on a rack in a shallow baking pan. Insert a meat thermometer in the center of the thickest portion of meat. Bake, uncovered, in a 325° oven for 1½ to 2 hours or till thermometer registers 140°.

Meanwhile, for glaze, in a small saucepan combine jelly, 2 *tablespoons* of the wine, and lemon juice. Cook and stir till jelly is melted. After ham has baked about 1¼ hours, brush with *half* of the glaze.

For sauce, in a small bowl stir together remaining wine, chicken broth, and cornstarch. Stir into remaining glaze in saucepan. Cook and stir till thickened and bubbly. Cook and stir for 2 minutes more.

Transfer ham to a serving platter. Garnish with green onion tops and orange peel in a crisscross pattern. Serve with lingonberries, if desired. Pass sauce. Makes 8 to 10 servings.

Microwave directions: Score ham as directed. Place ham, fat side down, in an 8x8x2-inch microwave-safe baking dish. Add ¼ cup *water*. Cover loosely with waxed paper. Micro-cook on 100% power (high) for 5 minutes. Cook on 50% power (medium) for 18 to 20 minutes or till heated through, shielding edges with foil if necessary to prevent overcooking. (Check your owner's manual to see if you can use foil in your oven.) Let stand while preparing glaze.

For glaze, in a small microwave-safe mixing bowl combine jelly, 2 *tablespoons* of the wine, and lemon juice. Cook, uncovered, on high for 1 to 2 minutes or till jelly is melted. Brush ham with *half* of the glaze.

For sauce, in a 2-cup microwave-safe measure stir together remaining wine, chicken broth, and *1 tablespoon* cornstarch. Stir in remaining glaze. Cook, uncovered, on high for 1 to 2 minutes or till thickened and bubbly, stirring every minute.

Transfer ham to a serving platter. Garnish as directed and pass sauce.

Nutrition information per serving: 193 cal., 22 g pro., 17 g carbo., 5 g fat, 53 mg chol., 930 mg sodium. U.S. RDA: 70% thiamine, 15% riboflavin, 28% niacin, 25% phosphorus.

OYSTER STEW WITH VEGETABLES

Nutrition tidbit: Oysters, like other fish and seafood, have omega-3 fatty acids that can lower blood cholesterol levels—

- ½ of 16-ounce package frozen mixed broccoli, cauliflower, and carrots (about 2 cups)
- 1 small onion, cut into thin wedges
- ½ cup water
- ½ teaspoon instant chicken bouillon granules
- ⅛ teaspoon white pepper
- 1 bay leaf
- 2 13-ounce cans (3⅓ cups total) evaporated skim milk
- 1 pint shucked oysters *or* two 8-ounce cans whole oysters

Cut up any large vegetables. In a 3-quart saucepan combine vegetables, onion, water, bouillon granules, white pepper, and bay leaf. Bring to boiling. Reduce heat. Cover and simmer for 5 to 7 minutes or till vegetables are crisp-tender. *Do not drain.*

Stir in the evaporated milk. Heat through. Add *undrained* oysters to vegetable mixture. Cook over medium heat about 5 minutes or till edges of oysters curl, stirring frequently. (If using canned oysters, just heat through.) Remove bay leaf. Makes 6 servings.

Microwave directions: Cut up any large vegetables. In a 2-quart microwave-safe casserole combine vegetables, water, bouillon granules, white pepper, and bay leaf. Micro-cook, covered, on 100% power (high) for 5 to 7 minutes or till vegetables are crisp-tender, stirring once. *Do not drain.*

Stir in evaporated milk. Cook, uncovered, on high for 4 to 6 minutes more or till heated through, stirring once. Add *undrained* oysters. Cook, uncovered, on high for 4 to 5 minutes more or till oysters begin to curl around the edges, stirring once. (If using canned oysters, cook 1 minute more or till heated through, stirring once.) Remove bay leaf.

Nutrition information per serving: 199 cal., 20 g pro., 23 g carbo., 3 g fat, 55 mg chol., and 612 mg sodium. U.S. RDA: 44% vit. A, 66% vit. C, 37% riboflavin, 40% calcium, 39% iron, and 40% phosphorus.

CAJUN PORK PINWHEELS

Spiced-up pork tenderloin—lean, luscious, and peppery hot—

- 2 ¾-pound pork tenderloins
- 2 small sweet red, yellow, *and/or* green peppers, seeded and finely chopped (1 cup)
- ½ cup finely chopped onion
- ½ cup finely chopped celery
- 1 teaspoon dried thyme, crushed
- ½ to 1 teaspoon ground red pepper
- ½ teaspoon garlic salt
- ½ teaspoon paprika
- 2 tablespoons cooking oil
- 1 tablespoon fennel seed
- 1 tablespoon pepper medley *or* lemon-pepper seasoning
- Sweet red, yellow, *and/or* green pepper slices (optional)
- Fresh dill (optional)

Remove fat and paper-thin membrane from surface of tenderloins. Use a sharp knife to cut *one* tenderloin lengthwise to, but not through, opposite side. Cover with clear plastic wrap. Use flat side of meat mallet to pound tenderloin, working from the center to edges, to make a 12x8-inch rectangle. Repeat with remaining pork.

In a medium skillet cook chopped sweet peppers, onion, celery, thyme, red pepper, garlic salt, and paprika in hot cooking oil about 5 minutes or till vegetables are tender, stirring often. Spread vegetable mixture evenly over tenderloins to within ½ inch of edge. Roll up from short sides.

Combine fennel seed and pepper medley or lemon-pepper seasoning. Crush finely. Press fennel mixture into the top and sides of *each* roll. Tie rolls with string, if necessary.

Place meat, seam side down, on a rack in a shallow roasting pan. Insert a meat thermometer in the center of one roll. Roast, uncovered, in a 325° oven for 1¼ to 1½ hours or till meat thermometer registers 170°.

Remove the strings. Slice meat. Transfer meat to a platter lined with pepper slices, if desired. Garnish with dill, if desired. Makes 6 servings.

Nutrition information per serving: 169 cal., 19 g pro., 5 g carbo., 8 g fat, 57 mg chol., 208 mg sodium. U.S. RDA: 42% vit. A, 76% vit. C, 42% thiamine, 16% riboflavin, 17% niacin, 14% iron, 20% phosphorus.

BEEF WITH LIGHT YORKSHIRE PUDDING

- Nonstick spray coating
- 2 eggs
- 2 egg whites
- 1½ cups all-purpose flour
- 1½ cups skim milk
- 2 tablespoons snipped parsley
- 1 3-pound boneless beef round rump roast *or* boneless rolled beef round tip roast
- 2 tablespoons cornstarch
- ¼ cup sliced green onion
- 1 teaspoon instant beef bouillon granules
- ¼ teaspoon pepper

Spray a 13x9x2-inch baking pan with nonstick spray coating. For Yorkshire pudding, in small mixer bowl beat eggs and egg whites with an electric mixer on high speed till well mixed. Add flour and milk. Beat on medium speed for 2 minutes, scraping sides of bowl occasionally. Stir in parsley. Pour into prepared pan. Bake in a 400° oven for 30 to 35 minutes or till golden brown. Let cool on a wire rack while meat roasts.

Trim any surface fat from meat. Place meat, fat side up, on a rack in a shallow roasting pan. Insert a meat thermometer. Roast, uncovered, in a 325° oven about 2 hours or till the thermometer reaches 150° (medium). Transfer meat to serving platter, reserving juices in roasting pan. Cover meat and keep warm. Return the Yorkshire pudding to the 325° oven for 10 minutes or till heated through.

Meanwhile, for gravy, add about ½ cup *water* to roasting pan, scraping up any crusty brown bits. Pour meat juices into a 2-cup measure. Skim off fat. Add enough water to make 2 cups. Return to the roasting pan. Stir 2 tablespoons *water* into cornstarch. Stir cornstarch mixture, green onion, bouillon granules, and pepper into reserved juices. Cook and stir till thickened and bubbly. Cook and stir for 2 minutes more. Cut Yorkshire pudding into squares. Slice meat. Arrange meat and Yorkshire pudding on a platter. Spoon gravy atop. Makes 8 servings.

Nutrition information per serving: 329 cal., 34 g pro., 23 g carbo., 10 g fat, 154 mg chol., and 163 mg sodium. U.S. RDA: 16% thiamine, 25% riboflavin, 31% niacin, 27% iron, and 32% phosphorus.

STAR-BURST FRUIT TRIFLE

You'll find convenient ladyfingers in one of three places: the refrigerator case, the cookie aisle, or the bakery—

½ cup jellied cranberry sauce
3 tablespoons water
1 4-serving-size package reduced-calorie *instant* vanilla pudding mix
1 cup skim milk
1 8-ounce carton low-fat vanilla, peach, *or* lemon yogurt
1 3-ounce package (12) lady-fingers, split
1½ cups frozen unsweetened peach slices, thawed and well drained
1½ to 2 cups halved fresh strawberries, orange sections, *or* halved grapes
Strawberry leaf (optional)

In a small saucepan heat cranberry sauce and water till melted. Use a wire whisk to beat till smooth. Let cool.

Prepare pudding mix according to package directions *except* use the skim milk and yogurt in place of whole milk.

In a 1½-quart soufflé dish or straight-sided serving bowl arrange enough of the split ladyfingers to cover bottom and sides of dish, reserving remaining ladyfingers for layering. Toss together *1 cup* of the peaches and *1 cup* of the strawberries, orange sections, or halved grapes.

Spoon *half* of the fruit mixture over ladyfingers in dish. Spread *half* of the pudding mixture over fruit. Top with *half* of the cranberry mixture. Arrange remaining ladyfingers atop. Repeat fruit and pudding layers. Spoon remaining cranberry mixture in center. Cover and chill at least 4 hours.

Just before serving, arrange remaining peach slices and strawberry halves, orange sections, or grapes on top. If desired, garnish with a strawberry leaf. Makes 8 servings.

Nutrition information per serving:
207 cal., 4 g pro., 46 g carbo., 1 g fat, 39 mg chol., 117 mg sodium. U.S. RDA: 122% vit. C, 11% riboflavin.

MERINGUE STARS

2 egg whites
½ teaspoon vanilla
¼ teaspoon cream of tartar
½ cup sugar
Small silver decorative candies, small multicolored decorative candies, ground cinnamon, colored sugar, *and/or* chopped almonds

Line a large cookie sheet with brown paper or foil. In a small mixer bowl beat egg whites, vanilla, and cream of tartar with an electric mixer on high speed till soft peaks form (tips curl). Gradually add sugar, beating till stiff peaks form (tips stand straight).

Put egg-white mixture into a decorating bag fitted with a ½-inch star tip. Squeeze the bag gently and make star shapes, releasing pressure as you pull up tip and placing stars about 1 inch apart. Decorate as desired with decorative candies, cinnamon, sugar, or nuts.

Bake in a 300° oven for 15 minutes. Turn off oven and let cookies dry in the oven with door closed for 30 minutes. Makes 40 cookies.

Nutrition information per cookie:
13 cal., 0 g pro., 3 g carbo., 0 g fat, 0 mg chol., 3 mg sodium.

YULETIDE LOG

This frosting made from whipped dessert topping mix and cocoa is lighter and easier to prepare than the traditional buttercream frosting—

Nonstick spray coating
½ cup all-purpose flour
1 teaspoon baking powder
¼ teaspoon salt
2 egg yolks
½ teaspoon vanilla
⅓ cup sugar
4 egg whites
½ cup sugar
Sifted powdered sugar
2 1.4-ounce envelopes whipped dessert topping mix
3 tablespoons unsweetened cocoa powder
¾ cup skim milk
1 teaspoon vanilla
Unsweetened cocoa powder (optional)

Spray a 15x10x1-inch jelly roll pan with nonstick spray coating. Line pan with waxed paper. Spray again with nonstick spray coating. Set aside.

Sift together the ½ cup flour, baking powder, and salt. In a small mixer bowl beat egg yolks and the ½ teaspoon vanilla with an electric mixer on high speed about 5 minutes or till thick and lemon colored. Gradually add the ⅓ cup sugar, beating till sugar is dissolved. Wash the beaters thoroughly.

In a large mixer bowl beat egg whites on medium speed till soft peaks form (tips curl). Gradually add the ½ cup sugar, beating on high speed till stiff peaks form (tips stand straight). Fold yolk mixture into beaten egg whites. Sprinkle flour mixture over egg mixture. Fold in gently. Spread in prepared pan. Bake in a 375° oven for 12 to 15 minutes or till wooden toothpick inserted in the center comes out clean.

Immediately loosen edges of cake from the pan and turn out onto a towel sprinkled with sifted powdered sugar. Peel off waxed paper. Roll up warm cake and towel together, jelly-roll style, starting from one of the short sides. Cool, seam side down, on a wire rack.

For frosting, in the small mixer bowl combine dessert topping mix and the 3 tablespoons cocoa powder. Add milk and the 1 teaspoon vanilla. Beat on high speed for 4 to 5 minutes or till soft peaks form and the mixture is light and fluffy.

Unroll cooled cake. Remove the towel. Spread with *half* of the frosting to within ½ inch of edges. Reroll cake. Transfer to a serving platter. Frost roll with remaining frosting. Using a knife or fork tines, draw lightly through frosting to give appearance of bark.

Use a serrated knife to cut a 1-inch slice from one end of cake roll. Place on top of the cake roll in the center. Chill until serving time. Sprinkle with cocoa powder. Makes 10 servings.

Nutrition information per serving:
167 cal., 4 g pro., 29 g carbo., 5 g fat, 55 mg chol., 136 mg sodium.

HONEY COOKIES

These fancy Christmas cookies have fewer calories than other cookies, and are easy to decorate with cookie stamps—

⅓ cup margarine
¼ cup sugar
2 tablespoons honey
1 teaspoon vanilla
1 teaspoon finely shredded lemon peel
1¼ cups all-purpose flour
¾ cup ground almonds
Colored sugar (optional)
Whole almonds *or* red cinnamon candies (optional)

In a large mixer bowl beat the margarine with an electric mixer on medium speed 30 seconds. Add the sugar, honey, vanilla, and lemon peel. Beat well. Add flour to mixture. Beat well. Stir in the ground almonds.

Shape the dough into 1-inch balls. Place balls 2 inches apart on ungreased cookie sheets. Using the bottom of a glass dipped in colored sugar or a cookie stamp dipped in flour, flatten the cookies to about ¼ inch thick. Press an almond or a red cinnamon candy into cookies, if desired.

Bake in a 325° oven for 8 to 9 minutes or till golden. Let cool on cookie sheet for 1 minute. Remove cookies from cookie sheet. Cool on a wire rack. Makes about 30 cookies.

Nutrition information per cookie:
60 cal., 1 g pro., 7 g carbo., 3 g fat, 0 mg chol., 25 mg sodium.

FESTIVE FRUITCAKE

Our version has 30 percent fewer calories than a traditional fruitcake—

Nonstick spray coating
1 cup all-purpose flour
1 teaspoon baking powder
½ teaspoon ground cinnamon
½ teaspoon ground nutmeg
1 6-ounce package mixed dried fruit bits
½ cup raisins
⅓ cup chopped pecans
¼ cup chopped maraschino cherries
1 tablespoon brandy
1 8-ounce can crushed pineapple (juice pack)
1 egg
1 egg white
¼ cup packed brown sugar
2 tablespoons molasses
2 tablespoons margarine, melted
Brandy (optional)
Powdered sugar (optional)

Spray an 8x4x2-inch loaf pan with nonstick spray coating. In a large mixing bowl combine flour, baking powder, cinnamon, and nutmeg; set aside.

In a medium mixing bowl combine fruit bits, raisins, pecans, cherries, and the 1 tablespoon brandy. Toss to coat. Drain pineapple well, reserving juice. Stir fruit mixture and pineapple into flour mixture. Set aside.

In a small mixing bowl beat egg and egg white till combined. Add *2 tablespoons* of the reserved pineapple juice, brown sugar, molasses, and margarine. Beat well. Stir into the fruit mixture.

Turn batter into prepared pan. Spread evenly. Bake in a 325° oven for 55 to 60 minutes or till a wooden toothpick inserted near the center comes out clean. Cool in pan on a wire rack.

Remove from the pan. Wrap cake in a cheesecloth soaked in remaining pineapple juice or brandy. Wrap in clear plastic wrap. Chill at least 24 hours or up to 2 weeks.

If desired, sprinkle with powdered sugar and garnish with an additional maraschino cherry and raisin. Makes 24 servings.

Nutrition information per serving:
117 cal., 2 g pro., 23 g carbo., 2 g fat, 12 mg chol., 35 mg sodium.

SWEET POTATO CHEESECAKE

Put this great make-ahead together in 20 minutes, bake, and chill—

1 cup fine gingersnap crumbs (15 cookies) *or* graham cracker crumbs (14 cracker squares)
3 tablespoons margarine, melted
2 8-ounce packages Neufchâtel cheese, softened
1 cup mashed cooked sweet potatoes
⅔ cup sugar
1½ teaspoons pumpkin pie spice
1 teaspoon finely shredded orange peel
1 teaspoon vanilla
5 egg whites
1 cup evaporated skim milk
Frozen whipped dessert topping, thawed (optional)
Gingersnaps, halved (optional)
Finely shredded orange peel (optional)

For crust, combine gingersnap or graham cracker crumbs and margarine. Press crumb mixture onto the bottom and 1 inch up sides of an 8-inch springform pan. Set aside.

For filling, in a large mixer bowl combine cheese, sweet potatoes, sugar, pumpkin pie spice, the 1 teaspoon orange peel, and vanilla. Beat with an electric mixer on medium speed till combined. Add the egg whites, beating on low speed just till combined. *Do not overbeat.* Stir in milk. Carefully pour filling into prepared pan.

Bake in a 350° oven for 60 to 70 minutes or till center appears set. Cool on a wire rack for 45 minutes. Cover and chill thoroughly. Remove sides of pan. Dollop with dessert topping, if desired. Garnish with gingersnap halves and additional orange peel, if desired. Makes 12 to 16 servings.

Nutrition information per serving:
242 cal., 8 g pro., 26 g carbo., 12 g fat, 32 mg chol., 273 mg sodium. U.S. RDA: 85% vit. A, 13% riboflavin, 10% calcium, 10% phosphorus.

INDEX

Index

O-Q

R-S

Index

Microwave Wattage

All microwave recipes were tested in countertop microwave ovens that operate on 625 to 700 watts. Cooking times are approximate because ovens often vary by manufacturer.

Nutrition Analysis

Some nutrient information is given by gram weight per serving. The United States Recommended Daily Allowances (U.S. RDAs) for selected vitamins and minerals are given in the recipes when the value exceeds 10 percent. The U.S. RDAs tell the amounts of certain nutrients necessary to meet the dietary needs of most healthy people.

To obtain the nutrition analysis of each recipe, the following guidelines were used:

● When ingredient options appear in a recipe, the analysis was calculated using the first ingredient choice.

● Optional ingredients were omitted in the analyses.

● The nutrition analyses for recipes calling for fresh ingredients were calculated using the measurements for raw fruits, vegetables, and meats.

● If a recipe gives optional serving sizes (such as "Makes 6 to 8 servings"), the nutrition analysis was calculated using the first choice.

Have BETTER HOMES AND GARDENS® magazine delivered to your door. For information, write to:
MR. ROBERT AUSTIN
P.O. BOX 4536
DES MOINES, IA 50336